Chronicle
of the year 1995

A DORLING KINDERSLEY BOOK

Managing Editor Jane Laing
Senior Editor Lee Stacy
Editor Christina Bankes
Managing Art Editor Ruth Shane
Designers Sue Caws, Jamie Hanson, Luke Herriott,
Tony Limerick, Rebecca Willis
Production Manager Ian Paton

Editorial and design by Brown Packaging Ltd
255-257 Liverpool Road, London N1 1LX
Authors Steve Adamson, Alison Ali, Nigel Cawthorne,
John Collis, Graham McColl, Henry Russell
Design Steve Wilson

US Editors Mary Sutherland,
Kathleen Kent, Michael T. Wise

First published in the United States in 1996
by Dorling Kindersley Publishing, Inc.
95 Madison Avenue, New York, NY 10016

A catalog record is available from the Library of Congress
ISBN 0-7894-0374-9

Reproduced by Kestrel Digital Colour Ltd., Chelmsford, Essex UK
Printed and bound in the United States by R.R. Donnelley & Sons

How to use this book

Chronicle of the Year 1995 reports the events of the year as though they had just happened. The weekly chronology summaries do not aim to cover all the most important events since these are reported in greater detail in the reports adjoining the summaries. The summaries include less important events and those leading up to the main events reported elsewhere or their consequences. These chains of development can be tracked through a system of cross-references that complements the index by pointing to the next link in the chain. Arrows indicating the next link appear at the end of the reports or summaries. They point only forward in time, but can lead to either an entry in the weekly summaries or to one of the fuller reports. They look like this: (→Feb 17).

Chronicle

of the year 1995

DORLING KINDERSLEY
LONDON • NEW YORK • STUTTGART

S	M	T	W	T	F	S
1	2	3	4	5	6	7
8	9	10	11	12	13	14
15	16	17	18	19	20	21
22	23	24	25	26	27	28
29	30	31				

Brasília, 1
Fernando Henrique Cardoso inaugurated as President of Brazil.

London, 1
Frederick West, accused of the murder of 12 young women, found hanged in his cell at Winson Green Prison, Birmingham. Suicide is suspected. (→ November 23)

Bosnia, 1
A cease-fire officially begins, amid widespread fears that it will be no more durable than its predecessors. (→ January 9)

Cairo, 2
Twelve people killed in gun battles between police and Islamic militants in the Nile Valley town of Mallawi.

Pasadena, 2
Penn State wins the Rose Bowl 38-20 against the favored Oregon team.

Jerusalem, 3
Israeli troops shoot three Palestinian policemen dead in an accidental exchange of fire that could have dire repercussions for the Middle East peace process.

Colombo, 3
The Tamil Tigers, the Sri Lankan separatist guerrillas, agree to a cease-fire with government forces.

Fort Lauderdale, 4
Prisoners in Florida dig a 60-ft (20-m) tunnel in an attempt to break out of jail.

Rome, 4
The Vatican announces that the Pope still intends to visit the Philippines later this month despite death threats from Muslim extremists.

Hamburg, 5
Günther Parche, the man who stabbed top women's tennis player, Monica Seles, goes on trial.

London, 5
Author Martin Amis hires US literary agent Andrew Wylie in the hopes of getting $750,000 for his next novel (→ January 11)

Deaths
Mohammed Siad Barre, former president of Somalia, at the age of 80, January 1.

Joe Slovo, leader of South Africa's Communist Party and long-time opponent of apartheid, January 5.

GROZNY, CHECHNYA, SUNDAY 1

Russians pound Grozny in a new offensive

A Chechen resistance fighter darts across open ground near the Presidential Palace, the focus of Russian assaults on this embattled city.

Russian forces have redoubled their efforts to take the city of Grozny, capital of the breakaway republic of Chechnya, where Chechen rebels are holding out despite the superiority of the Russian army. Fierce hand-to-hand fighting now rages in the streets, but the situation is too chaotic to judge who has the advantage.

The Russian offensive began on December 11 amid optimism that Yeltsin's troops would make light work of retaking the city. Facing the well-equipped Russian army there is, effectively, only a group of lightly armed guerrillas, but they are making the Russians fight every inch of the way. The conscripts who form the bulk of the Russian army proved to have little stomach for the early fighting, and their wrecked tanks still litter the streets. Artillery bombardment also failed to subdue the rebels. Today's offensive was preceded by a massive artillery assault, after which more tanks and special forces went in.

The objective of the Russian forces is the capture of the former Presidential Palace, a grim concrete symbol of the old regime but the very center of Chechen resistance and site of the underground bunker that is the headquarters of separatist leader Dzhokhar Dudayev. Unconfirmed reports say Dudayev has been forced out to the suburbs of the city.

In Moscow, President Yeltsin said that a main aim for 1995 was to bring peace to the republic. (→ January 19)

MEXICO CITY, MONDAY 2

New crisis for Mexican peso

International markets are preparing themselves for a new shock later today. With the country beset by massive debt, the Mexican peso is tottering. The Mexican president, Oscar Zedillo, is expected to make an announcement before the week is out, but without foreign financial support he is effectively powerless.

The activities of Zapatista guerrillas in the south of the country have deepened the crisis. Mexico's financial and political instability threaten to undo all the close trade links that have been established with the USA in recent years. (→ January 13)

Massachusetts, Sunday 1. Flowers on the pavement outside the abortion clinic in Brookline where "pro-life" campaigner John Salvi shot dead two women receptionists. Salvi also sprayed bullets into an abortion clinic in Virginia before being arrested.

Astronomers stretch the universe

Scientists operating the Keck telescope situated here on Mauna Kea mountain have found a galaxy more distant than any known before. They have prosaically named their discovery 8C 1435+63.

The new galaxy is calculated to be 15 billion light years away. This is more than 1 billion light years farther than anything seen before, and places it at the farthest edge of the universe.

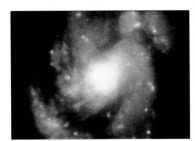

The new galaxy, seen through the Keck.

Murder rate falls in New York

Mayor Rudolph Giuliani proudly announced today that the murder rate in New York has fallen by one fifth. A total of 1,581 murders were recorded last year in the five boroughs of the city, as opposed to 1,946 two years ago.

Various factors account for the steady fall in homicides, which peaked at 2,245 in 1990. Principal among them is a significant drop in the population of teenage males living in the city, as this is the group that commits the highest proportion of murders. In addition, the crack epidemic of the 1980s began to ease in 1990, with a consequent decline in drug-related crime.

Mayor Giuliani called the figures a "very significant success," but stressed that despite the improvements, the city remained burdened with an image problem: "People outside New York City are very often almost shocked by the notion that it is not the most dangerous city in America," he said. "That's a reputation that the city, despite all the statistical evidence to the contrary, can't quite shake off."

New Congress has a different hue

The new Congress assembles outside the Capitol, committed to a radical program.

The new Congress that is to be sworn in today is very different from its predecessors. For the first time in 40 years it will be dominated by Republicans. The leader in the Senate will be Robert Dole, one of the best-known Republicans nationally. In the House of Representatives the new majority leader is Newton "Newt" Gingrich, whose flair for publicity and determination to stick to a clear and simple policy were key factors in the Republicans' election victories last autumn.

Gingrich now has the task of steering through the ten-point "Contract with America" that he persuaded all Republican candidates for the House to subscribe to, and which laid out a highly popular set of measures that, supposedly, all could understand. The Republicans are now committed to excising what they see as waste in the welfare system, to balancing the budget, to cutting taxes, and to a fierce drive against crime. Their measures may bring them into conflict with President Clinton, but Dole has no qualms about this. "We control the Congress now and we're going to set the agenda," he stated triumphantly. Or, as some car stickers proclaim: "Have a Happy Newt Year!"

Marion Barry comes back from the political dead

Mayor Barry makes his inaugural speech.

The checkered career of Marion Barry took another bizarre turn today when he was sworn in again as mayor of Washington DC. Barry has made no secret of the problems of his past. His conviction on drug charges in 1990 seemed to have ended his career, but toughness, honesty, and massive sympathy from the city's black population have enabled him to stage an amazing political recovery.

In his inauguration speech the new mayor pledged to "bring integrity back into government," and promised that he would restore Washington DC's position "from the ground up." He realises the enormity of the task ahead: "We have difficult days ahead of us … And we have some difficult decisions to make."

Saatchi forced out of his agency

Maurice Saatchi today stormed out of the agency he founded with his brother, sending an open letter to the staff in which he gave full vent to his feelings. "Saatchi & Saatchi has been taken over," he wrote. "No shareholder vote has been taken. But make no mistake – Saatchi & Saatchi is under new control." His anger is directed particularly at David Herro, 34-year-old American fund manager, who wanted Maurice replaced as chairman (offering him the honorary post of company president), and who urged the board to abandon Saatchi's lucrative share option package. The questions gripping the City are, will Saatchi set up a new company? And will he be able to take his blue-chip clients with him?

S	M	T	W	T	F	S
1	2	3	4	5	6	7
8	9	10	11	12	13	14
15	16	17	18	19	20	21
22	23	24	25	26	27	28
29	30	31				

New York, 8
Police arrest a man suspected of killing six people in Queens in what may be a drug-related attack.

Washington DC, 9
Newt Gingrich sacks an old friend from the position of historian of the House of Representatives weeks after appointing her, because of her revisionist views on the Holocaust.

Washington DC, 10
A new deal with Japan opens Japanese financial markets to American competition.

Johannesburg, 10
South Africa's police chief is to step down as the nation's police force is being overhauled because of its role in supporting apartheid.

La Jolla, California, 10
Scientists at the Scripps Research Institute have discovered a way of destroying cancers by cutting off the blood supply to them.

Paris, 10
The smart money in France is going on Edouard Balladur, the present prime minister, to win the race to become the country's president in the spring. (→ May 7)

London, 11
Martin Amis signs a deal with HarperCollins worth $700,000 for a novel and a book of short stories.

Beijing, 12
Deng Xiaoping's daughter admits her father's health is in sharp decline. (→February 1)

Mexico City, 13
Middle-class demonstrators clash with police in protests against the country's financial crisis. (→ January 21)

Warsaw, 13
The Polish government is rocked by the resignation of Foreign Minister Andrzej Olechowski, who claimed that the ideals of the ruling coalition were against the best interests of the people.

Deaths
Prince Souphanouvong, the "Red Prince" of Laos who fought against the US with the Vietcong and Pathet Lao, January 10.

Peter Cook, British satirist, in London, at the age of 57, January 9.

BELFAST, THURSDAY 12
End of daylight patrols in Belfast

In a move that is seen as proof of the strength of the peace process in Northern Ireland, it was announced today that troops will be withdrawn from the streets of Belfast during daylight hours for the first time in 25 years. Chief Constable Sir Hugh Annesley, head of the Royal Ulster Constabulary said that the situation would be kept under review.

Soldiers will continue to be seen in daytime in some of the more volatile areas of the province such as the border areas of South Armagh. But even here it is hoped to be able to reduce the military presence soon.

MADRID, TUESDAY 10
"Dirty war" allegations in Spain

Spain's opposition parties today called for the resignation of Prime Minister Felipe Gonzalez after his appearance on television last night. In a half-hour broadcast, Sr. Gonzalez angrily rebuffed allegations that he and his party were involved in a "dirty war" against Basque separatists. However, he has failed to convince his critics that the government was not behind death squads that killed 28 people during attacks on Basque separatists in southwestern France in the mid-1980s.

PALE, BOSNIA, MONDAY 9
No pullback from Sarajevo warns Mladic

General Mladic, accompanied by his translator, at the press conference.

In the Bosnian Serb capital of Pale tonight, Ratko Mladic, commander of the Bosnian Serb forces, said that he would not withdraw his forces from around the beleaguered city of Sarajevo unless the Muslim government troops abandon territory they hold on Mount Ignam, south of the city. This the government is unlikely to do as it would mean losing all the ground they gained in their assault last fall. This defiant stance by the Serbs threatens an already fragile cease-fire, which after only a week now appears even closer to collapse.

General Rose has assured General Mladic that the Muslims appear to have withdrawn from the demilitarized zone established on Mount Ignam, as was demanded by the Serbs as one of their conditions for releasing their stranglehold on access to the city. However, Mladic is now demanding complete Muslim withdrawal from the mountain. In the meantime, the blockade of Sarajevo remains and the threat of a Serb assault on the city is still a very real fear for the beleaguered inhabitants.

Fighting also continues around Bihac in the north of Bosnia where the Bosnian government is confronting rebel Muslim fighters who have joined nationalist Serbs from Croatia who did not agree to the cease-fire. (→ January 15)

Minneapolis, Thursday 12. Malcolm X's daughter, Qubilah Bahiyah Shabazz, after her arrest today, accused of trying to murder Louis Farrakhan. Ms Shabazz will face charges that she tried to hire a hit man to kill her father's one-time disciple but then rival.(→ May 1)

NEW YORK, MONDAY 9
Terror sheikh trial opens

Twelve mostly Arabic-speaking Muslims appeared in court in New York today at the opening of their trial for allegedly planning to blow up the Lincoln and Holland tunnels and several New York landmarks.

The group includes the blind religious leader Sheikh Omar Abdel Rahman, who is held by the prosecution to be the ringleader. The men are also charged with participating in or approving the 1993 World Trade Center bombing. Sheikh Rahman regularly preaches at a Jersey City mosque. (→ February 8)

LOS ANGELES, WEDNESDAY 11

Thirty-three rescued in California floods

Traffic grinds to a halt in a flooded California street as the flood waters reach record levels because of rainstorms from the Pacific.

Over $61 million worth of damage has been caused across California in the last three days by storms blowing in from the Pacific, with more expected. The storms have caused floods throughout the state, affecting areas stretching from the border with Oregon down to the edges of the deserts surrounding San Bernadino. So far, the death toll has reached eight, including an 11-year-old boy who drowned while crossing a creek in Orange County, and a marine officer who was swept out to sea while out on exercises. Other deaths have been caused by the high winds and by swollen rivers.

The heavy rains, mud, and wind have been disastrous for an agricultural industry that has, in any case, been plagued for a year by drought. Store prices are expected to rise steeply as a direct result.

President Clinton has issued a disaster declaration for 24 of the state's counties. James Bailey, assistant chief of the California Flood Center, said yesterday, "This is at least the storm of the decade." At present, few in California would disagree.

WASHINGTON DC, MONDAY 9

Dole threatens to curb Clinton

New Senate majority leader Robert Dole today suggested a Peace Powers Act that would severely limit presidential power in the use of armed forces. He is proposing that Congress would have to give its assent before forces could be committed by the President to any UN peacekeeping operation. The President would be obliged to present Congress with an estimate of the cost and to show where in the federal budget the funds would come from.

Dole's move reflects a widespread unease about US participation in UN operations. The intervention in Somalia has widely been held to have been unsuccessful. Currently there is considerable fear that the US could be sucked into the Bosnian conflict.

In 1973 Congress sought to limit to 90 days the time a president could commit troops without its agreement, but no president has accepted the resolution. (→ February 14)

Rome, Friday 13. Lamberto Dini, who today agreed to become Italy's prime minister. The position has been vacant since Silvio Berlusconi's resignation just before Christmas. Signor Dini was Director General of the Bank of Italy before becoming Berlusconi's treasury minister. It is hoped he can find a middle way in a country rocked by accusations of bribery and tax evasion.

MANILA, SATURDAY 14

Pope's success in Philippines

Even the arrest of two Arabs with bomb-making equipment and police fears that a 20-man hit squad is stalking him has not checked the Pope in his triumphant passage through the Philippines. The first leg of his four-nation tour opened in Manila to massive crowds. The Pope has made a special point of talking to the young. This culminates today, the last full day of his three-day tour, when he addresses a three-hour open-air mass being held to mark World Youth Day. A congregation of over three million is confidently anticipated.

The Pope arrives at Manila airport, to a rapturous welcome from Filipinos.

S	M	T	W	T	F	S
1	2	3	4	5	6	7
8	9	10	11	12	13	14
15	16	17	18	19	20	21
22	23	24	25	26	27	28
29	30	31				

Sarajevo, 15
Serb shelling of Bihac kills two teenage girls. (→ February 11)

Baghdad, 15
Fourteen senior officers of the Iraqi air force were executed today for attempting to assassinate Saddam Hussein.

Los Angeles, 16
Dispute between Faye Dunaway and Andrew Lloyd Webber over Dunaway's dissmissal from the musical *Sunset Boulevard* is settled out of court.

Strasbourg, 17
Jacques Delors chairs his last European Commission meeting, after ten years as its president.

Washington DC, 17
The *Washington Post* recounts how six CIA men escaped from Iraq in the build-up to the Gulf War, disguised as Polish workers, with the help of Polish intelligence officers.

Washington DC, 18
Democrats attack Newt Gingrich for agreeing to a book deal with one of Rupert Murdoch's companies.

Tucson, 18
Scientists studying the edge of the universe through the Hubble telescope have found clouds of ultrathin gas from the Big Bang.

Chechnya, 19
Russian forces capture the Presidential Palace in Grozny, the rebels' headquarters. (→ January 24)

Pretoria, 20
Nelson Mandela and F.W. De Klerk patch up their differences after a row over indemnity for past crimes.

Frankfurt, 21
A key Lockerbie bombing suspect, already jailed on terrorism charges, is freed by Germany and returned to Syria in a secret deal with Iran.

Mexico, 21
Mexican financial markets go into further fall as it appears US Congress will not back Clinton's plan to support the peso.

Death
Bishop David E. Johnson, age 61, leader of largest Episcopal diocese in the USA, found dead on Sunday 15 January at home in Boston, having apparently shot himself.

Mother accused of drowning her two children

Susan Smith entering the courtroom in Union, South Carolina.

A 23-year-old woman appeared in court today accused of the murder of her two sons, aged three and 14 months. Mrs. Susan V. Smith, who did not enter a plea, broke down in tears several times.

The story of the disappearance of the children caused nationwide alarm when it broke last October. Mrs. Smith claimed that a black man had stolen her car and kidnapped the boys. The prosecution claims that when after nine days the searches proved fruitless, Mrs. Smith admitted to police that she had let her car roll into a lake near Union with the two boys inside, strapped into their car seats. This horrific crime has shocked the nation.

Mrs. Smith was going through a divorce from the boys' father at the time of the boys' deaths. If found guilty she could face the electric chair, in which case she would be the first woman to be executed in the USA for ten years. (→ July 10)

Joe Slovo buried in Soweto

There were tears in his eyes as Nelson Mandela gave the main address at the state funeral of his old friend and white ally in the battle against apartheid, Joe Slovo. Slovo died of cancer ten days ago.

The measure of the new South Africa was shown by the fact that leaders of the Nationalist Party attended the funeral. Under the old regime, Slovo, the Lithuanian-born leader of South Africa's Communist Party, was regarded by the government as Public Enemy Number One. Soweto celebrated the life of the man who championed freedom and justice with dawn-to-dusk dancing in the streets.

Joe Slovo, late SA communist leader.

New cave art found in France

Cave paintings comparable in quality to those at Lascaux have been discovered in the Ardèche region of southern France. The paintings were found a week before Christmas, but the discovery was kept secret while the caves were made secure from intruders. The work is of extremely high quality and may well have been produced by a single person. "We have a selection of animals infinitely more varied than at the other sites and with exceptional features," said Geneviève Martin, of the Rhônes-Alpes archeological service.

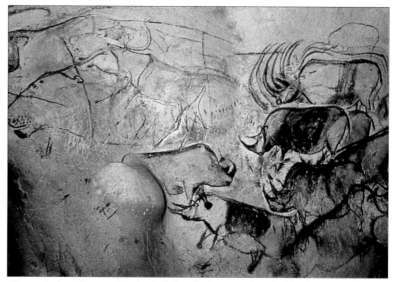

Cave paintings discovered in the Ardèche, after being undisturbed for thousands of years.

TOKYO, TUESDAY 17

Earthquake rocks Kobe

Fires fuelled by ruptured gas pipes rage out of control and destroy earthquake-shattered buildings in the Japanese city of Kobe.

Elevated roads buckled and collapsed during the tremor, killing hundreds of commuters.

A huge earthquake hit western Japan this morning, causing massive damage in the city of Kobe. A busy port near Osaka with a population of 1.4 million people, Kobe is situated in the heart of one of Japan's most important industrial areas.

The early reports of 300 dead have been constantly revised upward during the day to 2,700. Over 1,100 buildings collapsed, as did some overhead freeways, sending motorists plunging to their deaths. Fires raged across the city, fed by fractured gas pipes, as firemen struggled to reach them through blocked roads and over rubble. Fires also broke out in various other towns and cities across the region, including Osaka itself.

The earthquake hit at 5:46 a.m. local time. Measuring 7.2 on the Richter scale, it is Japan's worst earthquake since 1923, when Tokyo was destroyed, and 142,000 people killed. Near-freezing temperatures have made matters even worse for the thousands whose houses have been destroyed, and the hundreds of thousands whose homes now have no power or heating. (→ January 25)

WASHINGTON DC, FRIDAY 20

US lifts sanctions on North Korea

The US State Department has announced that the USA is partially lifting economic sanctions on North Korea that have been in place since the Korean War of 1950-53. A new trade pact has been agreed between the two countries which will allow American telecommunications companies to establish businesses in North Korea. In return North Korea will export magnesite, a mineral used in the manufacture of steel, to the US. American visitors to North Korea will also be able to use major credit cards in the country.

The sanctions were originally imposed under a "trading with the enemy" act. This thaw in relations follows the release of a US army pilot shot down in North Korea, and President Clinton's assurances that the US would help to meet some of the expenses incurred by the termination of North Korea's nuclear program. The North Korean government has now responded by agreeing to abandon work on two nuclear reactors it was building and to close a plutonium reprocessing plant.

Republicans expressed unhappiness with the move, as they claim it supports the current North Korean regime. As recently as last year, the then chairman of the Joint Chiefs of Staff, Colin Powell, said that US forces might at some time have to invade and fight in the country.

Idaho, Sunday 15. Four Canadian gray wolves released near the Salmon River are the first of 30 to be reintroduced into the Rocky Mountains.

S	M	T	W	T	F	S
1	2	3	4	5	6	7
8	9	10	11	12	13	14
15	16	17	18	19	20	21
22	23	24	25	26	27	28
29	30	31				

Los Angeles, 22
Tom Hanks takes the Golden Globe award for Best Actor and *Forrest Gump* for Best Picture. Hugh Grant picks up Best Actor in a Comedy.

London, 22
The Prince of Wales plans to sue his former housekeeper over a book about her years in his service.

Sarajevo, 23
The US embassy shows dissent from its government's new policy of direct talks with Bosnian Serbs.

Bangkok, 23
Burmese opposition leader Aung San Suu Kyi pledges no deal with the ruling junta to end her house arrest.

Chechnya, 24
Russian tanks and artillery bombard Grozny to prevent reinforcements from joining the remaining bands of Chechen rebels. (→ February 4)

Jerusalem, 25
The Israeli government overrides Palestinian protests by agreeing to the building of 3,000 new Jewish homes around East Jerusalem.

Dublin, 25
A gang steals over £3 million from a security depot in the Republic's biggest-ever cash robbery.

Tokyo, 25
Estimates of the cost of the damage caused by the Kobe earthquake rise to $100 billion.

Melbourne, 29
Andre Agassi beats Pete Sampras in the final of the Australian Open.

Algiers, 30
A car bomb believed to have been planted by Islamic extremists kills 38 and wounds 256 in central Algiers.

Washington DC, 31
Failing to get Congressional backing for his $40 billion rescue plan for the Mexican economy, Clinton instead pledges $20 billion on his own emergency authority.

London, 31
The leakage of plans for a joint North-South Irish authority causes alarm amongst Ulster Unionists.

Amsterdam, 31
More than 200,000 people are evacuated from their homes in eastern and central Holland as rising rivers burst their protective dykes.

CANBERRA, THURSDAY 26
Opposition leader quits in Australia

Alexander Downer, leader of the Federal Liberal Party, resigned today after just eight months in office. His resignation is widely seen as an act of sacrifice in order to keep his warring party together.

Downer is the sixth leader the Liberals have had since 1983, when Bob Hawke's Labour Party formed the first in what has since been an unbroken series of Labour administrations. John Howard is expected to take over as leader. Howard, 55, is one of the party's most respected figures, having previously held the post of Leader of the Opposition between 1985 and 1989.

LIMA, SUNDAY 29
Peru launches new attack on Ecuador

Four days of border clashes between Peru and Ecuador escalated today when the Peruvians launched a major offensive against their western neighbor. The fighting is along a 48-mile stretch of border in the Andes that has been in dispute since 1960. An earlier demarcation agreement determined the countries' mutual borders but in the last 30 years, Ecuador has chafed against being cut off from the Amazon. (→ February 16)

Massachusetts, Tuesday 24. Rose Kennedy, matriarch of the Kennedy clan, is buried at Brookline. She died on Sunday, at the age of 104.

TEL AVIV, SUNDAY 22
Suicide bomb attack near Tel Aviv kills 19

An Israeli soldier mourns his murdered comrades after the suicide bombing.

Nineteen people, mostly soldiers, were killed this morning and 61 injured in a double suicide bomb attack at Nordiya near the seaside town of Netanya. Islamic Jihad claimed responsibility, and said that two of its members blew themselves up in the attacks. The killings took place at 9:30 a.m. at a bus stop outside an army base. Rabbis wearing surgical gloves were still sorting through the remains several hours later trying to identify the victims.

The Israeli government responded to the attack by sealing off the occupied territories tonight, preventing Palestinians from entering the rest of the country.

WASHINGTON DC, TUESDAY 24
State of the Union address

President Clinton today delivered the longest-ever State of the Union address as he became the first Democratic president to face a Republican majority in both houses of Congress for 50 years. He emphasized conciliation and separation: conciliation in going along with the Republicans in reforming welfare, reducing government, cutting taxes, and clamping down on illegal immigration, and separation on the ways in which these should be done. He put himself forward as the champion of working Americans, seeking tax breaks on college fees for the middle classes, and a rise in the minimum wage from its current $5 an hour for blue collar workers. In a keynote passage he stated, "I am proud to say that I have made my mistakes, and I have learned again the importance of humility in all human endeavor. But I am also proud to say tonight that our country is stronger than it was two years ago."

LOS ANGELES, TUESDAY 24

O.J. Simpson trial begins

O.J. Simpson (right) makes a point to a defense attorney at the start of his trial for murder.

The trial of O.J. Simpson, accused of murdering his ex-wife and a friend, opened in a packed courtroom today. Chief Prosecutor Marcia Clark said that a trail of blood led from the house where Nicole Simpson was murdered, all the way to the bedroom of the former football star. The prosecution also alleged that Simpson is a deeply jealous man with a history of wife abuse, who regularly beat Nicole in the 15 years that they had known each other. The case had been scheduled to start yesterday, but last-minute arguments over admissability of evidence meant that opening statements had to be delayed. In a critical ruling Judge Lance A. Ito yesterday gave the defense permission to cross-examine key prosecution witness detective Mark Fuhrman for racial prejudice. (→ February 16)

WASHINGTON DC, MONDAY 23

US intelligence report that Iran paid $10 million for Lockerbie

A document released under the US Freedom of Information act casts doubt on the American and British governments' previous claims that only Libyan nationals were responsible for the Lockerbie bombing that killed 270 people when a Pan Am airliner exploded over Scotland in December 1988.

The document, a report compiled during the Gulf War by the US Air Force Signals Intelligence Unit, alleges that a minister in the Iranian government paid $10 million for the attack. The report accuses the minister of giving the same amount to the terrorist groups Abu Abbas and the PFLP-GC, led by Abu Nidal, for other terrorist activities. The document was obtained by the makers of a forthcoming television documentary about the Lockerbie bombing.

The governments of both the USA and the UK have maintained that Colonel Qaddafi, president of Libya, personally ordered the attack, and that it was carried out by two Libyans for whom American and Scottish courts have issued arrest warrants. The response of the British Foreign Office to the new report is that there is still a case for the Libyans to answer, and that it will continue to press for extradition. (→ February 4)

WASHINGTON DC, THURSDAY 26

House approves balanced budget bill

The first major victory of the new Republican majority in the House of Representatives was racked up today as the House voted an amendment of the Constitution that would prevent the federal government from spending more than it collects. Under its terms, by the year 2002 the government will have to work with annual budgets in which income is not exceeded by spending.

It is the fourth time since 1990 that conservatives have tried to get the House to accept such an amendment. Today's vote gave the bill's movers more than the two-thirds majority required for any amendment to the US constitution. All the Republicans bar two supported the measure, together with 72 democrats. The victory was a triumph for Speaker Newt Gingrich who had campaigned for the measure as part of his "Contract with America" to reduce excess government spending. Afterward he said, "It's a historic moment for the country. We kept our promise; we worked hard; we produced a real change." The amendment now has to be approved by the Senate, and if passed, it then goes to the state legislatures.

The requirement is not, however, a straitjacket. Deficit spending will still be allowed if supported by both houses of Congress, and the restriction could be suspended during a war.

Miami, Sunday 29. San Francisco 49ers' quarterback Steve Young celebrates his team's fifth title after their 49-26 Super Bowl victory over the San Diego Chargers. This was one of the most one-sided football finals in recent memory.

POLAND, FRIDAY 27

Ceremonies commemorate the liberation of Auschwitz

Fifty years ago today, advancing Soviet troops entered Auschwitz, in Poland, and liberated the survivors of the Nazis' largest factory of death. Both an extermination camp and a slave labor camp, Auschwitz has become the most potent symbol of the Holocaust.

Thirteen presidents, three kings, Nobel Peace Prize winners, camp survivors, and more than 10,000 mourners gathered at Auschwitz to commemorate the fiftieth anniversary of the liberation and the death of 1.5 million inmates, the majority of them Jews. A minute's silence was observed and prayers were offered in a moving ceremony for the dead.

The organization of the ceremony had provoked bitter controversy between Jewish groups and Polish Catholics. The Jews had feared that the commemorations, hosted by Polish president Lech Walesa, a committed Catholic, would downplay the specifically Jewish tragedy of the Holocaust. To Poles the camp is also a symbol of national suffering. But many Jews feel that the anti-Semitism prevalent in Poland contributed to the Holocaust.

Two days before the ceremony, Jewish activist and Nobel laureate Elie Wiesel, himself a camp survivor, made an impassioned attack on what he saw as complacent calls for a general spirit of reconciliation. Addressing a crowd of Auschwitz mourners, he said: "God, do not have mercy on those who have created this place. God of forgiveness, do not forgive those murderers of Jewish children here."

But in the event, the ceremony, which was attended by the German president, Helmut Kohl, was conducted with dignity and without dissent. As the world leaders toured Auschwitz's "bathhouses" for gassing prisoners, its corpse cellars, and its cremating ovens, none could remain unmoved by the evidence of what an agreed statement called "the biggest crime of the century."

Political and religious leaders attend the 50th anniversary commemorative service.

Memorial candles burn as a survivor mourns those who died in the camp.

Grim interior of an Auschwitz dormitory.

Faces and uniforms of some of the millions of victims displayed in the Auschwitz museum.

Joyous prisoners greet the Soviet army in 1945.

A funeral procession of prisoners after the liberation.

The children of Auschwitz look forward to freedom.

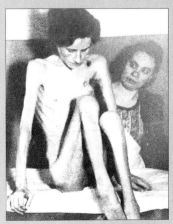

Many survivors were little more than skin and bones.

Concrete, barbed wire, and electrified fencing encircled the camp.

The anniversary was a time for solidarity.

S	M	T	W	T	F	S
			1	2	3	4
5	6	7	8	9	10	11
12	13	14	15	16	17	18
19	20	21	22	23	24	25
26	27	28				

Washington DC, 1
US State Department condemns human rights abuses in Russia and China. Moscow is accused of massive cruelty in Chechnya; Beijing is criticized for its crackdown in Tibet.

Washington DC, 1
Congress votes to make it harder for the Federal government to impose obligations on cities and states without providing necessary funds.

London, 1
A dispute over the export of live veal calves to Europe heats up after a protester is accidentally killed.

Washington DC, 1
American and European studies suggest that a new combination of drugs, including AZT, can suppress the AIDS virus.

Rome, 2
A third of the estate of Italian composer Giacomo Puccini is awarded to his son's illegitimate daughter after a wrangle with the family butler.

Oxford, 2
Britain's Oxford University drops its entrance exam, since it is thought to favor those from private schools.

Washington DC, 2
President Clinton meets with the federal mediator in an attempt to resolve the baseball dispute.
(→ March 29)

Paris, 2
Road deaths in France fell by 5.7% last year after new drunk-driving and seat-belt regulations.

Seattle, 2
Boeing cuts 7,000 jobs as airplane recession continues.

Chechnya, 4
Chechen rebels shoot down a Russian jet fighter in a defiant act as Russian shelling seals off the last roads into Grozny. (→ March 23)

Lockerbie, 4
Mystery about the 1988 Pan Am disaster over the Scottish town: The police surgeon issued 59 death certificates, but only 58 bodies were accounted for. (→ March 27)

Death
Fred Perry, British tennis champion in the 1930s and TV commentator, at age 85, February 2.

FRANKFURT, THURSDAY 2

International crisis in wake of peso bailout

The frenzied response of Mexican currency dealers to yesterday's deepening peso crisis.

Six European countries have refused to endorse President Clinton's plans to stabilize the Mexican peso, while in Washington DC, Alan Greenspan, Federal Reserve chairman, has described the current crisis as the worst in the world's currency dealings for 30 years.

Following Bill Clinton's personal commitment of US funds from the Exchange Stabilization Fund on Tuesday, the President today sought a package of $17.8 billion in loans for Mexico from the International Monetary Fund (IMF). Although the IMF agreed, Britain, Germany, Denmark, Switzerland, Belgium, and the Netherlands all abstained – an unprecedented public lack of support for US policy. Given only one hour to study the proposal, the Europeans felt that the IMF was being rushed into its largest-ever currency rescue operation, and that such action would deplete funds that would then be unavailable to support Eastern Europe and countries in the developing world.

Washington itself is unhappy with the bailout of Mexico. The President failed to get the approval of Congress to his original request for $40 billion. Even though Newt Gingrich and Bob Dole gave him their personal backing, they were not followed by fellow Republicans. (→ March 10)

BEIJING, WEDNESDAY 1

Jiang calls for talks with Taiwan

In a speech given to mark the Chinese New Year, President Jiang Zemin has called for talks with Taiwan to reunite it with mainland China. The call was given extensive coverage throughout official newspapers, where it was said that the ideas were "further elaboration" of Deng Xiaoping's views. Deng still wields enormous power in China, and the acknowledgment that his ideas are being developed by another political leader is not only unusual but reinforces Jiang's position as Deng's most likely successor.

London, Thursday 2. English character actor Donald Pleasence, 75, died today. His many films included *Hallowe'en* and *The Great Escape*.

LONDON, WEDNESDAY 1

Major moves to reassure Unionists

John Major endeavored tonight to reassure Ulster's Unionists that the government had their best interests at heart. This followed furious reactions to the news leaked yesterday that the British and Irish governments were planning a joint body that would have sweeping executive powers over the province. The British government then conceded that a framework document had been drawn up, but denied that it had been finally agreed. British Northern Ireland secretary, Sir Patrick Mayhew, repeated an earlier promise made by Mr. Major that no new agreements would be forced upon the people of Northern Ireland.

That Mr. Major made the appeal on nationwide television reflects the government's concern that Unionist hostility could derail the whole peace process. He urged Protestants to trust him and not to throw away the gains made by five months of peace. "Tonight I ask for time. And I ask for trust. And I promise to pursue a lasting peace."

NEW JERSEY, WEDNESDAY 1

Rutgers head made "racist" comments

Dr. Francis Lawrence, president of Rutgers University, has come under attack for his remarks at a faculty meeting in November. He is quoted as having said that "genetic hereditary background" made it harder for black students to pass entrance examinations. He claimed today that he had jumbled his words, but his defense does not satisfy students at a university that has one of the highest proportions of blacks in the country.

AMSTERDAM, WEDNESDAY 1

Europe hit by worst floods since 1945

Aerial view of flood-stricken Charleville-Mézières in northeast France.

Tonight, as flood waters rose across Holland, Belgium, France, and Germany, more people have fled their homes than at any time since World War II. More than 200,000 Dutch people have already abandoned their homes as water levels rose to danger levels in the south and east of the country. The situation is particularly bad near Ochten, in eastern Holland, where a dyke has already cracked, fueling fears that other dykes are weakening under the increased pressure from rising water. The situation remains highly unpredictable. "It is extremely difficult to make a reasonable estimate of the danger," said Interior Minister Hans Dijkstal.

Flooding and storms have left 29 dead across western Europe and have caused hundreds of millions of dollars' worth of damage. The low-lying area around Cologne in western Germany bordering on the swollen Rhine have been badly hit, as have parts of northern Belgium. The rainfall is now easing, and although a state of emergency has been declared in Holland, it is hoped that the worst has passed.

MOSCOW, THURSDAY 2

Moscow politician in "Mafia" shooting

Russian MP Sergei Skorochkin, 33, who took on the so-called Russian "Mafia," has been found murdered. He had been handcuffed and shot in the head.

As a businessman he refused to pay off local gangsters, and in May he shot dead a Georgian bandit who was threatening him. To ordinary Russians, Skorochkin became something of a hero as the first prominent politician to make a principled stand.

The influence of the Russian "Mafia" has been growing rapidly in recent years. However, in a country with endemic bureaucratic corruption that is still unused to entrepreneurial methods, it is often hard to distinguish between aggressive business methods and organized crime. Russian gang wars have spread far and wide, and murders as far away as London and New York have been attributed to them.

Skorochkin's body was found by the police in a village near Moscow. Four men claiming to be police officers seized him two days ago in a restaurant. Wearing masks and carrying automatic rifles, they told the customers they were looking for drugs and weapons. (→March 1)

Bootleg items are widely available in China.

WASHINGTON DC, SATURDAY 4

Trade war looms as US puts tariff on Chinese goods

President Bill Clinton has imposed punitive duties on over $1 billion worth of Chinese imports, winning praise from right-wing Republicans.

The move is in response to the failure of the Chinese to deal with alleged widespread piracy of software, movie, and music copyrights. "The Chinese have a habit of stealing our intellectual property rights," said Newt Gingrich. "They can't cheat us and expect to have our market open." The tariffs will be levied at 100 percent of the price of the goods, and will be imposed on a range of items from silk clothing to cellular telephones. The sanctions are designed to hit only goods that can be obtained elsewhere, so as not to deprive American consumers or businesses of important commodities. Some companies said immediately that they would purchase these goods elsewhere in Asia. However, some business people are nervous about the prospect of a trade war with the world's third largest economy.

There are three weeks to go before the sanctions are enforced, giving China time to reconsider. The issue has been a sore point for some time, since inexpensive copies of American electronic, video, and audio products are sold widely throughout Asia. The issue was taken up with China in 1992, at which point the country passed stringent laws against copyright piracy. But China has failed to enforce the laws, even against state-owned industries. American determination will be noted in other countries where piracy of intellectual property is common. (→February 26)

Miami Beach, Wednesday 1. George Abbott, Broadway producer of *Pal Joey*, *The Pajama Game*, and *A Funny Thing Happened on the Way to the Forum*, has died at age 107.

S	M	T	W	T	F	S
			1	2	3	4
5	6	7	8	9	10	11
12	13	14	15	16	17	18
19	20	21	22	23	24	25
26	27	28				

Sicily, 5
The Mafia's first "godmother" is arrested by the Italian police. She became a "woman of honor" two years ago after her clan-chief husband was jailed for 21 years for murder.

Washington DC, 6
Four Catholic priests have been sacked after admitting sexual abuse of an altar boy.

Dallas, 6
Mark Thatcher is named in a lawsuit arising from his takeover of an aviation fuel company. The petitioner is asking for $21 million compensation. (→ April 8)

New York, 6
In the World Trade Center terrorist trial, one defendant pleads guilty of conspiring to assassinate President Mubarak of Egypt and turns state's evidence. (→ February 8)

Washington DC, 6
Republicans press to revive "Star Wars" defensive system, albeit on a smaller scale.

Johannesburg, 7
ANC leader Dr. Allan Boesak embezzled funds during the apartheid years, an inquiry finds.

Washington DC, 7
The White House says that Michael P.C. Carns, a retired Air Force general, will be the next CIA head.

Crimea, 8
Russia and Ukraine settle their dispute over the future of the Black Sea fleet. Russia rents part of Sebastopol, which will remain a Russian base.

Colombia, 8
At least 23 people are killed and 200 injured in an earthquake. Worst hit is the city of Pereira.

India, 8
India's ruling Congress (I) party faces defeat at poll in the crucial western state of Maharastra.

Washington DC, 9
Former vice-president Dan Quayle drops out of the 1996 Presidential race, stating lack of funds.

Death
J. William Fulbright, senator who opposed the Vietnam War, at age 89, February 9.

HOUSTON, MONDAY 6
Mir and Discovery meet in space

The US space shuttle *Discovery* flew within 33 ft (10 m) of Russia's *Mir* space station in a rehearsal for the planned docking of the two craft in June. Earlier the Russians banned the shuttle from coming within 1,000 ft (300 m) of *Mir*, because they were concerned about a leaking thruster and feared that chunks of frozen nitrogen might damage the space station's solar panels. But American scientists were able to convince them that the danger was nonexistent.

This was the first rendezvous between US and Russian spacecraft for 20 years, and both crews agreed that the fly-by − at 17,500 mph (28,000 kmph), 315 miles (500 km) above South America − was one of the most beautiful things they had ever seen. (→ March 16)

Right: Mir *seen from* Discovery.

Below: The crew of the US space shuttle Discovery *pose for publicity photographs before taking off on their latest mission.*

Los Angeles, Monday 6. Actor Doug McClure, 59, has died. He first achieved fame as Trampas in the TV series *The Virginian* and went on to star in B-movies such as *The Land that Time Forgot*.

LONDON, WEDNESDAY 8
"Coal first used 74,000 years ago"

Cavemen came home to real coal fires, according to an article this week in the prestigious British science journal *Nature*. An article supplied by French researchers claims that Stone Age man was burning coal nearly 74,000 years ago. Previously, the use of coal as a fuel had been traced back only 18,000 years.

Isabelle Thery and a team from the University of Montpellier have unearthed evidence from fossils in hearths at Les Canalettes and Les Usclades in the southern Massif Central in France. These showed that early man had collected coal from local outcrops during periods when firewood was scarce.

Coal outcrops are not confined to that area of France, and the use of coal as a fuel could have been widespread from even earlier times. The advantages to early humans would have been manifold. Coal provides higher temperatures and a more constant heat than wood and is of particular value in cooking.

The discovery indicates that early humans were more sophisticated than had previously been believed. It is possible that they found other technological uses for the greater heat obtained from coal fires. How they first came to realize that coal was combustible, and how they lit their fires, are still mysteries.

BOSNIA, SATURDAY 11
Bosnian cease-fire violations threaten latest peace plan

The designated Muslim safe havens are under increased pressure from the Bosnian Serbs.

The recent cease-fire in Bosnia seems to be going the way of all the others as tension mounts on five fronts. Heavy fighting has taken place throughout the last week in the so-called safe haven of Bihac, while there have also been hostilities in the enclaves at Srebenica and Gorazde. Government troops are massing by the Posavina Corridor in the northeast, where Serb positions are vulnerable. Most

ominously, President Tudjman of Croatia has asked the UN to remove its troops from his country, implying that he is about to attack Krajina, the region lost to the Serbs in 1991.

The UN has recorded 62 helicopter flights in five days as Serbia moves military supplies to Bosnia in flat violation of Serbian president Milosevic's purported blockade of the Bosnian Serbs. (→ March 6)

WASHINGTON DC, WEDNESDAY 8
House aims to cut death row appeals

In a victory for supporters of the death penalty, the House of Representatives today voted to reduce the time allowed to prisoners on death row to appeal against their executions. By a majority of 297 to 132 the House voted to restrict the use of habeas corpus appeals by state prisoners, allowing them only one petition, which must be made within six months of their exhausting their state appeals.

In a simultaneous move, the House approved a measure that would allow prosecutors to use in-court evidence seized illegally, including evidence obtained without a search warrant. Supporters of the bill claim it will prevent guilty people from escaping conviction on technicalities, while opponents say that the bill violates the rights of the accused, specifically the Fourth Amendment protection against unreasonable seizure.

The electric chair.

Paris, Tuesday 7. Work began on a much-needed new coat of paint for the city's 106-year-old Eiffel Tower. It is expected that the job will take around three years to complete.

ISLAMABAD, WEDNESDAY 8
Bombing suspect extradited

Ramzi Ahmed Yousef, the man suspected of masterminding the 1993 bombing of the World Trade Center in New York, was arrested by Pakistani authorities and handed over to the FBI, who immeditely flew him to New York, where he arrived this evening. It is believed that Yousef was personally responsible for the making of the World Trade Center bomb.

Yousef, who has been on the FBI's Most Wanted List since shortly after the bombing, disappeared despite a massive international manhunt. He was indicted *in absentia* on 11 felony counts, along with four other defendants, all of whom were tried and convicted and then given sentences that totaled 240 years in jail. Recent sightings of the 27-year-old Yousef were reported in various places round the world.

Filipino police, who believed he was behind a failed plot to kill the Pope during his visit to the Philippines last month, called the FBI, but on arrival there US federal agents were unable to locate him. An informer tipped off the Pakistanis that Yousef was in their capital; they then seized him in a surprise raid. President Clinton has hailed the arrest as a major breakthrough in the fight against terrorism. (→ April 3)

BONN, MONDAY 6
German metalworkers plan nationwide strike

German metalworkers go out on a one-day strike in support of their pay claim.

The massive German engineering union, IG Metall, is preparing for a nationwide strike. The union's three million members are threatening to withdraw their labor if employers do not accede to their demands for a 6 percent pay increase. The union has warned that employees' patience is wearing thin. Some 247,000 have already walked out in one-day local strikes over the past weeks.

Employers want cost-cutting measures to be included in wage talks. But the union is adamant that it has not received a suitable response to its pay claim. It says that talks are now over and that it will soon be holding a strike ballot.

S	M	T	W	T	F	S
			1	2	3	4
5	6	7	8	9	10	11
12	13	14	15	16	17	18
19	20	21	22	23	24	25
26	27	28				

Pretoria, 12
President Mandela tells his estranged wife, Winnie, to apologize or resign after she criticized his government, of which she is a member. (→ March 1)

Angola, 12
A congress of Unita rebel leaders accepts the terms of a peace treaty drawn up in November 1994.

Zaire, 13
Médecins Sans Frontières pulls out of refugee camps around Rwanda, fearing that its presence strengthens the Hutu militia.

Mexico City, 13
Two thousand troops begin searching for "Marcos," the elusive guerrilla leader of the Zapatista rebels.

Algiers, 13
Muslim fundamentalists kill the director of Algeria's national theater.

Israel, 13
Israel and the PLO agree to resume talks in the face of suicide attacks by Palestine extremists.

Washington DC, 14
Congress starts work on a bill meant to reduce the President's power to send troops on UN missions.

Islamabad, 14
Prime Minister Benazir Bhutto confirms the death penalty imposed on a 14-year-old for blasphemy.

Karachi, 14
Sectarian fighting in Karachi leaves 20 dead, bringing the death toll in the city this month to 83.

Italy, 14
A 5,300-year-old mummified man found in the Alps is to go on display in a museum in the Italy.

Washington DC, 16
President Clinton asks Congress for more money to stop illegal immigration from Mexico.

Montgomery, 16
Tornado kills three in Alabama.

Los Angeles, 16
Key witness in the O.J. Simpson trial, Rosa Lopez, leaves the country and returns to El Salvador. (→ March 1)

London, 17
UK government starts to lift orders banning Irish Republicans from mainland Britain.

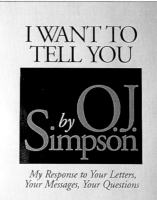

I WANT TO TELL YOU

S. *by* O.J. Simpson

My Response to Your Letters, Your Messages, Your Questions

New York, Wednesday 15. O. J. Simpson's recently penned life story, *I Want To Tell You*, tops the *New York Times'* best-seller list.

JERUSALEM, TUESDAY 14
Anniversary of Israel massacre

At least one Palestinian was killed and scores were injured today as rioting broke out across the West Bank on the first anniversary of the massacre of 29 Muslims by Baruch Goldstein, a Jewish settler. A general strike brought the town of Hebron to a standstill, and Israeli security forces were put on full alert amid fears of attacks on military bases.

WASHINGTON DC, MONDAY 13
Clinton's new surgeon general comes under fire

The White House attempted today to fight off right-wing critics of President Clinton's choice for Surgeon General, Dr. Henry W. Foster Jr. Opponents of the nominee claim that he is unsuitable for the post, having performed a number of abortions and for having sterilized severely mentally retarded black women over 20 years ago.

A beleaguered White House Chief of Staff, Leon E. Panetta, said that Foster's critics are a coalition of opportunistic extremists and anti-abortionists "who are basically saying, 'We want to make illegal a woman's right to choose.'" He made it clear that the President was committed to the nomination, although many Democrats think the President has made a mistake and may have to back down.

The issue of abortion has maintained a high profile since the killing of two women receptionists at a Massachussetts abortion clinic last year. The "pro-life" lobby has kept up its pressure, and the President's proposed appointment has given them a new target.

Palestinians praying at the spot where 29 were killed by an Israeli gunman in 1994.

New York, Thursday 16. Governor Pataki displays the new law that sees the return of the death penalty to New York State after 33 years. The Congress, Senate, and Governor of the state today agreed that judicial execution should be reintroduced, although it is expected to be ten years before the first sentence is carried out.

BOSTON, MONDAY 13
Low sperm counts fear

Average sperm counts are down by 2.1 per cent over a 20-year period, says a report published in the *New England Journal of Medicine*. Based on a survey of Parisian men carried out between 1973 and 1992, the report confirms widespread suspicions of a decline in male fertility across the western world.

Various theories have been put forward to explain the decline. Many scientists now believe that the reason is that more substances containing the female hormone estrogen are being produced and finding their way into the food cycle. Estrogen would have a direct bearing on the production of male hormones. Another explanation blames the tightness of modern trousers.

SOUTH AMERICA, THURSDAY 16

Peru and Ecuador end border fighting

Ecuadorian troops at a checkpoint on their way to the disputed border region.

After three weeks of border skirmishes, Peru and Ecuador signed a cease-fire today in the Brazilian capital. The agreement, which followed a plan drawn up by Argentina, Brazil, Chile, and the US, will be monitored by international observers along the 48-mile (77-km) stretch of the Andes that has been the scene of fighting since January 26.

The dispute stems from the 1942 Rio Protocol – of which the US is a guarantor – that regulates the border areas between the two countries, but which failed to provide proper demarcation of the disputed area. Ecuador rejected the Protocol as long ago as 1960 and has been pursuing its claim ever since. The Ecuadorian grievance is that the treaty effectively cut the country off from access to the Amazon and deprived it of several tracts of territory that previously belonged to it.

Observers will be in place along the border within 48 hours and will stay initially for 90 days. During that time a demilitarized zone will be established and bilateral negotiations will begin. President Alberto Fujimori of Peru, up for reelection later this year, said that the agreement was "broadly acceptable."

BOSTON, MONDAY 13

Reconciliation speech in Dresden

In a candlelit ceremony in Dresden, Germany's president Roman Herzog gave a powerful speech on the fiftieth anniversary of the night on which the greater part of this historic city was destroyed by concerted Allied fire-bomb attacks.

Representatives of the British, American, and German governments heard him call for an end to "bookkeeping exercises in monstrosity," in which historians tried to adjudicate between the sides and apportion degrees of blame for the crimes against humanity committed during World War II.

The tone of the President's speech, and indeed the atmosphere of the whole nocturnal ceremony, were of healing and reconciliation.

MINEOLA, NEW YORK, FRIDAY 17

Jamaican convicted of Railroad Massacre

Colin Ferguson, convicted murderer.

Jamaican immigrant Colin Ferguson was today convicted of the "Long Island Railroad Massacre," in which six people were gunned down on an evening commuter train. He was also found guilty on a further 22 counts of attempted murder, possession of illegal weapons, and endangerment of life. He was cleared on 25 counts of civil rights' violations.

Ferguson's defense, which he largely conducted himself, involved him in personal cross-examination of a number of individuals who he had tried to kill during his rampage through the train. The court announced that he will be sentenced on March 22. (→ March 22)

Manila, Monday 13. The ownership of the idyllic Spratly Islands, which barely rise above the surface of the South China Sea, is under dispute. President Fidel Ramos of the Philippines has ordered large numbers of troops to protect the islands against possible invasion in response to recent increases in the Chinese naval presence in the area.

S	M	T	W	T	F	S
			1	2	3	4
5	6	7	8	9	10	11
12	13	14	15	16	17	18
19	20	21	22	23	24	25
26	27	28				

Atlanta, 19
The American Association for the Advancement of Science is told by the director of the Alaskan Native Language Center that between 5% and 10% of the world's 6,000 languages will die out during the next century, due to the spread of English.

Brussels, 19
NATO Secretary General Willy Claes denies receiving bribes for an Italian helicopter contract in 1988 when he was Minister for Economic Affairs for Belgium. (→ October 20)

Washington DC, 19
The National Association for the Advancement of Colored People votes out its leader William Gibson and replaces him with Myrlie Evers-William, widow of the murdered civil rights activist Medger Evers.

France, 20
The fossilized remains of a previously unknown species of two-legged dinosaur have been unearthed in southeastern France.

Paris, 20
A senior French policeman resigns over the wiretapping of a politician authorized by Prime Minister Edouard Balladur.

Seoul, 20
Reports state that North Korea has testfired a missile that has a range of 937 miles (1,500 km) – enough to reach Japan.

San Francisco, 21
AIDS patients with only three months to live are to be experimentally injected with bone marrow cells from baboons immune to the HIV virus.

Hanoi, 23
Vietnam speeds up repatriation of boat people, aiming to empty the refugee camps in Hong Kong and Southeast Asia by the end of the year.

New York, 23
The Dow Jones industrial average breaks 4,000 for the first time.

Beijing, 26
China agrees to crack down on copyright infringement, ending its dispute with the US.

Malaysia, 26
A 14-year-old boy who ran away from his London home with his father's passport and two of his credit cards is found.

MOGADISHU, MONDAY 20

Marines land in Somalia

Déjà vu – Marines land on the beach at Mogadishu, to assist in the withdrawal of UN forces.

Marines have again stormed the beach at Mogadishu, in a rerun of the US landing here two years ago. But this time their aim is not to aid the Somali people. The task force of 2,500 US Marines and 500 Italian marines backed by helicopters, gunships, and a fleet of 18 vessels is here to oversee the withdrawal of the remaining 2,500 UN troops who have been stuck in the midst of the Somali civil war. The beachhead is a tiny area of land where both the city's port and airport are located. It is now surrounded by razor wire bearing notices warning Somalis not to cross it. Eighty armored vehicles are being brought ashore, along with a force of 14,000 American, British, Italian, French, and Malaysian troops. They will form a rearguard as the remains of the failed UN peacekeeping force are withdrawn.

Two years ago 28,000 US troops landed in the same spot to try to restore order and end the famine in this lawless country. Now Somalia has been given up as a lost cause, and the country, torn apart by clan violence, is to be left to its own devices.

NEW HAMPSHIRE, SUNDAY 19

Dole emerges as early front runner for Republicans

Bob Dole addresses Republicans.

The 1996 presidential election campaign opened in Manchester, NH, a full year before the first primary. At a fund-raising dinner given by the New Hampshire Republican Party nine "wannabes" presented their cases for becoming the next US president. Each was allowed eight minutes to address next year's voters, and most of them struck favorite Republican themes – cutting back on government and reducing taxes.

First polls in the state show Bob Dole, the Kansan majority leader in the Senate, to be the man to beat. But Phil Gramm of Texas, former governor of Tennessee Lamar Alexander, and Pennsylvanian Arlen Specter also made strong claims.

Beijing, Sunday 19. Swedish group Roxette becomes the first major rock band to play China in ten years after Wham! had displeased Chinese authorities.

RANGOON, TUESDAY 21
Last rebel stronghold falls in Burma

Hundreds of Karen guerrillas are pouring across the border into Thailand after Kawmoora, their last outpost in Burma (Myanmar), fell to government troops. The Karen have been fighting for independence for over 50 years. They first split from Rangoon during World War II, when they were allies of the British against the Japanese. However, the writing has been on the wall for the Karen separatists since other Burmese ethnic minorities signed a cease-fire with the military government in 1992, leaving them isolated. Their position was further weakened last December, when 500 Buddhist Karen mutinied against the Christian leadership of their 4,000-strong army.

Rebel spokesmen say that several Karen soldiers were rendered unconscious by shells that contained outlawed gases. The government denies using chemical weapons as well as allegations that they executed wounded prisoners.

Burmese government troops displaying captured Karen arms.

HONG KONG, MONDAY 20
Chinese business scandal shock waves reach Hong Kong

A senior Chinese businessman and personal friend of Deng Xiaoping is under suspicion of corruption, while his son has been arrested for "commercial crimes." Five companies connected with the individuals suspended trading on the Hong Kong Stock Exchange today.

Zhou Guanwu, 77, chairman of one of the largest state-owned enterprises in China, the Capital Iron and Steel Corporation, resigned suddenly last Tuesday. Then it was announced during the weekend that Zhou Beifang, his 41-year-old son, chairman of Capital Iron and Steel's Hong Kong affiliate, had been detained for "economic crimes." The elder Mr. Zhou has known Deng since the 1940s.

The Hong Kong Stock Exchange.

LONDON, MONDAY 27
Collapse of British bank

One of the City of London's most revered merchant banks has collapsed, following dramatic losses in Singapore. Barings Bank, which was founded in 1767, faces losses of over $1.2 billion as the result of trading by one of its employees, Nick Leeson. Twenty-eight-year-old Leeson gambled huge sums on the Japanese futures market over a two-month period, and lost. Leeson, who is now on the run, is believed to have left Singapore.

Frantic efforts are taking place to find a buyer for the bank. If none comes forward some 4,000 jobs will be at risk, and all deposits will be frozen. These include $1.5 million belonging to the Prince's Trust, a charity established by Prince Charles, the heir to the British throne. The London stock market fell sharply at the news. (→ March 5)

Moscow, Monday 27. Cranach's *The Fall of Man* is one of the works on show in an exhibition of paintings looted by the Nazis. It is the first time they have been seen in public since the Second World War.

PARIS, WEDNESDAY 22
Five US citizens expelled from France for spying

An American woman, said to be working undercover in Paris, and four US embassy officials, including the CIA's Paris bureau chief, are being expelled from France for industrial espionage. The incident marks the lowest point in Franco-US relations for 20 years.

In 1992–3 the US and France were at loggerheads on the General Agreement on Tariffs and Trade (GATT), when the French refused to remove controls on the number of American movies and television programs allowed to be broadcast in the country. According to the French, the CIA tried to bribe a senior adviser to prime minister Edouard Balladur and a Cultural Ministry official with access to key communications. The CIA was hoping they would divulge information on France's negotiating position on the issue. The French claim to have photographic evidence to support these allegations, along with credit card receipts in false names.

MISSISSIPPI, WEDNESDAY 22
Legal ruling opens door to massive suits against tobacco companies

A judge in Mississippi has undermined cigarette companies' classic defense against claims for damages for their products' effects on health. Traditionally they argue that individuals choose to smoke of their own free will, but the Judge has ruled that this has no validity in a case brought by the State of Mississippi for compensation for tax payers' money spent on the health care costs of people who could not afford private insurance.

The ruling opens the door to other claims across the US, with the prospect of the tobacco companies being presented with a massive total bill.

S	M	T	W	T	F	S
			1	2	3	4
5	6	7	8	9	10	11
12	13	14	15	16	17	18
19	20	21	22	23	24	25
26	27	28	29	30	31	

Moscow, 1
Boris Yeltsin sacks Moscow's police chief and its public prosecutor because of the spate of Mafia killings.

Soweto, 1
Winnie Mandela's home is raided by the police, looking for evidence of fraud and corruption. (→ March 27)

Batavia, Illinois, 2
Physicists find the "top quark," a vital sub-proton particle predicted by theory but never before observed.

Palermo, 2
Former Italian Prime Minister Giulio Andreotti is indicted on a charge of protecting the Mafia while in office.

Indianapolis, 2
Officers of a company making turboprops admit they missed the significance of evidence that their planes became unstable when iced, but deny any design fault.

Mogadishu, 3
The last US troops pull out of Somalia.

Washington DC, 3
The Justice Department says it is bringing a suit against Illinois State University for running a janitor training program that discriminates against white males.

Mexico City, 3
Former president Carlos Salinas de Gortari goes on a hunger strike protesting both claims that he covered up the assassination of his main political rival and the arrest of his brother on another murder charge, then calls it off after a few hours.

Rome, 3
The Pope reschedules to this fall his postponed visit to Newark, New York, and Baltimore. (→ October 4)

Washington DC, 3
President Clinton offers qualified support to Boris Yeltsin and counters Bob Dole's argument two days ago that he should distance himself on account of the Chechnya conflict.

Los Alamos, 4
Scientists speculate that a proposed underground dump for atomic waste in Nevada might blow up.

DENVER, WEDNESDAY 1
Denver airport opens – finally

With a United Airlines flight to Kansas City at 6 a.m., the most modern airport in the US opened this morning, amid continuing controversy over its cost. The final check for Denver airport runs to $4.9 billion, some $2 billion over budget. The airport is also opening 16 months later than scheduled.

With its gleaming white roof like a row of tents, the airport certainly looks the part, and its state-of-the-art landing systems mean that it is the only airport in the world where three airplanes can land simultaneously in bad weather. On the other hand, its $193 million baggage handling system had to be overhauled when it started to rip the suitcases.

An inquiry into the building costs and the financing of the airport is being conducted by the Federal Aviation Administration, the local US Attorney, and three other bodies.

The gleaming white roofs of the terminal top the first major new US airport for 21 years.

Los Angeles, Thursday 2. Sheryl Crow wins three Grammys: the record of the year for "All I Wanna Do," Best Female Pop Vocal Performance, and Best New Artist. Also in the awards are Bruce Springsteen, writer of the Best Song, "Streets of Philadelphia," and the Rolling Stones (Best Rock album).

LOS ANGELES, FRIDAY 3
Man gets 25 years for stealing pizza

California's "three strikes and you're out" law exacted a tough punishment on Jerry Dewayne Williams, 27, today. He was sentenced to 25 years-to-life for stealing a slice of pizza.

Williams had taken the pizza from four children who were eating it at Redondo Beach. As he had five previous convictions for drug possession and robbery, he met the law's requirement for a lengthy sentence for anyone convicted of two previous felonies. The case has reopened the controversy about the law, designed to reduce crime in the state. Allan Parachini, of the American Civil Liberties Union, said, "No matter how many pizza thieves it sends to prison this law is not going to make our streets safer." The prosecuting attorney, Bill Gravlin, defended the law: "The people of California are sick of revolving-door justice and they're sick of judges who are soft on crime."

Ironically, Williams threw the pizza into the sea because it contained pepperoni, which he does not like.

LOS ANGELES, WEDNESDAY 1
New O.J. trial problem as juror is dismissed

A 46-year-old black man has been dismissed from the O.J. Simpson jury following accusations that he showed overt support for Simpson during the jury's visit to the former football star's home. He becomes the fourth juror to be dismissed.

The man wore a San Francisco 49ers cap on the visit (the 49ers were O.J.'s last team as a professional), and was alleged to have lingered over photos of O.J. in the house, despite the judge's order to ignore them. He is also said to have omitted to put on the jury questionnaire previous experience with domestic violence.

The juror is alleged to have made a bet with a colleague before the trial that Simpson would be acquitted. He is also alleged to have said that a book he planned to write about the trial would be more successful if there were a hung jury. Judge Ito did not give his reasons for the dismissal.

LONDON, WEDNESDAY 1
Top Tory rebels against Major

The Conservative government in Britain is furious over the decision by the former Chancellor of the Exchequer, Norman Lamont, to side with the opposition in a crucial vote. Labour leader Tony Blair has tabled a motion criticizing the government's stance on Europe. Norman Lamont, who was fired by John Major two years ago, voted for the motion. The government, however, managed to scrape through the vote. Mr. Lamont was believed to be exacting retribution for his dismissal.

WASHINGTON DC, THURSDAY 2

Democrats narrowly halt balanced budget measure

Senate Republican leader Bob Dole at his Washington press conference after the balanced budget amendment fails.

Senate Democrats are celebrating tonight after inflicting their first reverse on the Republicans' Contract with America, having defeated by a single vote a constitutional amendment to enforce a balanced federal budget by the year 2002. Bob Dole, the Republican leader in the Senate, had been trying for three days to get the two-thirds majority necessary to pass a constitutional amendment, but with Republican Senator Mark Hatfield of Oregon intransigent in his opposition to the measure he eventually had to give up. Fourteen Democrats supported the amendment, but amid bitter exchanges and recriminations, no others could be found to vote with them.

The amendment would probably have been passed if the Republicans had added a wording barring the use of the Social Security trust fund to help reduce the deficit. An opinion poll last week showed wide support among the population for balancing the budget, but only if it was not at the cost of cutting Social Security.

WASHINGTON DC, FRIDAY 3

Senator switches to Republicans

Senator Ben Nighthorse Campbell.

Bob Dole has welcomed a notable convert from the Democrats. The first Native American to serve as a senator in 60 years, Ben Nighthorse Campbell, a 63-year-old Cheyenne, told the President that he was defecting to join the Republicans, out of sympathy with their campaign to reduce the power of government.

MIDLAND, MICHIGAN, FRIDAY 3

Neo-Nazis charged with murder of parents in Pennsylvania

Bryan and David Freeman, in police custody on suspicion of murdering their parents.

Two teenage skinheads have been charged with murdering their parents and their younger brother at their home in Salisbury Township, Pennsylvania. Following a traced call, the FBI were waiting for them when they arrived at a house in Hope, Michigan, two days after the bodies were found.

Bryan Freeman, 17, and David Freeman, 15, both weighing over 225 lbs (101 kg), are covered with neo-Nazi tattoos. Both are followers of the Pennsylvania-based Christian Identity Movement cult, which preaches that God will instruct whites to kill all non-Aryans at the Apocalypse, starting in the US.

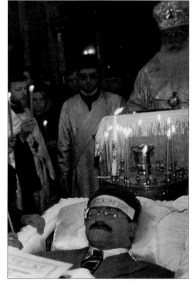

Moscow, Saturday 4. The body of the chief of one of Russia's main TV channels, Vladislav Listyev, 38, lies in his coffin before his funeral. He was shot outside his home on Monday. Listyev, a popular public figure, was waging a campaign to stamp out corruption in the press and TV.

London, 5
The Dutch banking group ING buys the collapsed Barings merchant bank for £1, but will inject capital of $1 billion.

Beijing, 5
Chinese Premier Li Peng admits that the country's economic boom has brought in its wake high inflation, corruption, and increased crime.

Tokyo, 5
Arguments rage among members of the Japanese parliament over whether the country should apologize to other Asian nations for World War II.

San Diego, 5
Australia's America's Cup contender, a favorite for the finals, sinks.

Copenhagen, 6
UN World Summit on Social Development opens. About 100 world leaders will discuss poverty, unemployment, civil unrest, and uncontrolled migration.

Zagreb, 6
Croatia and Bosnia sign a pact establishing a common military front against the Serbs. (→ March 27)

New York, 7
New York State Governor Pataki signs the death penalty bill into law. The law will take effect on September 1.

Karachi, 8
Two Americans are killed and one injured as gunmen open fire on their van from a taxi during the rush hour.

Washington DC, 8
A CIA report says that 90% of "ethnic cleansing" in the former Yugoslavia was carried out by Serbs, and that leading politicians were certainly involved.

Washington DC, 10
The jobless rate unexpectedly falls to a four-year low of 5.4%.

Deaths
Edward L. Bernays, widely regarded as the "father of public relations," at age 103 in Cambridge, Massachusett, March 9.

Ian Ballantine, pioneering paperback publisher, at age 79 in New York State, March 9.

LOS ANGELES, WEDNESDAY 8

Hamburgers cause more pollution than buses in Los Angeles

A McDonalds in the Los Angeles suburbs. Are such fast-food outlets major polluters?

Researchers at the University of California have found that fast foods such as hamburgers produce nine times more pollution in Los Angeles than the city's buses, and could be a major contributor to poor health.

The leader of the research team said that pollution was mainly created by the broiling, in which fat drips out of the hamburgers and is burned off at high temperatures. The researchers estimate that fast-food restaurants account for 13.7 tons of smoke every day, and 19 tons of organic compounds. These reflect sunlight, adding to the smog which has become synonymous with the city. They could also increase the risk of cancer and respiratory problems.

Environmental officials in California are now pressing for legislation to force fast-food restaurants to change the fare they serve, or else to install pollution control devices. Restaurateurs are challenging the experiment's findings.

The researchers cooked thousands of hamburgers and hundreds of fish, beef, and chicken products every day during the program.

WASHINGTON DC, FRIDAY 10

CIA nominee withdraws

Another White House nomination for office crashed to the ground today as retired US Air Force General Michael Carns withdrew his name for the post of Director of the CIA. Previously regarded as upright and honorable, Carns has been rocked by accusations of impropriety leveled by a Filipino he brought as a youth to the United States in the early 1980s and treated as an adopted son. Carns has denied the allegations, calling them "groundless, outrageous tabloid charges," but he has admitted that he mishandled the affair. Mr. Clinton has asked Deputy Defense Secretary John Deutch to head the agency.

GENEVA, WEDNESDAY 8

UN shirks China rights criticism

For the first time ever, the United Nations agreed to consider a motion criticizing China on its human rights record. However, the UN Human Rights Commission then voted against the motion, which would have required the commission to investigate rights in China, by 21 votes to 20. In the past China has succeeded in preventing such motions, but a similar attempt earlier in the day to block a French resolution was defeated by one vote.

WASHINGTON DC, WEDNESDAY 8

Dollar's four-day plunge

A four-day fall in the value of the dollar has seen it drop to 1.37 German marks from 1.46, and to 90.05 Japanese yen from 96.7. Overall the dollar has declined in value by 10 percent against the mark since the beginning of the year. The decline was halted today when Alan Greenspan, chairman of the Federal Reserve, hinted at a possible hike in interest rates. The fall may have been triggered by Mr. Greenspan's earlier suggestions that interest rates would fall. He linked the weakness to the government deficit. (→ March 23)

San Francisco, Sunday 5. The top two men's tennis players in the world, Pete Sampras and Andre Agassi, surprise passersby in San Francisco by playing a game of tennis in the street. The stunt is a fund-raising ploy for charity.

Spain sends gunboat to confront Canada

A week of conflict in the North Atlantic came to a head today as Spain sent a gunboat to protect its trawlers fishing in international waters off Newfoundland. Canadian coastguardsmen are already patrolling the area on the lookout for Spanish fishing vessels, and one Spanish trawler has been seized and is on its way to Canada, following a four-hour chase by three Canadian ships.

The argument is over Greenland halibut. A meeting last month of the North Atlantic Fisheries Organization ruled that Europe's share should be only 3,400 tons, compared with last year's catch of 40,000. Canada's permitted amount increased more than four times. The European Commission lodged an objection but, citing the need to protect fish stocks, Canada ordered all EU trawlers out of the area, which is in international waters. (→ March 14)

New austerity measures from Mexican Government

Guillermo Ortiz fighting for the peso.

As the peso fell to another new low on international exchanges, Mexico's Treasury Secretary, Guillermo Ortiz, has announced a package of emergency measures. Increases in the minimum wage will not exceed 10 percent, while the sales tax will rise five percent to 10 percent, and electricity and gas prices will rise by 35 percent. Other wage rises are not restricted, but subsidies of basic foodstuffs will increase to try to protect the poor. Inflation is expected to level out, according to Señor Ortiz, at 42 percent by the end of the year.

New York, Tuesday 7. Carol Shaya-Castro is dismissed from her job as a New York police-woman for posing both nude and in her uniform in *Playboy*, who paid her $100,000.

O.J.'s defense presents theory

O.J. Simpson's chief defense lawyer, Johnnie L. Cochran Jr., has been elaborating a theory that Nicole Simpson and Ronald Goldman were mistakenly killed by drug dealers. Cross-examining detective Tom Lange, he argued that the police had willfully ignored any evidence that pointed elsewhere than to O.J., and that the real murderers were drug dealers who had come to the house for a friend of Mrs. Simpson's who had briefly been living with her. The friend, he said, was behind on cocaine payments, and the brutality of the murders indicated a Colombian revenge killing. Mr. Lange said that the methods used were too messy for drug gangsters. (→ March 13)

Afghan government attacks last rebel stronghold in Kabul

Government forces loading artillery in Afghanistan's three-year-long civil war.

Government forces in the Afghan capital launched an all-out attack today on the last rebel stronghold in the city. After rocket attacks, air strikes, and artillery shelling, ground forces captured positions in the rebel enclave of Karte Se.

Rebel forces have responded with rocket attacks on the government-held sectors of the city. Hospitals on both sides of the fighting have been hit, and the Red Cross in the city reports numerous civilian casualties. Many foreign aid workers are trapped in the battle zone.

The civil war has lasted for three years, but the UN is attempting to arrange a peaceful transfer of power on March 21. A UN delegation was to have landed in Kabul today, but was prevented from doing so by the fighting. It is unclear what effect the government attack will have on the prospects for peace. (→March 19)

Scotland, Thursday 9. Far from being gentle and peaceful, dolphins are shown in a BBC Television Scotland program to attack and kill porpoises in the Moray Firth. They do not eat them, but batter them and toy with them for up to 45 minutes before they die.

Las Vegas, 12
Riddick Bowe leaves town to discuss a possible bout with Mike Tyson, having taken the WBO heavyweight title from Briton Herbie Hide.

Copenhagen, 12
After talks with US officials, Croatian President Franjo Tudjman withdraws his demand that UN forces leave his country.

New York, 13
The UN Security Council votes to maintain sanctions against Iraq, imposed at the time of the invasion of Kuwait.

New York, 14
Ex-President of Mexico, Carlos Salinas, appears in Manhattan denying he has been exiled from his country.

Newfoundland, 14
Spanish trawlers return to contested fishing grounds, watched by Canadian planes. (→April 16)

Washington DC, 14
Conoco pulls out of an agreement to develop two off-shore oilfields for Iran, following a threat from the White House to block the deal.

Istanbul, 15
Three days of rioting by the moderate Islamic Alawite sect end when four people are killed and 25 injured.

Philippines, 16
Vietnamese boat people facing deportation are threatening to kill themselves rather than be returned.

Moscow, 16
Astronaut Dr. Norman Thagard is given a traditional Russian welcome of bread and salt on becoming the first American to enter the Russian space station *Mir*.

Deaths
Carlos Facundo Menem, 26-year-old son of the Argentinian president, is killed when his helicopter crashes into power cables, March 16.

Notorious gangster Ronnie Kray dies in prison from a heart attack, at age 61 in London, March 17.

Adams visits White House

Gerry Adams speaking at a press conference during his week-long American visit.

This year's St. Patrick's Day celebrations have been given a special significance with an historic handshake between President Clinton and Gerry Adams, leader of Sinn Fein, the political wing of the Irish Republican Army (IRA). Although he had invited Mr. Adams to the White House luncheon, it was doubtful that the President would actually embrace the Irish Republican in any way, and he did avoid contact with the Sinn Fein leader while there were photographers present. However, those at the luncheon – mainly Irish-American members of Congress – said that the private handshake was warm and enthusiastic. The two men spoke with each other for five minutes.

President Clinton has been under pressure from the British government, which is openly unhappy about the visit and the official reception accorded to Mr. Adams. John Major, the British Prime Minister, is refusing to enter into further talks with Sinn Fein until the IRA have handed in their arms.

Mr. Adams is in America for a week-long visit, which started on Sunday with Sinn Fein's first-ever legal fund-raising event in the US, held in Queens. Mr. Adams announced at the event that Sinn Fein would be opening an office in Washington. During his visit he has also met with Governor Pataki of New York, and will be at the White House again on Friday for a reception in honor of the Irish Prime Minister, John Bruton.

The President is reported as having told Mr. Adams that he is committed to the peace process, and insisted that it would be successful. (→April 4)

Two US citizens arrested in Iraq

Two Americans have been arrested and accused of spying in Iraq after straying across the border with Kuwait. William Barloon, 39, and David Daliberti, 41, were reported to have lost their way when visiting friends in the demilitarized zone. They were arrested at a military checkpoint and accused of espionage. US sources fear that Iraq will attempt to use the two men as bargaining chips to overturn the sanctions imposed after the invasion of Kuwait in 1990. (→ March 25)

New songs from surviving Beatles

Paul McCartney has announced that he, Ringo Starr, and George Harrison have been working together to record new songs. The three have been meeting in secret in a studio in London to record what McCartney described as "a couple of tracks" that will be released this November on *The Beatles Anthology*. Last year it transpired that the three surviving Beatles had been adding to the vocals of a John Lennon song that Lennon's widow, Yoko Ono, had on tape. (→ November 20)

O.J. cop quizzed

Lawyers in confrontation at the O.J. trial.

Defense lawyers in the O.J. Simpson trial have been given the go-ahead to quiz Detective Mark Fuhrman over his alleged racism. They claim that Fuhrman tampered with evidence and that racism could supply the motive for his actions. (→ March 27)

ATLANTA, TUESDAY 14

Pat Buchanan announces he will run for White House again

The man regarded in some quarters of the Republican Party as having lost them the presidency in 1992 has announced that he is to run again for his party's nomination. Pat Buchanan, the right-wing political commentator, told viewers of the *Larry King Live* show on CNN that he thought that his brand of conservatism was what America needed.

Buchanan has been accused in the past of anti-semitism, and the charge is likely to be leveled again. He said on the program, "I believe that Christianity is the truth that makes men free, and I believe Western culture and Western civilization are the greatest this world has ever produced, bar none." It was this kind of outspoken affirmation of right-wing principles from Mr. Buchanan that is thought to have lost George Bush support from some Republicans for seeming too liberal in contrast.

Mr. Buchanan is also an isolationist, critical of both the GATT and NAFTA agreements and against US troops taking peace-keeping roles overseas.

Political commentator Pat Buchanan, heading again for a role in the electoral drama.

Madrid, Saturday 18. Spain comes to a halt for three hours as almost the entire population watches on television the wedding of King Juan Carlos' daughter Elena to Jaime de Marichalar Saez de Tejada. In Seville hundreds of thousands of people line the route to the cathedral, where the wedding takes place.

Iwo Jima, Tuesday 14. Fifty years after the fierce battle for the Pacific island Japanese and American veterans meet to share a moment's silence.

TOKYO, WEDNESDAY 15

Eleven Japanese gangsters arrested for profiteering from Kobe earthquake

Eleven gangsters were arrested earlier today on charges of profiteering from the recent earthquake in Kobe. The January quake not only claimed 5,500 lives, but also caused massive devastation and made hundreds of thousands homeless. Relief operations are still going on. The police claim that the gangsters pretended to be victims of the quake in order to be awarded relief loans of 4.6 million yen ($51,000) from a social welfare office in the city.

One of the eleven arrested is believed to be the head of a gang that is affiliated to the largest of Japan's crime syndicates, the Yamaguchi-gumi, which is estimated to have a membership of 30,000. In a country which has an enviably low crime rate, members of organized gangs, or *yakuza*, are responsible for a large proportion of the crimes that are committed. Indeed, *yakuza* members account for about two out of three prisoners in the country's jails.

Frauds such as the alleged one at Kobe are favorite ploys of Japan's gangsters. They rarely target individuals, and attacks on the public, especially those involving physical assault, are rare in Japan. Fighting between opposing gangs is, however, more common.

Bonn, Friday 17. Fashion designer Karl Lagerfeld's injunction prevents the showing of Altman's film *Prêt à Porter* on the grounds of libel.

Kabul, 19
The Afghan army reenters the capital, having driven out the rebel Taliban Islamic movement to lines 19 miles from Kabul.

Los Angeles, 20
Judge James Bascue, supervising judge of the criminal courts of Los Angeles County, says that civil trials are being jeopardized by the backlog of criminal cases due to the "three strikes" law.

Ankara, 20
Thirty-five thousand Turkish troops enter northern Iraq looking for Kurdish separatists. (→ May 4)

St. Andrews, 22
University professor reports that the spread of flowering plants in the Arctic proves global warming.

Washington DC, 22
Record US trade deficit is posted for January, soaring to $12.23 billion.

Mineola, New York, 22
Colin Ferguson, the Long Island Rail Road murderer, is sentenced to 200 years.

Washington DC, 23
Veterans are told that the "VJ" Day designation will not be replaced by "VP Day," despite Japanese protests.

Moscow, 23
The Russian commander forecasts a long war in Chechnya, at the same time as the Chechen leader appears on TV saying only mutual discussion can end the conflict. (→ April 18)

Washington DC, 23
A Senate committee proposes outlawing pornography on the Internet. (→ September 14)

Nigeria, 24
A report published by the Human Rights Watch says that the Nigerian military government is deliberately persecuting and killing the Ogoni people in the south. (→ July 12)

Baghdad, 25
Two Americans who strayed into Iraq are sentenced to eight years each for spying. (→ July 16)

Death
Irving Shulman, author of *The Amboy Dukes* and the original treatment of *Rebel without a Cause*, at age 81.

Nerve gas attack on Tokyo subway

Rescuers help victims of the nerve gas attack outside a subway station in Tokyo.

A guerrilla-style attack paralyzed Tokyo this morning at the height of the rush hour as a deadly nerve gas was released in the subway system. Ten people have died, and 5,500 others have been injured, many of them critically. It appears that up to 15 canisters were left at important stations on three of the subway system's lines, and were timed to release the gas more or less simultaneously.

First tests indicate that the gas was sarin, a poison gas developed by the Nazis, but never used by them. Passengers reported seeing a liquid oozing from lunch boxes that had been wrapped in newspapers. "I saw no gas, but I saw a transparent liquid spreading on the floor, and people falling on the ground one by one," reported one woman.

Passengers staggered onto the platforms from the trains, and many collapsed. Several had bubbles coming from their mouths, and others were bleeding from the nose. A similar incident, but without fatalities, took place on the Yokohama subway earlier this month, while last June seven people died mysteriously from gas poisoning in Matsumoto in central Japan. Sarin was suspected then. No group has claimed responsibility for today's attack, but police attention has focused on the Aum Supreme Truth cult. (→ March 30)

Tighter rules for commuter planes

In the hope of cutting around ten accidents a year, the Department of Transportation is planning to subject small commuter planes to the same level of standards that currently apply to the main airlines. Transportation Secretary Federico F. Peña is honoring a pledge he made last December following the crash of a commuter plane in North Carolina, when he promised that within 100 days he would bring in tougher rules covering both operating practices and equipment. The new rules, he estimates, will typically add between 68 cents and $2 to the price of a one-way commuter ticket.

New York, Sunday 19. Breeders are petitioning for official status for the Munchkin cat, after its appearance at the International Cat Show. The cat, named after the characters in *The Wizard of Oz*, has exceptionally short legs and can turn quickly and run backward.

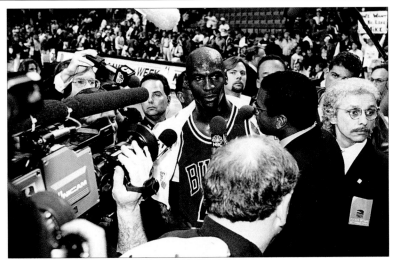

Indianapolis, Sunday 19. Michael Jordan's comeback to professional basketball attracted massive media attention. He scored 19 points, but the Chicago Bulls lost 103–96 to Indianapolis. He criticized some players: "The younger guys aren't taking responsibility."

GARY, INDIANA, SATURDAY 25
Mike Tyson released from jail

After serving three years of his ten-year sentence for the rape in 1991 of a teenage beauty queen, Mike Tyson was released from the Indiana Youth Correction Center this morning into a cold dawn. Four years of his sentence were suspended and he was excused three years for good behavior. Wearing a white Islamic skullcap and surrounded by Black Muslim bodyguards, Tyson refused to talk to the waiting reporters.

However, a written statement was handed out in which he said, "I'm very happy to be out and on my way home." He was met by boxing promoter Don King and it is expected that the fit-looking boxer will shortly be back in the ring. (→ August 19)

Mike Tyson, with Don King, leaving jail.

BONN, SATURDAY 25
Border controls removed in EU

French customs man: a thing of the past?

At midnight tonight seven of the 15 members of the European Union offically remove the border controls between themselves. The move, hailed by German Foreign Minister Klaus Kinkel as the "precursor to complete freedom of movement in all of Europe," is highly symbolic for those who want closer European integration. The seven countries, known as the "Schengen group," include Germany, France, Holland, and Spain. It excludes Great Britain, which is opposed to the arrangement on the grounds that laxer border controls will make crime too easy for terrorists and drug smugglers.

WASHINGTON DC, FRIDAY 24
House of Representatives cuts $69 million from welfare over five years

Social welfare principles that had operated for decades were deliberately abandoned today at the House of Representatives. Voting much on party lines, the House agreed on a measure to cut welfare spending by $69 billion, or between 6 and 11 per cent of what the spend would otherwise be, over the next five years. They are also giving the states more discretion over how they spend federal money earmarked for the poor. The bill now passes to the Senate.

Citing the proposed five-year limit on how long anyone can receive cash benefits, Republicans claim the bill will liberate people from dependence on welfare. Democrats argue that that the replacement of child-care and school-meal subsidies with lump sum payments to states to spend as they wish is cruel to children.

WASHINGTON DC, THURSDAY 23
Senate gives President item veto on budget and tax bills

The Senate voted by a clear majority today to give the President new powers to veto specific items in budget bills, controlling both spending and taxing. The bill passed earlier by the House had some differences, and these will have to be ironed out by a conference committee before it passes to the White House, but President Clinton has indicated that he will sign the measure.

The bill empowers the President to strike specific proposals from financial bills. Mr. Clinton welcomed the 69-to-29 vote: "The Senate tonight has taken another step toward passing strong line-item legislation. I hope the House and Senate will now get together quickly to resolve their differences and pass the strongest possible bill." Acknowledging one of the reasons why Congress should hand a President from another party such powers, he went on: "The sooner such a bill reaches my desk, the sooner I can take further steps to cut the deficit."

Behind the bill is not only the Republicans' hope of co-opting the President in reducing the federal deficit. They also have their eyes on 1996, when they hope to see the Republican Party recapture the White House.

TORONTO, SUNDAY 19
Cancer supergun unveiled

Some 6,000 attendees at the American Association for Cancer Research have been told of a new treatment for cancer that has halted tumor growth in tests on mice. The secret is a hand-held gun that shoots microscopic gold bullets into the patient. The bullets are coated with genetic material that enters the cancers and stimulates the body's immune system to fight them.

Cape Town, Monday 20. The British Queen arrives here for the first royal visit to South Africa for nearly 50 years.

S	M	T	W	T	F	S
			1	2	3	4
5	6	7	8	9	10	11
12	13	14	15	16	17	18
19	20	21	22	23	24	25
26	27	28	29	30	31	

Beijing, 26
The Chinese government introduces a five-day work week for government employees to reduce unemployment.

Sarajevo, 27
The United Nations threatens air strikes against the Bosnian Serbs unless they stop shelling the UN "safe areas." (→May 2)

Algiers, 27
Between 300 and 600 Islamic militants have been killed in six days as Algerian government forces step up their campaign against the rebels.

Los Angeles, 27
An important prosecution witness in the O.J. Simpson trial is ruled "hostile," allowing the prosecution to cross-examine him. (→ May 1)

Tokyo, 28
The world's largest bank is to be created by the merger of the Bank of Tokyo and the Mitsubishi Bank. It will have assets of $819 billion.

Washington DC, 28
Lobbying Congress in person, the King of Jordan gets a cool reception to his request for the US to honor its pledge to forgive his country's debt.

New York, 29
The baseball players' union says they will return to work if a judge forces owners to restore salary arbitration. (→ April 2)

Washington DC, 29
Republican motions to limit members of Congress to 12 years in office are defeated in the House.

Paris, 30
A 24-hour strike by transport unions in support of a pay raise brings chaos to France.

Tokyo, 30
Japan's top policeman is shot outside his home, following warnings from the Aum Supreme Truth cult. (→ April 13)

New York, 30
A federal judge rules that a government policy, enacted last year, discriminates illegally against homosexuals in the armed forces.

Burundi, 31
An estimated 20,000 Hutu refugees flee for Tanzania after several of them are attacked and killed.

MANILA, SUNDAY 26
Imelda Marcos campaigns to be elected to Filipino Congress

Imelda Marcos addressing a crowd on her home island of Leyte, where she is still sure of finding faithful supporters.

Despite being on bail as she appeals the corruption conviction that sentenced her to life imprisonment, Imelda Marcos, widow of the deposed president of the Philippines, is not giving up her fight to reenter Filipino politics. She is currently campaigning in the villages on the island of Leyte in order to drum up support for her candidacy in the elections this May to the country's Congress. Leyte is Mrs. Marcos's home island, and she is treated like royalty wherever she goes.

Mrs. Marcos, who came fifth of the seven candidates in the 1992 presidential election, is campaigning on a platform of restoring the Philippines to what she still sees as an international respectability enjoyed during her husband's tenure of office.

ROME, THURSDAY 30
Pope's "Gospel of Life"

In a newly published encyclical, Pope John Paul II has taken his strongest-ever stand against abortion and euthanasia. He condemns them as "crimes which no human law can claim to legitimize." The encyclical, *Evangelium Vitae* (which means "The Gospel of Life") urges Catholics everywhere to fight any laws that sanction either abortion or euthanasia, on the basis that there is "no obligation in conscience to obey such laws."

The Pope restates the Church's traditional stand against contraception and comes down against experiments on human embryos. The encyclical also condemns capital punishment except in cases so rare as to be "practically nonexistent."

HOLLYWOOD, MONDAY 27
Forrest Gump sweeps board at Oscars

The feel-good factor triumphed at the Academy Awards as *Forrest Gump*, the tale of a simple man caught up in national events, garnered six Oscars. Its star, Tom Hanks, won Best Actor, Robert Zemeckis won Best Director, and the film was judged Best Picture. It also won the awards for Best Editing, Best Visual Effects, and Best Adapted Screenplay. Star Tom Hanks let his emotions show as he collected his second Best-Actor award in successive years.

Jessica Lange gained the Best-Actress award for her performance in *Blue Sky*. Dianne Wiest was Best Supporting Actress, in *Bullets Over Broadway*, and Martin Landau Best Supporting Actor, for his portrayal of Bela Lugosi in *Ed Wood*. Quentin Tarantino was rewarded with Best Screenplay Oscar for *Pulp Fiction*.

Tom Hanks with his Oscar for Best Actor.

PORT-AU-PRINCE, TUESDAY 28

Aristide opponent shot and killed

President Jean-Bertrand Aristide of Haiti.

A prominent opponent of Haitian President Jean-Bertrand Aristide has been assassinated. Ms. Mireille Durocher Bertin, a 33-year-old lawyer and head of a leading opposition political party, was shot in her car by gunmen who fired from a taxi. The assassination follows three weeks of political violence in which more than 30 have died and comes only one day before President Clinton is due to visit the island. President Aristide has condemned the killing.

WASHINGTON DC, MONDAY 27

US urges Libya oil embargo

The American government is calling for a worldwide ban on importing Libyan oil. The Clinton administration is trying to force Colonel Qaddafi to hand over two Libyans suspected of planting the bomb that destroyed Pan Am flight 103 over the Scottish town of Lockerbie in December 1988.

Oil, of which Libya produces 1.4 million barrels a day, is the mainstay of the Libyan economy. However, calls for a ban are unlikely to get the support needed in the United Nations. The US's Arab allies, Egypt, Saudi Arabia, and Kuwait, are unlikely to support the call, as are Italy and Germany, major customers for Libya's oil.

Some sanctions are already in force against Libya, and have been since 1992 when Colonel Qaddafi first refused to hand over the suspects. One of these is to ban civilian flights to and from the country. Colonel Qaddafi has said he will defy these by running a flight to take pilgrims to Mecca. If the plane is downed when visiting Islam's holiest shrine, he said, this would show that the shrine "is under US domination and Saudi Arabia is not independent."

BUCHAREST, FRIDAY 31

59 die in Romanian airbus crash

Wreckage from the plane operated by Romanian airline Tarom in a field near Bucharest.

An Airbus operated by the Romanian national airline, Tarom, crashed into a field only three minutes after taking off from Bucharest airport today. All 59 people on board, 32 of them Belgian, are believed to have died. The Brussels-bound plane, an A310-300 Airbus, was found 18 miles from Bucharest airport, shattered into tiny pieces, of which the largest is only just six and a half feet long. The cause of the crash is not known, but sabotage has not been ruled out.

Witnesses reported hearing an explosion before the plane hit the ground, and two weeks ago a similar Tarom flight to Brussels made an emergency landing after someone called the airline saying there was a bomb on board. None was found. Moreover, the weather conditions today were good. On the other hand, another Tarom Airbus nearly crashed recently over Paris when it nosedived after the automatic pilot suddenly malfunctioned.

Johannesburg, Monday 27. Winnie Mandela is defiant following her dismissal by her husband from the government for her repeated attacks on it.

WASHINGTON DC, FRIDAY 31

Dollar falls to new low against the yen

The dollar hit a post-war low against the Japanese yen today as shares and bonds on both sides of the Atlantic plummeted in response to fears that the weak US currency would lead to a renewed bout of inflation. After standing at 89.54 yen the previous day, the dollar ended the month at 86.60 yen.

In a volatile trading day the dollar failed to benefit from an overnight cut in Japanese short-term interest rates. Against the pound it closed three cents down at $1.6280 and against the deutschmark it dropped to 1.3870 from 1.4110.

In early trading the Dow Jones industrial average plunged 60 points before the market settled down later in the day. The Dow closed 14.87 points down at 4157.69.

Currency analysts said that the drastic fall indicated that rate moves by Germany and Japan had been insufficient to alter the "negative fundamentals" of the US currency. Neil MacKinnon, chief currency economist at Citibank, said he expected the dollar soon to hit 75 yen.

The slump of the dollar came in spite of a revised assessment of US economic growth in the final quarter of 1994, which was up to an annualised 5.1 percent, well ahead of the expected 4.6 percent. Together, the day's events fueled renewed speculation that the Federal Reserve would intervene to raise interest rates.

Milan, Tuesday 28. Maurizio Gucci, 45, grandson of the founder of the luxury leather goods company and himself head of the company until 1993, has been shot dead by a gunman outside his office in downtown Milan.

S	M	T	W	T	F	S
						1
2	3	4	5	6	7	8
9	10	11	12	13	14	15
16	17	18	19	20	21	22
23	24	25	26	27	28	29
30						

Gaza Strip, 2
Eight people are killed by a bomb explosion in an area renowned as a stronghold of the Palestinian separatist group Hamas. A spokesman for the PLO said they believed it was an accident as Hamas members were preparing a bomb. (→ April 9)

London, 3
A judge rules that UK premier John Major cannot make a scheduled broadcast because it may interfere with Scottish local elections.

Virginia, 3
William Aramony, the former head of the United Way of America, is found guilty of stealing $600,000 from the charity.

Seattle, 3
The UCLA Bruins defeat the Arkansas Razorbacks to take the NCAA basketball championship.

Burundi, 3
Robert Krueger, the US ambassador to Burundi, says that hundreds of Hutus have been massacred over the past weeks.

Bosnia, 4
As the weather improves, heavy fighting breaks out near the town of Tuzla in northern Bosnia, as Bosnian government forces attack Serb positions. (→ April 24)

Washington DC, 4
President Clinton backs John Major in calling for the IRA to give up their arms. (→ May 10)

Washington DC, 5
The House of Representatives votes for a big package of tax cuts, the core of Newt Gingrich's "Contract with America." The radical proposals now go to the Senate.

Washington DC, 6
Senator Alfonse M. D'Amato apologizes on the floor of the Senate for racist remarks he made about O.J. trial Judge Ito on a radio show.

Hollywood, 6
The distilling company Seagram buys 80% of MCA from Matsushita.

LOS ANGELES, THURSDAY 6
Judge Ito orders investigation into jury misconduct

Questions have been raised about whether jurors in the O.J. Simpson trial have lied to serve in the case, were prematurely discussing the case among themselves, and were circumventing sequestration by making unsupervised phone calls. The questions were prompted by the comments of Jeanette Harris, excused from the jury by Judge Ito yesterday, after it came to light that she had made misrepresentations on her jury questionnaire about her experiences of domestic violence – a central issue in the case. Judge Ito today ordered an investigation into the allegations made by Harris in a TV interview. (→ May 1)

MANILA, MONDAY 3
Six linked to World Trade Center bomb arrested

The World Trade Center bombing, 1993.

Six Arabs, said to be linked to the man accused of carrying out the 1993 bombing of the World Trade Center in New York, were arrested yesterday in the Philippine capital, Manila.

Police seized guns, explosives, timing devices, and computer disks in the raid on a suburban apartment. They believe that the arrested men have ties to Ramzi Ahmed Yousef, who has now been extradited from Pakistan to the US to face charges that he masterminded the 1993 bombing.

Philippine police also say that Yousef plotted to assassinate the Pope during his Asian tour in January. Yousef narrowly escaped arrest in the Philippines during the papal visit.

WASHINGTON DC, SUNDAY 2
Water in liquid form found on Mars

Scientists claim that meteorite debris shows humans can create a second world on Mars.

One of the greatest obstacles to establishing life on Mars has been removed, with the crucial discovery that water in liquid form exists on the planet's surface. The finding also increases the probability that primitive life already exists on Mars, although this has yet to be proved.

Last week, Professor Thomas Donahue of the University of Michigan explained how studies of meteorites which have fallen to Earth from Mars show that the air in the thin Martian atmosphere is interacting with water at its surface.

"If water was spread on the surface uniformly," said Donahue, "it would cover Mars to a depth of 80 ft (24 m). All that colonists on Mars will need to do is sink wells to get it out. This will make establishing settlements easier and cheaper than was previously thought."

He added that, in theory, microbial creatures could already exist there.

DALLAS, SATURDAY 8
Thatcher's son faces US revenue suit

As his Texan business empire crumbles, Mark Thatcher, son of former UK premier Lady Thatcher, is coming under fierce attack from those who claim they were deceived by his companies. The aggrieved include former business associates, investors, and employees, as well as the US government, which claims that he may have evaded US taxes totaling almost $3 million. Thatcher faces a jury trial on the evasion charges, which he denies along with the other allegations. The Internal Revenue Service has been investigating his Texas-based Grantham Company.

Mark Thatcher, under IRS investigation.

Los Angeles, Monday 3. The actress Glenn Close has fallen out with Sir Andrew Lloyd Webber over his musical *Sunset Boulevard*, claiming that his company has lied about box-office takings.

CHICAGO, SUNDAY 2

Baseball strike called off after 234 days

Major league baseball owners today accepted the players' offer to return to work, ending the longest work stoppage in professional sports history on the day the 1995 season was supposed to open.

The owners' decision, announced after a four-and-half-hour meeting, ended the players' strike, which has lasted 234 days. The players will go back to work without a new collective bargaining agreement, but with the protection of an injunction forcing the owners to reinstate elements of the expired agreement, including salary arbitration, individual bargaining between clubs and players, and the anti-collusion provision of the free-agency rules.

Players can begin reporting for spring training on Wednesday..

President Clinton intervenes in the long-running baseball strike.

NEPAL, MONDAY 3

First Lady meets namesake in Asia

Hillary Clinton met the man responsible for making her a Hillary with two l's today, marking the end of her day off sandwiched between 12 days of visits to schools, clinics, and the leaders of five nations in South Asia.

At an airstrip in Katmandu, Nepal, Mrs. Clinton shook hands with Sir Edmund Hillary, the New Zealander who conquered Everest in 1953. She told reporters that her mother, Dorothy Rodham, had read an article about Hillary when she was pregnant with her daughter in 1947: "It had two l's, which is how she thought she should spell Hillary. When I was born, she called me Hillary, and always said it's because of Sir Edmund Hillary."

The rest of Mrs. Clinton's trip was concerned with the vitally important task of helping to encourage the education of girls and women in Asia.

Mrs. Clinton meets Sir Edmund Hillary.

LONDON, SATURDAY 1

Bosnia airlift girl loses fight for life

Irma Hadzimuratovic, the severely injured Bosnian girl whose plight inspired a mission to airlift wounded children from Bosnia, has died in her sleep at Great Ormond Street children's hospital, London.

She arrived in London in August 1993, at age five. The mortar shell that exploded in a Sarajevo market killed her mother and left Irma badly injured in her stomach, spine, and brain. After a tearful TV appeal from her surgeon, Irma was flown to Great Ormond Street where she was operated on. Irma gradually grew stronger, before suffering complications which prevented her from eating and finally led to her death.

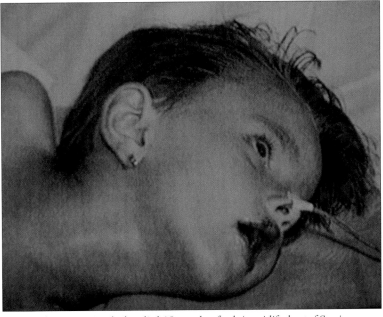

Irma Hadzimuratovic, who has died 18 months after being airlifted out of Sarajevo.

WASHINGTON DC, MONDAY 3

Gingrich ties tax relief to deficit cuts

Speaker Newt Gingrich agreed with dissident Republicans today to loosely tie his tax relief legislation to future reductions in the huge Federal deficit, removing a big barrier to passage of the tax bill in the House of Representatives later this week.

The dissidents had held the bill hostage for two weeks and threatened to block the final vote. With today's accord, Republican leaders escaped that threat and received assurance that their five-year, $189 billion package of tax cuts will pass an increasingly skeptical House.

Gingrich has called the bill the "pièce de résistance" of the Contract with America. It will reduce capital gains tax, eliminate the alternative minimum tax, and award a $500-per-child tax credit to tax-paying households earning $200,000 or less.

In return, the agreement requires Congress to approve 1996 budget legislation with a "clear path" toward erasing the Federal deficit before tax relief becomes law. However, the notion of suspending tax cuts if Congress fails to follow through with deficit cuts has been dropped, meaning there is nothing actually guaranteed in the accord.

April

S	M	T	W	T	F	S
						1
2	3	4	5	6	7	8
9	10	11	12	13	14	15
16	17	18	19	20	21	22
23	24	25	26	27	28	29
30						

Tajikistan, 9
Tajikistan appeals for international help after its border guards are fired on from Afghanistan.

Augusta, Georgia, 9
Bob Crenshaw wins the US Masters for a second time.

Tokyo, 9
Voters in Japan make some surprise choices in selecting television personalities for the governorships of Tokyo and Osaka.

New York, 11
Donald Trump is selling control of the Plaza Hotel to a consortium backed by money from Saudi Arabia and Singapore.

Boston, 12
An in-depth academic study by Dr. Alberto Ascherio of the Harvard School of Public Health has found that the amount of fish that men eat does affect their susceptibility to heart disease.

Detroit, 12
Billionaire investor Kirk Kerkorian, already the biggest single shareholder in Chrysler, says that he will make a bid for the entire company. (→ April 24)

Washington DC, 13
Vietnamese claiming to be commandos who served with US forces in Vietnam have had applications for asylum turned down.

Tokyo, 13
Japanese police set up roadblocks and search cars as they hunt for leaders of the Aum Supreme Truth sect, who are thought responsible for last month's nerve gas attack on the Tokyo subway system. (→ April 14)

Rome, 14
The Pope leads the Good Friday procession as usual, but, for the first time, does not carry the wooden cross. (→ April 16)

Deaths
Maraji Desai, former Indian prime minister, April 10 in Bombay at age 99.

Annie Fisher, classical pianist, in Budapest, April 10, at age 81.

Hamburg, Saturday 15. Fifty years ago today, British soldiers of the Allied forces entered the concentration camp of Belsen. Most camps were located further east, and this was the first time that troops of the western allies had come across such scenes of horror.

TOKYO, FRIDAY 14
Easter alert in Tokyo after sect phone threats

Police are out in force in and around Tokyo. Shoko Asahara, leader of the Aum Supreme Truth sect, prophesied that a terrible disaster will befall the city on the Easter weekend, worse than the Kobe earthquake of January.

Asahara's sect is held to be responsible for devastating nerve gas attacks on the Tokyo underground system. The fear is that Asahara's followers will use their stocks of nerve gas to make an attack on the Shinjuku entertainment district. A woman whose daughter joined the cult said her daughter had phoned her and warned her not to go to Shinjuku.

Police have set up road blocks in the capital, to stop cars and search motorists. Wearing chemical-warfare clothing, they have also raided centers known to be used by the cult. (→ April 21)

NEW YORK, MONDAY 10
Smoking ban in New York restaurants comes into force

An endangered species: the smoker.

The anti-smoking lobby is celebrating a significant victory. Regulations that seriously limit smoking in New York's restaurants go into effect today. The new rules essentially ban smoking in dining areas where there are seats for more than 35 people.

Smoking is permitted in a bar area or separate lounge only if dining tables are at least 6 ft (1.8 m) away. Many restaurant owners believe that without the opportunity to relax and smoke before or after their meal, diners will spend less on drink, and profits will fall heavily.

KANSAS, MONDAY 10
Bob Dole makes formal his bid for presidency

"We need a president who shares our values, embraces our agenda, and who will lead the fight for the fundamental change America chose last November." These words from Bob Dole were greeted with enormous enthusiasm by thousands of his supporters who had crowded into the Landon Arena in Topeka. In making his formal bid for the presidency in his home state, Senator Dole was ensuring himself of a large and sympathetic audience.

This is the Senate majority leader's third bid for the highest office of state: he also campaigned in 1980 and 1988. Compared to his campaign in 1988, however, he now sounds a lot tougher on government spending and taxation. In particular, it was widely thought that his failure to rule out raising taxes contributed greatly to his heavy defeat by George Bush in the 1988 New Hampshire primary. The new Dole put his position squarely and openly: "Let me make one fundamental belief crystal clear. We can cut taxes and balance the budget all at the same time. Middle-class families are forced to send too much of their hard-earned money to Washington." Senator Dole also signed a "taxpayer protection pledge" – something he had been unwilling to do in 1988.

New York, Friday 14. Burl Ives, much loved singer of American folk ballads, dies at age 85. He was also a successful actor on stage and screen.

TEL AVIV, SUNDAY 9

Suicide bombers kill seven in Gaza Strip

One of the wounded Israeli soldiers hit by the suicide bomb blast near Kfar Darom. More than 45 people were injured in two attacks.

The prospects for a lasting peace in Israel were jolted when Palestinian suicide bombers struck at Israeli targets within the Gaza Strip today.

In the first attack, which took place near Kfar Darom, a van drove next to a bus carrying Israeli soldiers back from their weekend leave. The driver activated the explosive killing himself and seven Israeli soldiers in the blast. There were also nine casualties.

The second attack took place on a convoy near the town of Netzarim. In this, a car pulled up near a security convoy and exploded. Five Israeli policemen were injured. Israel's premier, Yitzhak Rabin, was clearly shocked by the attacks, but vowed that he would not abandon the peace negotiations with the Palestinians and neighboring Arab states. He did, however, warn: "The Palestinian authority must prove that it can act against these groups." (→ April 16)

WASHINGTON DC, THURSDAY 13

US to threaten Japan with sanctions

Frustrated by lack of progress in lengthy free trade negotiations with Japan, the White House has decided to impose punitive tariffs on the Japanese unless they agree to open up their domestic market to US automobiles and auto parts. The tariffs will come into effect if no clear progress has been made within the next three weeks.

The situation is exacerbated by the recent drastic fall in the value of the dollar against the yen, and that has convinced US administration officials that they cannot afford to delay action any longer. (→ May 16)

Athens, Monday 10. In a three-month experiment to try to solve the city's enormous pollution problems, the government has banned traffic from the historically important Ermou area.

WASHINGTON DC, SUNDAY 9

McNamara admits his Vietnam policy was wrong

During a TV interview to publicize his new book *In Retrospect: The Tragedy and Lessons of Vietnam*, Robert McNamara was in tears as he described how he now believed that he should shoulder much of the blame for the tragedy of the Vietnam War. It is now almost 20 years ago – April 30, 1975 – when the last Marines escaped from the embassy compound in Saigon as North Vietnamese tanks drove into the city. McNamara believes, however, that it is important to be aware of the mistakes that he and others made in the 1960s, if only to try to avoid repeating them in the future: "We owe it to future generations," he stated.

McNamara was defense secretary from 1961 to 1968. He says that he underestimated the importance of Ho Chi Minh as a nationalist leader, and that the Pentagon, which he controlled, failed to understand that hi-tech weaponry was not suited to a war in a peasant society.

LIMA, SUNDAY 9

Fujimori easily re-elected in Peru

Fujimori supporters celebrate victory.

Alberto Fujimori, the incumbent president of Peru, has been reelected by a large majority in today's election. His majority will probably be close to 60 percent, which means that there will be no need for a second round of voting.

President Fujimori's main rival was Javier Pérez de Cuéllar, former secretary general of the United Nations. He has polled 22 percent of the votes. Pérez de Cuéllar has complained about election fraud, but the result is unlikely to be overturned.

Turkey, 16
A 25,000-strong Turkish force moves against Kurdish areas in the mountainous Tunceli province in the east of the country.

London, 17
Auction house Sotheby's announce that one of the world's biggest flawless diamonds will go on sale in a month's time.

Singapore, 17
The trial of Briton John Scripps, accused of international serial killing begins in Singapore. (→ November 10)

Teheran, 17
Iran bans the use of TV satellite dishes, and announces that US TV program *Baywatch* is a corrupting influence.

Washington DC, 17
President Clinton signs executive order ensuring that all government documents, even classified ones, will normally be released after 25 years, with very few exceptions.

Sri Lanka, 19
The latest ceasefire in this troubled island comes to a halt as Tamil Tigers attack a government naval base.

Athens, 20
Two men die in a terrorist bomb blast – a naval officer and almost certainly the terrorist himself. Police said the explosives were similar to those used by terrorists in attacks over the past few months.

Yokohama, 21
There is a further gas attack on the underground system in the city. The Aum Supreme Truth cult is again suspected of having planned the attack, after which 300 people were taken to hospital. (→ April 23)

Washington DC, 21
US State Department formally complains to Saudi authorities about their failure earlier in the month to cooperate in catching Imad Mugniyeh, one of the world's most dangerous terrorists.

Death
Milovan Djilas, Yugoslav dissident, April 20, in Belgrade, at age 83.

HEBRON, SUNDAY 16
Israel shoots three Hamas fighters

Israeli security forces killed three members of the Palestinian separatist group Hamas today. Dressed as Palestinians, the Israelis ambushed the Hamas men in an olive grove. After the shooting, the Israelis imposed a curfew on Hebron.

The Israelis maintained that the three men had been on their way to attempt a terrorist attack. The dead included two men who had been wanted for previous attacks. During the past six months, more than 60 Israelis have died in terrorist attacks, as Hamas militants have made a determined attempt to derail the peace process. (→ May 8)

NEW YORK, MONDAY 17
Beijing sells nuclear secrets to Iran

The US secretary of state, Warren Christopher, had two hours of talks with the Chinese foreign minister, Qian Qichen, in an attempt to persuade the Chinese that its nuclear cooperation with Iran is a threat to world peace. The Chinese agree in principle that there should be no spread of nuclear weapons, but are giving the Iranians know-how on nuclear reactors that could very easily be turned to military use.

TORONTO, SUNDAY 16
Agreement in Canadian fishing dispute

Spanish trawlers seized by the Canadian authorities during the dispute.

After a long period in which it looked as though they would fail, the negotiations between the European Union and Canada over fishing rights on the Grand Banks came to a successful conclusion this weekend. Agreement was reached on Saturday night and endorsed by the EU in Brussels today.

The key to the agreement is that there will be close inspection of fishing on the Grand Banks. Independent monitors will be present on all vessels fishing there, and they will inspect both the fishing gear used and the catch records. Satellites will track fishing vessels in the area.

This dispute, over what the Canadians saw as the over-fishing of the Greenland halibut by Spanish fishing vessels, threatened to set Canada against the EU, but the Canadians are happy that the new deal will keep fish stocks safe.

TAHITI, SUNDAY 16
Brando's daughter commits suicide

Cheyenne Brando.

Cheyenne Brando, daughter of film star Marlon Brando, committed suicide in her brother's home in Tahiti. She hanged herself after her mother left the house to go to church.

Cheyenne, Marlon Brando's daughter by his third wife, Tarita Teriipia, had led a troubled life. In May 1990, her brother Christian shot and killed Cheyenne's Tahitian lover, Dag Drollet; she was charged with complicity, but the charges were dropped in 1993. Cheyenne had a son by Drollet, born after his father's death. A drug addict, who needed to have plates implanted in her head after a car accident, she had twice tried to commit suicide before.

Florida, Friday 21. Tessie O'Shea, popular singer and variety performer, died at Leesburg, age 81. Her ample frame earned her the nickname of "Two Ton Tessie."

CHECHNYA, WEDNESDAY 19

Russians claim capture of last Chechen stronghold

Colonel General Anatoly Kulikov, commanding Russian forces in the breakaway republic of Chechnya, today claimed a significant breakthrough in his troops' operations. He announced that the town of Bamut was now in his hands. If so, this will mean that the last rebel stronghold in the lowlands has fallen, and the whole of the built-up north and west of the republic is under Russian control.

This success does not mean that the rebel forces of Dzokhar Dudayev are finally defeated, but it does mean that they are no longer able to put up significant resistance in the most populous areas of Chechnya – a far cry from early 1995, when they held up the Russian army in savage street fighting in the center of the capital, Grozny. Their best recourse is now to fight a small-scale guerrilla struggle in the mountains, attempting to wear the Russians out. (→ May 7)

Russian troops in relaxed mood as their offensive meets with success at last, after months of frustration and low morale.

KIGALI, RWANDA, FRIDAY 21

Hutus killed as Rwandans close refugee camp

Refugee camps have mushroomed across central Africa because of the Tutsi-Hutu conflict.

There was more death and misery in this ravaged nation today, when soldiers of the Rwandan Patriotic Army, mainly Tutsis, tried to close the Kibeho camp, containing thousands of displaced Hutus. The camp had been surrounded by government soldiers since Tuesday, and the refugees feared an attack. Government soldiers fired into the air and ordered the Hutus to return to their homes. Trucks were available to take Hutus back to their homes from the camp, but the operation was proceeding slowly. According to a UN spokesman, soldiers began to fire into the crowd when one of the refugees tried to grab a rifle. At least 13 people died in the subsequent shooting.

The government believes that the refugee camps harbor many of the militiamen responsible for the mass slaughter of Tutsis in 1994, and has ordered the closure of all camps in southwest Rwanda, which contain up to 250,000 people. (→ April 23)

CHECHNYA, TUESDAY 18

US disaster relief expert missing

It was announced today that Frederick C. Cuny, US disaster relief expert working in Chechnya, has disappeared, together with five Russian aid workers. Mr. Cuny had experience working in disaster relief in Bosnia, Biafra, and Somalia, and had been hired by the Soros Foundation in New York to help the civilian population of Chechnya, particularly those displaced by the fighting or those who had remained in built-up areas that had suffered severely from shelling. His immediate concern was to reestablish safe water supplies – cholera from contaminated water is now a threat throughout the region.

A State Department spokeswoman said that they feared he was dead, injured, or detained by one of the sides in the conflict. Mr. Cuny's party, which included an interpreter and two doctors, has not been heard from for nine days. An experienced operative, he had stayed in regular contact with Soros Foundation representatives in Moscow via a satellite telephone link. (→ April 19)

Rome, Sunday 16. In his Easter message, the Pope urged the Palestinians and the Kurds to renounce violence.

NEW YORK, THURSDAY 20

Declining dollar upsets IMF

There is a major dispute between the members of the International Monetary Fund. IMF Managing Director Michael Camdessus wants the dollar to be propped up: "A country which is responsible for the key currency of the world has the responsibility of maintaining reasonable stability of it," he stated. The Japanese especially fear that the weak dollar (which this week hit a new low against the yen and the mark) is slowing their recovery and hurting their exports. But the US economy is performing so well that the long-term trend is unlikely to change.

OKLAHOMA CITY, WEDNESDAY 19 – SUNDAY 23

Oklahoma terror bombing shocks a nation

At 9:02 a.m. on Wednesday April 19, a car bomb exploded immediately outside the Alfred P. Murrah building in Oklahoma City, which housed Federal government offices. It left a gaping, nine-story hole on the north face, festooned with trails of cable, masonry, and office equipment. Hundreds of people were buried in the rubble.

As the papers went to press that evening, 26 deaths were confirmed, including 12 children who had just been dropped off by their parents at a second-floor day center. Federal authorities began their investigations on the assumption that Muslim extremists had carried out the attack.

A day later, however, with the death toll at 53, two white males were named as suspects: they had rented a truck 245 miles north of Oklahoma City using false papers. On Friday, two men described as army deserters, Timothy McVeigh and Terry Nichols, were arrested. The theory was that a white supremacist militia was seeking revenge for the FBI assault on the Branch Davidian sect in Waco, Texas, exactly two years earlier. Later, Nichols's brother James was also brought in for questioning, and McVeigh was charged with malicious damage and destruction of Federal property.

On Sunday 23, with the death toll nearing 80, and with 100 still missing, the nation found itself united in grief as a national day of mourning was proclaimed. At an emotional memorial service for the victims of the bombing, held at the State Fairgrounds Arena, President Clinton addressed 10,000 mourners who were paying their respects to friends and relatives, innocent victims of the horrifying terrorist attack. He pledged to seek powers for a domestic counter-terrorism agency.

The Reverend Billy Graham summed up the general bewilderment over the bombing when he asked:"Why would God allow this to happen?" (→ April 25)

Rescue workers dig through the devastation the day after the bomb blast.

A blood-spattered victim is helped away from the Federal building for medical attention.

Oklahoma's feelings were plain to see.

The grim rescue

Twenty-month-old bomb victim P.J.Allen recovers from burns and other injuries as her grandmother, Doris Watson, waits in anguish.

An aerial view of the devastated Federal building.

A rescue worker searches through the wreckage.

Sniffer dogs are employed to seek out the missing.

Rescue workers take a break from their grim task.

Some of the 10,000-strong crowd who gathered at the Oklahoma State Fairgrounds Arena, April 23, to mourn the victims.

Oklahoma, 23
President Clinton vows to ask Congress for greater powers to combat the rise of terrorism.

Rwanda, 23
It is revealed that an estimated 2,000 Hutus have been massacred in Kibeho in the past few days.

The Hague, 24
The International Tribunal for the former Yugoslavia names Radovan Karadzic and Ratko Mladic as war crimes suspects. (→ May 2)

Detroit, 24
Chrysler rejects Kirk Kerkorian's bid to buy the entire company.

New York, 24
The Dow Jones industrial average hits a new record high of 4303.98.

Washington DC, 25
Finance ministers of the group of seven leading industrial nations announce that the decline in the dollar on international exchanges has gone far enough, but there is no promise of definite action.

Kurdistan, 25
Turkey pulls 20,000 troops out of northern Iraq, where they have been hunting members of the Kurdish Workers Party.

Buenos Aires, 25
The Argentine army admits that it sanctioned the killing and torture of civilians during the "dirty war" against leftist guerrillas in the 1970s.

San Francisco, 27
An antitrust lawsuit is filed against by the Justice Department to prevent Microsoft's $2 billion takeover of Intuit Inc., the makers of Quicken, a personal finance software package.

Los Angeles, 27
Robert L. Citron, former treasurer of Orange County, pleads guilty to six charges, including misappropriation of millions of dollars.

Deaths
Democrat John C. Stennis, 41 years Senator for Mississippi, Sunday 23 at age 93.

Sports broadcaster, Howard Cosell, Sunday 23, at age 77.

NEW YORK, THURSDAY 27

Unabomber claims 16th victim

A serial bomber has now described his motives in greater detail than ever after his sixteenth attack in 17 years killed an executive in California earlier this week. The FBI said that the man, known as Unabomber, sent three letters that were delivered on Monday, shortly before a package bomb explosion killed Gilbert Murray, president of the pro-logging California Forestry Association.

Two letters went to survivors of previous bombs. In the third, to the *New York Times*, he repeated claims to be a member of an anarchist group and defined his targets as leaders in technical fields considered destructive to the environment. He added he would stop killing people if a publication with nationwide circulation printed an article written by him.

Federal investigators who have spent years trying to break the case believe Unabomber is a man in his forties who acts alone. (→ September 19)

Police at the California Forestry Association, scene of the Unabomber's latest crime.

WASHINGTON DC, TUESDAY 25

Two brothers accused of conspiring with Oklahoma bomb suspect

As investigations continue into the the bombing in Oklahoma City last week, two brothers were charged today with engaging in a bomb-building conspiracy with Timothy J. McVeigh, the man accused of setting the blast. James D. Nichols, 41, and Terry L. Nichols, 40, are not yet linked directly with the Oklahoma bombing. They are accused of building bottle bombs and experimenting with explosives in 1992 and 1994 with former Army sergeant McVeigh. The conspiracy charges are intended to keep them in custody while investigators dig deeper. Investigators believe the bomb was planted to seek revenge for the Branch Davidian sect deaths at the hands of the FBI. (→ May 6)

Terry Nichols, above, and James D. Nichols, right.

WASHINGTON DC, SUNDAY 30

White House aide murder claim

Vincent Foster, the deputy White House counsel, was probably murdered and his body carried into a park as part of a staged suicide, according to a team of independent crime-scene investigators who were employed to look into the death by the Western Journalism Center, a California group that supports investigative journalism.

The private report is being taken seriously by the official investigation of special counsel Kenneth Starr, claim sources close to the inquiry.

The US Park Police concluded that Foster shot himself in the mouth on July 20, 1993. Two subsequent inquiries endorsed the suicide verdict, but Starr has reopened the investigation and has called witnesses for the first time before a federal grand jury.

The new report said that the lack of blood on the front of the body was inconsistent with death by a gunshot wound through the mouth, raising the possibility that Foster's heart had stopped before the gun was fired.

Las Vegas, Sunday 23. George Foreman, 46, raised his fist in jubilation late last night after retaining his IBF World Heavyweight Championship. He beat the 26-year-old German Axel Schultz in a hard-fought contest whose result was in doubt until the very end.

LONDON, SATURDAY 29
Blair wins vote to rewrite Clause 4

Tony Blair today won an important victory in the campaign to modernize the Labour Party, securing an overwhelming majority in favor of ditching the party's 77-year commitment to nationalization.

Delegates at the special conference held in Westminster's Methodist Central Hall, London, cast 65.23 percent of the votes in favor of rewriting Clause 4 of Labour's constitution, despite stiff opposition from the largest union affiliate, the Transport and General Workers' Union.

Blair, who greeted the result with an emotional speech, thanked delegates for their support and said: "I'm proud to be the leader and it's the party I'll always live in and die in." In an attempt to appease union critics, he said Labour would fight to keep the railroads under public control and would "renationalize" the National Health Service. (→ May 4)

PARIS, MONDAY 24
Jospin tops first round of French poll

Socialist candidate Jospin, dazed by his success in the first round of presidential voting.

The Socialist candidate in the French presidential election, Lionel Jospin, confounded all predictions to come in on top in yesterday's first round of voting. The result was a blow for the Gaullist, Jacques Chirac, who had been expecting an easy win.

Late-night estimates gave Jospin 23.3 percent of the vote, Chirac 20.1 percent and the other Gaullist, Edouard Balladur, 18.8 percent, which knocks him out of the race.

A left-right struggle will now ensue, as Chirac and Jospin scramble for the votes of the defeated candidates in the second round on May 7, though initial estimates last night were that Chirac would still win.

Balladur urged his supporters to vote for Chirac, who will also be hoping to pick up votes which went to the far-right candidates, such as Jean-Marie Le Pen, who won 15 percent in the first round. Jospin will be chasing the votes cast for the far Left: 8.7 percent Communist, 5 percent Trotskyist and 3 percent Green. (→ May 7)

SEOUL, FRIDAY 28
Gas explosion in Korea kills 100

A gas explosion beneath a crowded road in the South Korean town of Teagu killed ten children on their way to a school picnic. Over 100 commuters are also feared dead.

A spark, possibly caused by tunneling drills being used to construct an underground railway system, ignited a leak from a gas pipe at 7:30 a.m., blasting to pieces a 300 yd (274 m) stretch of road and hurling cars and buses into the air. A vast fireball erupted from below the ground, killing rush-hour commuters and pupils crossing the road to their school. The ten children and one teacher were the only confirmed dead, though with dozens of people buried beneath the debris, this number is certain to rise.

Almost 4,000 soldiers, police, and firemen were rushed to the scene to begin the rescue operation.

The devastation wreaked on the Taegu road by a gas explosion.

TOKYO, SUNDAY 23
Aum cult leader murdered in Tokyo

A leader of the Aum Supreme Truth cult was killed today by a man claiming to be a right-wing activist.

Hideo Murai, 36, head of Aum's "Science and Technology Agency," which operated secret laboratories where sarin and other poisons are thought to have been made, was stabbed in the stomach outside the sect headquarters in Tokyo. He died in hospital a few hours later.

His assailant, identified as Hiroyuki Jo, 29, said he was a rightist who wanted to exact revenge on the cult, accused of killing 12 commuters and injuring more than 5,000 others in a subway nerve gas attack on March 20.

The stabbing was filmed by many camera crews who have been covering the sect, and was shown repeatedly on television. (→ May 3)

Los Angeles, Tuesday 25. Ginger Rogers, the world-famous dancer and actress who starred in 80 films and regularly partnered Fred Astaire, has died at home in California, at age 83.

S	M	T	W	T	F	S
	1	2	3	4	5	6
7	8	9	10	11	12	13
14	15	16	17	18	19	20
21	22	23	24	25	26	27
28	29	30	31			

Los Angeles, 1
Judge Ito excuses yet another juror, the seventh so far, in the O.J. Simpson trial. (→ May 8)

Washington DC, 1
US secretary of state, Warren Christopher, claims Iran has been trying for a decade to develop nuclear weapons.

Minneapolis, 1
Malcolm X's daughter, Qubilah Shabazz, accepts "responsibility" for her role in a murder plot against Louis Farrakahn, leader of the Nation of Islam. Murder charges are dropped but no deatils of the settlement are released.

New York, 2
Sixteen Bronx policemen are arrested after a two-year undercover investigation by the Bureau of Internal Affairs.

Beijing, 3
Japanese premier, Tomiichi Murayama, pledges to make "peace last forever" on a historic visit to Beijing.

Washington DC, 3
The Senate Select Committee on Intelligence confirms the appointment of John M. Deutch as director of the CIA.

Alabama, 3
Chain gangs return to Alabama as 400 chained prisoners are put to work by the side of the state's busiest road, Interstate 65.

Tokyo, 3
Police arrest the "justice minister" of the Aum Supreme Truth cult, suspected of the gas attack on the Tokyo subway that killed 12 people and injured more than 5,000. (→ May 11)

London, 4
Britain's Labour Party wins an overwhelming victory in local government elections.

Ankara, 4
Turkish troops withdraw from northern Iraq after a six-week search-and-destroy mission against rebel Kurd bases.

Copenhagen, 6
A ten-year study claims that moderate consumption of wine can enhance longevity.

ZAGREB, CROATIA, TUESDAY 2
Fresh fighting between Serbs and Croats: Zagreb shelled

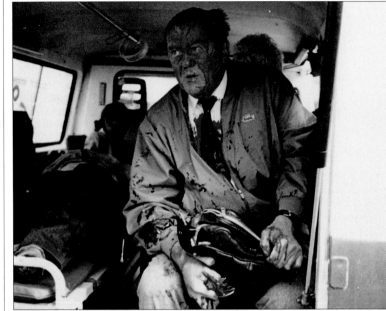
A blood-spattered victim of the rocket attack in Zagreb waits to be taken to hospital.

Five people died and 121 were injured when five rebel Serb rocket-propelled cluster bombs exploded the busy center of the Croatian capital Zagreb today.

The attack arrived without warning in the midmorning. The bombs smashed into houses and a school playground in this busy area, spreading panic and shock. Many passersby were injured by the flying shrapnel released from the warheads. One rocket landed only 100 yd (91 m) away from the US Embassy.

The attack was launched from rebel Serb positions about 25 miles away. It appears to have been in retaliation for yesterday's successful completion of the Croatian military operation to capture territory in Slavonia, which the Serbs also claim.

US, British, and German citizens were warned to leave the city in case of further attacks. (→ May 7)

The war in former Yugoslavia hits the civilians of Zagreb, capital of Croatia.

BOSTON, THURSDAY 4
Harvard professor under investigation

A three-man committee at Harvard Medical School is investigating the academic standards of psychiatry professor Dr. John Mack, author of the best-selling book *Abduction: Human Encounters with Aliens*.

In his book, and also in his appearances on TV talk shows, Dr. Mack deals sympathetically with the claims of people who say they have been adbucted by aliens and, in many cases, forced to have sex with them.

Dr. Mack's acceptance of his patients' stories as the truth has attracted criticism from some members of the academic community. As a result, his work is under investigation with a view to establishing whether it meets Harvard's standards of research. Other academics claim the inquiry is an attack on academic freedom.

WASHINGTON DC, TUESDAY 2
US to return refugees to Cuba

Cuban refugees wait at Guantánamo.

The White House today announced that it would start returning Cuban boat people to their homes, ending 35 years of preferential treatment for refugees from the Castro regime. An exception is to be made for a final group of 20,000 refugees held at the US Guantánamo Bay Naval Station.

The agreement with Cuba to return future refugees was described as "totally unacceptable" by Jorge Mas Canosa, chairman of the influential Cuban American National Foundation.

Clinton attacks militias

Uniformed members of the Michigan militia making their point at a gun-rights demonstration.

In the wake of the Oklahoma bombing, President Clinton is preparing tough new legislation to help fight terrorism and the threat of militia organizations. A raft of laws would give federal agents sweeping new powers to investigate suspected terrorists. A key element in the package is the relaxation of rules on using electronic bugs and wiretaps.

Under the five-year, $1.5 billion plan, more than 1,000 new agents and other law enforcement personnel would be hired to investigate terrorist activity. A national Domestic Counterterrorism Center, headed by the FBI, would be established to coordinate all counterterrorist activity.

Other proposals include measures to make mandatory the inclusion of tracing material in all explosives, and new powers for federal agents to check credit card, hotel, and travel records of suspected terrorists.

But the plan has not met with unanimous support. Doubts have been raised over the relaxation of rules on electronic surveillance. Senator Daniel P. Moynihan of New York has expressed concern that the legislation might infringe on the Fourth Amendment, which protects against unreasonable searches and seizures. The proposals are certain to come under much closer scrutiny before becoming law.

Oklahoma search called off

The search for victims of the Oklahoma City bombing has been abandoned, with no hope of finding further bodies.

The death toll stands at 158, with nine still missing. Jon A. Hansen, assistant chief of the Oklahoma City Fire Department, admitted that there was no hope of finding further bodies.

The search has been hampered in the past two weeks by high winds and rain that made the building dangerous. Rescuers have worked around the clock for 16 days but now the state of the building makes further work too hazardous. (→ May 13)

Tragic debris of the Oklahoma bombing.

Berlin, Tuesday 2. New evidence proves that Hitler did commit suicide with his lover Eva Braun in April 1945. The evidence also reveals that Hitler's remains were not destroyed until 1970. (Shown above, left, Hitler's jacket and, right, a Soviet intelligence report.)

Dallas elects first black mayor

Ron Kirk, a 40-year-old Democrat, has become the first black mayor of a major Texan city. Mr. Kirk won the race against two opponents in convincing fashion, gaining over 60 percent of the vote.

Mr. Kirk, a former Texas secretary of state, expressed surprise at winning on the first ballot: "Not in my wildest dreams did I believe we were going to get this concluded tonight," he said. Mr. Kirk gained the majority of the black vote, but also had strong endorsement from leading figures in the business, real estate, and sports communities.

West Africa, Monday 1. Rebel forces in Sierra Leone have cut off the capital, Freetown, from the rest of the country.

S	M	T	W	T	F	S
	1	2	3	4	5	6
7	8	9	10	11	12	13
14	15	16	17	18	19	20
21	22	23	24	25	26	27
28	29	30	31			

Rio de Janeiro, 8
Police shoot dead 14 drug pushers in a gun battle in Nova Brasília, a shantytown north of the city.

Detroit, 8
Dr. Jack Kevorkian assists in a suicide for the 22nd time.

New Orleans, 8
Severe flooding in New Orleans, with 19 inches of rain in one day, causes five deaths.

Rome, 8
Former prime minister Silvio Berlusconi sees his Freedom Front Party suffer heavy losses in Italian local elections.

Los Angeles, 8
The O.J. Simpson murder trial reaches a crucial stage as the prosecution introduces results of DNA tests. (→ May 18)

West Orange, New Jersey, 8
Israeli prime minister, Yitzhak Rabin, visits the family of Alisa M. Flatlow, who died in a terrorist attack in the Gaza Strip in April.

Washington DC, 9
Charges are brought by federal prosecutors in Oklahoma City against Terry Lynn Nichols in connection with the bombing of the Federal building there in April.

New York, 11
The Japanese owners of the Rockefeller Center, the Mitsubishi Estate Company, have forced it to file for bankruptcy protection.

New York, 11
A 35-year-old male teacher and his 15-year-old female pupil and lover are on the run from police in California after fleeing there from New York.

Johannesburg, 11
A runaway locomotive crushes over to death more than 100 workers in a Transvaal mine.

Tokyo, 11
Masami Tsuchiya of the Aum Supreme Truth cult confesses to making the nerve gas sarin for the cult's terror campaign. (→ May 16)

Oatman, Arizona, 13
A third suspect in the Oklahoma bombing, 35-year-old Steven Colbern, is arrested. (→ May 23)

PARIS, SUNDAY 7

Chirac elected French president on second ballot

The new French president, Jacques Chirac, waves to supporters.

Jacques Chirac has become French president after achieving a narrow victory over the Socialist candidate Lionel Jospin. A nerve-racking campaign ended with his garnering 52.7 percent to Jospin's unexpectedly high 47.3 percent before the votes in France's overseas territories had been counted. Chirac had previously contested the 1981 and 1988 presidential elections but despite his defeats in those contests and his unpopularity in presidential election polls taken earlier this year, the conservative mayor of Paris had remained single-minded in pursuit of France's highest political office.

BELFAST, WEDNESDAY 10

Ministers in first Sinn Fein meeting for 23 years

Michael Ancram, British Northern Ireland Minister, yesterday met representatives of Sinn Fein. It was the first official encounter between the two sides for 23 years but it ended in deadlock after they found little room for agreement on vital aspects of the Irish peace process. The talks are a turning point, however: after eight months of the IRA cease-fire, Britain has finally recognized Sinn Fein, the IRA's political wing. (→ June 17)

CHECHNYA, SUNDAY 7

Proof emerges of Russian Chechen atrocity

Details of a horrific massacre of civilians by 3,000 Russian troops in the conflict in the former Soviet territory of Chechnya have come to light. Over 100 inhabitants of the village of Samashki – women, children, and old people – were killed in cold blood by Russian troops last month. Soldiers, some of whom were said to be drunk, tossed grenades at the civilians and fired rounds of ammunition at them indiscriminately. (→ May 15)

JERUSALEM, MONDAY 8

Israeli PM announces release of 250 Palestinian prisoners

Israel made a further conciliatory gesture toward the Palestinians yesterday when it started the release of 250 prisoners. The freed Palestinians signed documents promising not to take part in further attacks on Israel. The gesture was timed to coincide with the Islamic festival of Eid al-Alha and drew criticism from some quarters. Israel's justice minister, David Libai, expressed doubts over whether the gesture could be justified on legal grounds. Also, the right-wing Israeli party, B'Tdezek, went to court in a failed effort to stop the action. A further 200 prisoners, held following violence that was directed at Israelis, are also expected to be released by the Palestinian Authority in Gaza and Jericho. (→ May 22)

Kashmir, Thursday 11.
A two-month siege of Muslim separatist guerrillas was ended when Indian troops stormed them and killed 42 at the site of an Islamic shrine.

WASHINGTON DC, WEDNESDAY 10

Senate is trumped by Republicans

A draft proposal to eradicate the Federal deficit, which was released yesterday by Republicans in the House of Representatives, promises bigger savings than a budget that was previously proposed by the Senate. The House proposal aims to cut $340 billion in taxes while the Senate proposes no tax cuts. And at $1.4 trillion, the savings projected by the House are approximately 50 percent more than those put forward by the Senate. Both sets of figures are envisioned as working over six years, and both aim to have the deficit eliminated by 2002. (→ May 18)

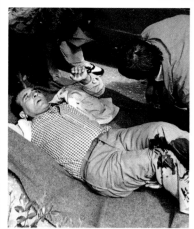

Sarajevo, Sunday 7. The latest Serb mortar attack on the beleagured city of Sarajevo has killed at least nine people and wounded 15. The attack hit the suburb of Butmir. (→ May 26)

Ebola outbreak in Zaire

A new outbreak of the deadly Ebola virus in Zaire has struck Kikwit, south of the capital Kinshasa. The town has now been quarantined. A total of 49 people have died in a month after this latest manifestation of the virus, which is regarded by scientists as a Level 4 pathogen, making it more dangerous than AIDS, which has a Level 3 classification. (→ May 24)

New York, Tuesday 9. A portrait of a Spanish anarchist, Angel Fernandez de Soto, painted by Picasso was sold for over $40 million at Sotheby's.

Russia celebrates VE Day with massive show of strength in Red Square

Presidents Clinton and Yeltsin share a toast to peace.

President Clinton was in Russia yesterday for that country's VE Day celebrations, but the military parade, the centerpiece of the Russians' celebrations, went ahead without him. The President decided to boycott what proved, as predicted, to be a powerful display of post-Soviet strength on the part of the Russian military.

With the eyes of the world upon them, the Russians made the most of the opportunity to show that they remain a force to be reckoned with. Pavel Grachev, the Russian Defense Minister, gave voice to the philosophy behind the Russians' display of military might. "The military threat still exists, and as long as it exists we would keep strengthening and modernizing our armed forces," he explained to 10,000 members of the Russian army on the Hill of Tributes.

Although President Clinton and Prime Minister John Major both absented themselves from the Red Square parade, they did attend an earlier Red Square event, during which Russian World War veterans marched past the visiting dignitaries. The atmosphere was markedly different there from the one at the later parade. President Yeltsin paid a sincere tribute to the Allied forces who had fought in tandem with Russian troops dur-

Ceremonials in Red Square to mark the fiftieth anniversary of VE Day.

ing World War II to defeat the threat of Nazism. "Who knows how many lives were saved by the establishment of the anti-Hitler coalition, uniting its efforts for a common goal?" he said.

However, the touching sight of the veteran troops commemorating a victory over fascism was later supplanted by the appearance on the scene of another type of veteran: Russian troops fresh from the Chechen front. President Clinton had earlier told the Russians he would not be seen to endorse that campaign. (→ May 15)

Dharamsala, 14
The Dalai Lama names a six-year-old as the reincarnation of the Panchen Lama, the second highest figure in Tibetan Buddhism. The last Panchen Lama died in 1989.

Buenos Aires, 14
President Carlos Menem is reelected president of Argentina, with just under half of the votes cast. He has more than a 10% lead over both his rivals.

Southern California, 14
New Zealand's yacht *Black Magic* wins its fifth consecutive race against *Young America* to take the America's Cup to New Zealand for the first time. It is only the second time that the Cup has left the US.

Cairo, 15
Egypt's Antiquities Council announces that US archaeologists have found the largest ancient Egyptian tomb yet discovered. It was built for the 50 sons of Ramses II and has 67 chambers.

Chechnya, 15
Russian troops resume their offensive, attacking villages near the border with Dagestan. A body believed to be that of missing US aid worker Frederick C. Cuny is found in a village south of Grozny. (→June 14)

Beijing, 15
In defiance of international opposition, China conducts an underground nuclear test, four days after signing an extension of the nuclear nonproliferation treaty.

Washington DC, 17
The Senate votes to establish a Whitewater committee to investigate President Clinton's affairs while he was governor of Arkansas.

Rio de Janeiro, 17
The Brazilian government appoints a retired general, 64-year-old Nilton Cerqueira, as Public Security Secretary, to spearhead a new drive against organized crime in the city.

Paris, 18
The new French premier, Alain Juppé, has named a cabinet that includes 12 women.

Washington to impose 100 percent tariff on Japanese cars in trade dispute

Once again, brinkmanship is the order of the day in trade negotiations between the US and Japan. Thirteen models of Japanese car will be subject to a 100 percent tariff from Sunday, May 28. The cars are all luxury models, and include the key flagship automobiles from Toyota, Lexus, and Nissan. Customs has been instructed to double the wholesale cost of all the listed models coming into the US.

The rise in prices will make these cars all but unsellable, and if the tariff actually comes into force, the Japanese will lose business that last year led to sales of $5.9 billion.

The US negotiators have decided to take a tough line because they see no sign of the Japanese committing to make their domestic market more open to foreign vehicles. US trade representative Mickey Kantor insis-ted that, "the US is not going to stand by and watch its workers and its products unfairly treated."

Those Japanese cars that are partly or wholly produced in the US will not be affected by the tariff, and Kantor claimed that among American workers, "very, very few people will be hurt." It is expected that some kind of compromise will be reached before June 28. (→ June 28)

House agrees to balance budget; Senate debates it

Bob Dole: Senate debate is under way.

In a historic decision, the House today voted by 238 votes to 193 to put into operation one of the central planks of the "Contract with America." The plan is for the Federal budget to be balanced by the year 2002, and involves cutting $1.5 trillion from government spending during the intervening years. The Senate began debate on its version of the measure today.

There are some differences between the houses of Congress, in that the Senate measure does not contain any provision for tax cuts, whereas the House voted for a detailed plan that includes $350 billion in tax breaks for individuals and businesses. At some point in the near future there needs to be a resolution of these differences, but there is no doubt that the Republican Party is keeping its pledges and pushing ahead with the radical program it promised during last year's elections. (→ June 7)

Senator Bob Packwood accused of sexual misconduct

The Chairman of the powerful Senate Finance Committee, Oregon Republican Bob Packwood, was today facing political ruin. The Senate Ethics Committee accused him of discrediting the Senate and endorsed claims that he had indulged in sexual misconduct, had enlisted lobbyists to help his wife get a job, and had tampered with evidence.

The sexual misconduct charges relate to 18 complaints by women, and he is also accused of altering his diaries when he found that the committee would subpoena them to use in its investigations. At a meeting with the press, Senator Packwood declined to comment on the charges themselves. (→ September 7)

Tokyo, Tuesday 16. Aum sect leader, Shoko Asahara, is arrested on suspicion of organizing the Tokyo subway gas attack. (→ June 22)

San Diego, Wednesday 17. Paramedics treat Shawn Nelson, shot by police after he stole a National Guard tank and went on the rampage through the streets of the city, crushing at least 30 vehicles.

LOS ANGELES, THURSDAY 18

O.J. trial: State DNA expert questioned about blood samples

The defense team began its cross examination of the DNA expert, chemist Gary Sims of the California Justice Department, and it pushed its questioning along the path that it has chosen as its main shield for the sports and TV star – that the evidence could not be trusted because of mistakes made by those involved in examining and processing it in the

course of the investigation. The defense lawyer who questioned Mr. Sims was Barry Scheck, and he led the witness through a series of questions concerning what might have happened had certain mistakes been made – if, for example, the custody of blood samples had been negligent, or the lab technicians did not change gloves between handling different

samples. Mr. Scheck has a history of being sceptical about DNA samples in previous trials. He faces an uphill task with Gary Sims, however, who, under cross examination from the prosecution, stated that he believed the odds were 240,000 to one that blood samples found near the bodies came from a black American other than the defendant. (→ June 5)

ROME, SATURDAY 20

Prosecutors apply for Berlusconi trial

Silvio Berlusconi: under investigation.

Magistrates today decided to press for the trial of former prime minister, Silvio Berlusconi, on corruption charges. They claim that $180,000 in bribes was paid to government officials to secure favorable tax breaks for his business empire.

Signor Berlusconi has admitted that directors of his companies may have made such payments, but his defence is that in the prevailing atmosphere of the time and under pressure from tax inspectors who were themselves corrupt, the men who ran his companies had little choice but to comply.

The future of Berlusconi's holding company, Fininvest, which currently owns three television stations, hangs in the balance, in any case. The Italian Parliament is debating whether to hold a referendum on limiting the ownership of television stations to one per owner.

Los Angeles, Thursday 18. The star of the TV series *Bewitched,* Elizabeth Montgomery, died today at age 57.

WASHINGTON DC, SUNDAY 14

New York police officers in drunken spree

Washington hoteliers are complaining bitterly about the behavior of New York's finest. Visiting the Federal capital for a ceremony to honor fallen comrades, at which President Clinton was present, the representatives of the NYPD drank to excess, let off fire extinguishers, stole license plates, set off fire alarms, and fired weapons into the air. Investigations continue. (→ June 8)

Washington DC, Saturday 20. Pennsylvania Avenue has been closed to traffic on the recommendation of White House security advisors.

S	M	T	W	T	F	S
	1	2	3	4	5	6
7	8	9	10	11	12	13
14	15	16	17	18	19	20
21	22	23	24	25	26	27
28	29	30	31			

Kashmir, 21
Twenty-two people die in violent protests against the policies of the Indian government.

Germany, 21
HIV-infected prisoners escape from jail and are involved in a police chase across northern Germany.

Barcelona, 21
Two paintings and a sketch bought in a Barcelona flea market are authenticated as genuine Picassos.

Washington DC, 22
Officials anounce that a visa will be granted to the President of Taiwan, a move that reverses a 16-year-old policy and will bring fury from Beijing. (→ August 23)

Oklahoma, 23
The ruins of the federal building are finally demolished.

Germany, 23
Germany's highest court rules that former East German spymasters cannot now be prosecuted, but those already serving sentences are not to be freed.

Zaire, 24
Deaths from the latest outbreak of the deadly Ebola virus reach 108.

South Africa, 25
The opening match of the rugby world cup is a triumph for South Africa as they defeat Australia 27-18.

Washington DC, 26
Congress votes to cut federal government spending by $1 trillion over the next seven years.

Moscow, 26
A Russian scientist claims that the body of Lenin, preserved and on display in his mausoleum, is spreading satanic energy.

London, 31
The trial for fraud of the sons of newspaper magnate, Robert Maxwell, opens today. Maxwell died in mysterious circumstances aboard his yacht in 1991.

Death
Les Aspin, former Democratic secretary of defense, May 22 at age 56.

SAKHALIN, RUSSIA, SUNDAY 28
2,500 feared dead in Russian earthquake

The inhabitants of Neftegorsk search for their belongings in the devastated town.

Thousands of people are still unaccounted for after an earthquake measuring 7.5 on the Richter scale flattened the town of Neftegorsk in the north of Sakhalin Island during the early hours of the morning.

The disaster was made worse by two factors. Firstly, a series of aftershocks made rescue work difficult, and, secondly, the geographical position of Neftegorsk, tucked away in the north of Sakhalin Island and thousands of miles away from Moscow in Russia's far east, meant that rescue workers and equipment had to fly in from long distances.

Three hundred deaths were registered soon after the first shock, but it is feared that the final casualty toll may well approach 2,500. In addition, massive ecological damage is feared as the earthquake also damaged an oil pipeline.

LONDON, MONDAY 22
Surgeon saves air passenger's life

Professor Angus Wallace saved the life of a fellow on a Hong Kong to London flight today. The drama began when the passenger, Pauline Dixon, began complaining of pains in her arm. She soon had difficulty breathing, and Wallace diagnosed a collapsed lung. Operating with a coat hanger, a pair of scissors, an oxygen mask, and a plastic bottle, all sterilised in five-star brandy, he saved his the passenger's life – and then drank the rest of the brandy.

Professor Wallace with improvized tools.

LONDON, WEDNESDAY 24
Death of former UK premier

One of the leading lights of post-war British politics died today, when Lord Wilson, 13 years Labour Party leader and victor in four of the five general elections he contested, passed away in his sleep.

There were tributes from all sides of the political divide. The Conservative prime minister, John Major, said Wilson was "one of the most brilliant men of his generation".

Wilson held his first cabinet post at the age of 31 (the youngest cabinet member since 1806), and became leader of the Labour Party in 1963

Harold Wilson at a party conference.

and prime minister in 1964. He resigned as prime minister in 1976, and later entered the upper house as Lord Wilson of Rievaulx.

NEW YORK, FRIDAY 26
Philip Morris decides to recall eight billion cigarettes

The tobacco industry faced another crisis today, as Philip Morris was forced to recall packs of many of its major brands. The problem is that defective filters have been detected in some cigarettes. Philip Morris believes that the percentage involved is very small, but the group is taking no chances in a political environment that has become increasingly hostile to cigarette manufacturers. It is thought that something approaching eight billion cigarettes will be recalled. The brands involved include the best-selling Marlboro. News of the recall took the stock market by surprise, and there was an immediate drop in the Philip Morris share price. The company's share price fell $2 on the day at the close of trading. The recall will affect profits, but will do no long-term damage to the company.

BOSNIA, FRIDAY 26

Serbs take UN troops hostage in retaliation for NATO air strikes

Some of the 200 UN troops taken hostage by Bosnian Serb forces are paraded for the TV cameras.

The atmosphere is tense in Bosnia, as the Bosnian Serb forces under Ratko Mladic seem, once again, to have outsmarted the international community. NATO air strikes were ordered against the Bosnian Serb capital of Pale on Thursday, to try to force the Serbs to pull their heavy guns back from around Sarajevo and other designated safe havens. International outrage was fuelled by a Serb shell that killed 71 Bosnians in Tuzla on Thursday. At first, the bombing was seen as a welcome show of resolution from the Western powers, which have watched with fuming impotence as the Bosnian Serbs have ignored all ultimatums to make them draw back.

In a sudden move, however, the Bosnian Serbs dramatically turned the tables by taking members of the UN peacekeeping forces hostage, and showing them on television. Nearly 200 soldiers have been taken by the Serbs, who now have the upper hand. In the game of bluff and double bluff, it is now up to the UN and NATO to formulate an effective response in a situation where they have once again lost the initiative. Further air strikes have been called off for the moment. (→ June 7)

JERUSALEM, MONDAY 22

Israel retreats on Jerusalem land annexation

The Israeli government of Yitzhak Rabin today effectively abandoned controversial proposals to annex Palestinian land in East Jerusalem. In total, an area of about 130 acres had been earmarked to be expropriated. It has been a feature of Israeli policy toward Jerusalem that it has never agreed that Palestinians have land rights in the historical capital of the Jewish state.

The proposal to expropriate the land was defeated by what was, in any reckoning, an unlikely alliance. The small Israeli Arab parties within the Knesset (which usually support the Labour government) tabled a motion of no confidence over the issue. Right-wing parties, including the Likud, threatened to support the motion because the combined votes would have brought down Rabin's government. Paradoxically, Likud supports land annexation in East Jerusalem. (→ June 25)

Virginia, Monday 29. Actor **Christopher Reeve,** star of the **Superman** series of films, was today seriously injured in a fall from a horse while competing in an equestrian competition at Charlottesville. Reeve was thrown when his horse refused a jump. He has badly injured his neck and back and may be paralyzed. (→ October 17)

North Sea, Tuesday 23. Greenpeace activists occupying the **Brent Spar rig** were brought ashore. They were protesting the plans to sink the rig in the mid-Atlantic. (→ June 16)

WASHINGTON DC, TUESDAY 23

Gunman shot and wounded in White House grounds

There was drama at the White House today when secret servicemen shot and wounded an intruder who had climbed the security fence.

Leland William Modjeski, 37, sometime psychology student but more recently fired as a pizza delivery man, got over the fence armed with a .38 revolver, later found to be unloaded. He refused to stop when ordered, and headed toward the Jacqueline Kennedy Garden, getting to within 30 yd (27 m) of the White House. One guard moved to stop him, but when other officers noticed that Modjeski was carrying a weapon, they opened fire, hitting him in the arm, but also wounding one secret serviceman. This is the fourth time in recent months that an intruder has attempted to get into the presidential residence.

June

BELGRADE, WEDNESDAY 7
Serbs release most UN hostages

United Nations troops in Pale following their release by the Bosnian Serbs.

The application of international pressure on the Serbs following the hostage taking of over 320 UN troops late last month continues to bear fruit. A Serbian official announced here today that a further 108 soldiers had been released, following the 121 set free last Friday. One hundred and forty-nine remain in Serb hands, but according to a spokesman for the Serbian president, Slobodan Milosevic, who has joined the calls for their release, the others should be freed soon. The Bosnian Serbs captured the soldiers following NATO air strikes on their positions, and they are insisting that there should be no more NATO attacks. (→ June 8)

CAPE CANAVERAL, THURSDAY 1
Woodpeckers delay launch of space shuttle

The latest problem to hit the troubled space shuttle program has emerged from the air. Woodpeckers have been found pecking away at the craft, causing sufficient damage to call into question next week's planned launch.

The birds have been chipping away into the insulating foam around the launcher's fuel tank. Seventy-one separate holes have been found in the insulating material.

NASA scientists have been experimenting with low-tech ways of detering this natural hazard. So far they have resorted to blowing air horns in the hope that the noise will drive off the birds. They have also placed decoy owls around the launch-pad in order to see if these will frighten away the woodpeckers.

Netherlands, Monday 5.
Ethiopian Haile Gebresilasie knocks nine seconds off the world 10,000 meters record.

TOKYO, TUESDAY 6
Japanese express remorse over war

After weeks of arguing, the Japanese government agreed tonight on a motion making an apology of sorts for its conduct during World War II. The depth of the apology depends on how one translates the word "*hansei*," which can mean either "remorse" or "reflection." Giving the word its stronger meaning, the motion says, "Recalling many acts of aggression and colonial rule in modern world history, we recognize and express deep remorse for these kinds of actions carried out by our country in the past."

HONG KONG, THURSDAY 8
Boat people riot in Hong Kong

Vietnamese boat people protest in Hong Kong against repatriation.

Over 800 rounds of tear gas were fired by police this morning at 50 Vietnamese protesting against their imminent deportation from a detention center in Hong Kong back to Vietnam.

The rioters attacked the police with spears and handmade weapons and set fire to the administration block in the camp, apparently in the hope of destroying the records necessary to their deportation. However, the papers were elsewhere.

The violence follows a riot last month in Hong Kong and another one four days ago at a camp in Malaysia, when 1,000 people broke out and had to be turned back by water cannon. Hong Kong officials are worried that the resistance will make the planned repatriations impossible to effect.

AVIANO, ITALY, THURSDAY 8
Downed US pilot rescued in Bosnia

Happy to be going home: Captain Scott O'Grady with a fellow officer after his rescue.

A US Air Force pilot is safely back with his comrades at their Italian base in Aviano after spending six days in Bosnia following the downing of his F-16C fighter by a Serb missile. In a daring, textbook mission he was picked up by US marines right in the heart of Serb-held territory in the north of Bosnia.

Captain Scott O'Grady had been moving around in wooded terrain since he bailed out. An F-16 pilot heard a radio message sent out by Scott calling for help. Within five hours a rescue helicopter, supported by three others and two jet fighters, released a team of marines who pulled him on board. There were no casualties during the raid, although the mission was shot at by the Serbs. The success of the rescue, and Scott's hero status, has helped to temporarily head off public criticism of the administration for US involvement in the Bosnian conflict. (→ June 13)

Washington DC, Sunday 4. Bob Dole's wife pledges to sell her shares in Disney after discovering one of its subsidiaries distributes *Priest*, a film branded as immoral by her husband.

MISSOURI, SATURDAY 10
"Smoker's gene"

Scientists at the Washington University School of Medicine in Missouri have published the findings of research that suggest that the propensity to smoke could be genetic. They have been examining over 2,000 pairs of twins, half of whom are identical and half fraternal. The identical twins, who have the same genes, were found to have far more similar smoking habits than the fraternal twins, whose genes are different. Personality characteristics were found to be much less important. One of the team, Dr. Pamela Madden, said, "Our evidence indicates that strong genetic effects are responsible for both starting smoking and for long-term smoking."

MEXICO CITY, THURSDAY 1
Mexico commits to new round of privatization

The Mexican government is planning a huge sell-off of state-owned enterprises. This will be the country's third round of major privatizations in ten years. There has been the distinct odor of a fire sale about the previous rounds, so observers will be watching this latest one to see if the government has learned from its mistakes.

This time the come-on items in the sale are the airports, communication satellites, and railroad system. Mexico has been under a lot of pressure from creditor nations, especially the US, to cut public spending and to raise cash. The previous sales have concentrated on the money raised, rather than the nature of the services that the nation requires. For example, the telephone system was sold as a single concern to a monopoly that has left the service in just as poor a state as it was in before.

A government official admitted that the same mistakes could be made again: "The pressure for that kind of thing to continue is pretty strong."

BRADFORD, ENGLAND, SATURDAY 10
Asians riot in English rust-belt city

An Asian man shows his anger during the street violence in this industrial city.

Riots have broken out on the streets of the northern English city of Bradford for two nights in a row as Asian youths clashed with police. About 1,000 youths went on a rampage, throwing Molotov cocktails and stones and setting fire to cars and furniture. Ironically, the riots are taking place in a district where community leaders and young people have in recent weeks been working closely with the police, in order to tackle a notorious prostitution problem.

The rioting started on Friday night when a 15-year-old who had been playing soccer in an alleyway had an altercation with the occupants of a police patrol car and was handcuffed by them. When another Asian protested he was arrested. Local people are claiming that the police responded insensitively to the incident. A spokesman for the community called for calm: "We want the situation defused as much as anyone. The economic prosperity of this community is being damaged and we don't want it to go on."

New York, Sunday 4. *Sunset Boulevard* wins its star Glenn Close and Sir Andrew Lloyd Webber seven Tony Awards, including the one for best musical.

June

Colombia, 11
A bomb kills 28 people, many of them children, at a music festival in Medellin.

New York, 11
IBM is successful in its bid for the Lotus software corporation, after raising its price to over $3.5 billion

Bosnia, 13
Bosnian Serbs free all but 26 of the remaining hostages. (→ June 18)

Los Fresnos, Texas, 13
A mysterious virus is attacking the US's largest shrimp farms and has detroyed $11 million worth of shrimp in a few days.

London, 13
President of the Board of Trade, Michael Heseltine, orders an official inquiry into possible Iranian arms deals by a company of which a fellow government minister was a director.

Budapest, 16
The International Olympic Committee designates Salt Lake City as the host of the 2002 Winter Olympics.

England, 16
Working with the FBI, British police find forged US gold and silver deposit certificates worth $700 million in a house in the Midlands.

Hamburg, 16
A Shell gas station is firebombed and thousands of others boycotted in protests against the company's planned dumping of the Brent Spar oil platform in the North Sea.
(→ June 20)

New York, 16
The Dow Jones Index breaks through 4,500 for the first time.

Madrid, 17
Felipe González, Spanish prime minister, finds himself in the center of a dispute over the tapping of the phones of many top people in Spain, including the king, Juan Carlos.

Death
Arturo Benedetti Michelangeli, brilliant but temperamental concert pianist, in Switzerland, at age 75, June 12.

PARIS, TUESDAY 13

France announces resumption of nuclear tests in Pacific

The New Zealand government has reacted angrily to an announcement by newly elected French president Jacques Chirac that France will resume nuclear testing in the South Pacific. Monsieur Chirac said that the first of eight tests would be in September, and that they would continue until May 1996, whereupon France would sign a comprehensive test ban treaty.

Monsieur Chirac had attacked the decision by François Mitterand to agree to a moratorium in 1992, and in the election campaign he was critical of his rival, Edouard Balladur, for agreeing to the moratorium. He said tonight, "I have consulted all the military and civil experts. They were unanimous in telling me that if we wanted to guarantee the sureness, safety, and reliability of our nuclear force, we were obliged to complete this series of tests." (→ September 10)

London, Saturday 17. Henry Kissinger is knighted by Queen Elizabeth II for his contribution to Anglo-American relations.

BELFAST, SATURDAY 17

Adams pulls Sinn Fein from preliminary talks

Sinn Fein leader Gerry Adams.

Gerry Adams today warned that violence could reerupt, as he pulled Sinn Fein, the political wing of the IRA, out of preliminary talks with the British government.

Speaking on BBC Radio from South Africa, where he is scheduled to meet President Mandela, he said that as far as he was concerned exploratory talks had finished. They have been going on for six months, but Sinn Fein now wants to conduct a formal meeting with Sir Patrick Mayhew, the Secretary of State for Northern Ireland.

But Sir Patrick has turned down the request, as the IRA has not responded to the government on the issue of decommissioning its weapons. "There is always a danger, unless we deal with the root causes of conflict, that the danger of slipping back into conflict remains," Mr. Adams warned. (→ July 3)

LOS ANGELES, THURSDAY 15

O.J. struggles to fit incriminating gloves

The attention in the O.J. Simpson trial today concentrated on his hands, as the prosecution insisted that he try on a pair of gloves tendered in evidence. One of the bloodstained gloves was found at the scene of the murder, the other, according to the prosecution, on a path at O.J.'s home.

O.J. struggled with the leather gloves, having manifest difficulty in getting them on, and muttering, "too tight, too tight," as he tried. A defense lawyer claimed they were obviously too small.

However, he did eventually get them on, and some spectators considered them a very snug fit. The gloves are crucial to the prosecution's case. The former football star has exceptionally large hands, and the gloves are extra large in size. A buyer at Bloomingdale's testified that Nicole Simpson bought such a pair of gloves from her department in December 1990. (→ July 27)

Does the evidence fit O.J. like a glove? The jury has to decide whether they are "too tight."

MOSCOW, WEDNESDAY 14

Chechen rebels take 2,000 hostages in hospital

Chechen gunmen earlier today swept through a town in southern Russia, and occupied a hospital, taking around 2,000 patients and staff hostage. Earlier in the day 37 policemen and soldiers, plus an unknown number of civilians, were killed as the men fought their way through the town of Budyonnovsk, some 70 miles (110 km) north of the Chechen border. According to various reports the gang numbers between 50 and 250; they are led by Shamil Basayev, third in the rebel Chechen hierarchy.

The raid answers Russian fears that the fighting would spread from Chechnya into Russia itself, now that the rebels have been driven into hiding. The gunmen have threatened the lives of the hostages, saying that ten hostages will be killed for every gunman, and five killed for every Chechen injury. The rebels are demanding that Russia withdraws from Chechnya, that President Yeltsin enters into negotiations with the Chechen leader, and that they are allowed to talk to reporters. Moscow is now gripped by fears of terrorist attack. (→ June 20)

Rebels and hostages in the hospital of the southern Russian town of Budyonnovsk.

WASHINGTON DC, MONDAY 12

Supreme Court narrows application of race law

Opponents of affirmative action were given a blow today by a Supreme Court ruling that calls into question the legality of Federal programs that favor businesses on racial criteria. By a vote of only five to four, the Court redefined the rules in a case occasioned by the requirement that a minimum of 10 percent of Federal money spent on highway projects should go to companies owned by "disadvantaged individuals." The Court ruled that any Federal program classifying people according to race must have "a compelling governmental interest." This judgment falls short of calling the program illegal, but places a hurdle so high it will prove very hard to clear. The District Court will now judge whether this particular case satisfies the criterion.

Houston, Wednesday 14. The Houston Rockets, anchored by their center Hakeem Olajuwon, celebrate after taking their second successive National Basketball Association championship, beating Orlando Magic 113 points to 101.

WASHINGTON DC, WEDNESDAY 14

Senate votes to outlaw computer pornography

Brushing aside arguments that regulation would be an infringement of freedom of speech, and could limit the growth of computer networks, the Senate today voted in favor of imposing heavy fines or prison sentences on anyone convicted of distributing pornographic material through cyberspace. Senators were considering an amendment to a telecommunications bill that will in most respects deregulate the telecommunications industry. However, talk of some of the material available on the networks won the Senators over to agreeing to fines of up to $100,000 and prison sentences of up to two years for those found guilty of transmitting obscene material that could be accessed by people under 18 years of age.

S	M	T	W	T	F	S
				1	2	3
4	5	6	7	8	9	10
11	12	13	14	15	16	17
18	19	20	21	22	23	24
25	26	27	28	29	30	

Sarajevo, 18
The Serbs free the last 26 UN peace-keepers held hostage. (→ June 25)

New Delhi, 18
The latest deaths in northern India's hottest weather this century bring the death toll to 525 as temperatures hit 113° F (45° C).

Luxembourg, 19
European finance ministers agree to drop their target date of 1997 for the introduction of a single European currency. Under the Maastricht treaty it will be introduced by the beginning of 1999.

Havana, 19
Cuba now says it will not extradite fugitive financier Robert Vesco.

France, 19
Municipal elections give the National Front control of three towns in southern France, including the port city Toulon.

Washington DC, 19
The Supreme Court rules that the organizers of the St. Patrick Day's parade in Boston had the constitutional right to exclude marchers parading under pro-gay banners.

Moscow, 20
Chechen rebels release their remaining hostages, used as human shields on journey to safe territory in Chechnya. (→ July 30)

Washington DC, 20
The Senate votes to allow individual states to set their own speed limits.

Washington DC, 21
The CIA asserts that China has sold vital components for missile systems to Iran and Pakistan.

Washington DC, 21
The US April trade deficit swells to $11.37 billion, the highest ever.

New York, 23
Scientists report that they have isolated a gene that predisposes some people to cancers.

London, 23
Douglas Hurd announces that he is resigning as the UK's foreign secretary.

Death
Jonas Salk, pioneer discoverer of the first polio vaccine, in California at age 80, June 23.

Senate finally blocks Clinton's nomination for surgeon general

Dr. Henry W. Foster Jr., now no longer in line to be surgeon general.

Republicans in the Senate have rebuffed President Clinton's choice of Dr. Henry W. Foster Jr. as surgeon general. A motion to end a Republican filibuster preventing the nomination being considered failed by just three votes.

A similar vote took place yesterday, and it had been agreed under the rules which Senate majority leader Bob Dole had proposed for the debate, that after two failures the motion would fall.

Dr. Foster, a 61-year-old obstetrician and gynecologist from Nashville, had been criticized by the Right for performing a number of abortions and for not having been open in admitting them.

However, he claimed that he was the victim of power play among Republican presidential hopefuls. Prominent among his opponents were Bob Dole, Phil Gramm of Texas, and Arlen Specter of Pennsylvania, all of whom are actively seeking the Republican nomination for 1996.

Corey Pavin wins US Open

Corey Pavin said goodbye to the label of being one of the finest golf players never to have won a major title when he completed the final round of the US Open in 68 today.

While finishing top of the leaderboard was a first for this determined 35-year-old competitor, it was yet another disappointment for the runner-up, Greg Norman, who started the day in the lead. It is the sixth time that Norman has found himself in this situation at the end of a major championship.

Corey Pavin is presented with the trophy after winning the US Open golf championship.

Jackson to alter anti–Semitic lyrics

Michael Jackson apologizes for lyrics.

Finding himself in a storm of anger over the lyrics of one of the songs on his latest album, Michael Jackson first apologized for their allegedly anti-Semitic content and has now agreed to alter them on all future pressings of the album. Jackson claims that he did not intend the words "Jew me, sue me, everybody do me; Kick me, kike me, don't you black and white me" to be offensive to Jews. He has been attacked by a range of commentators, including his friend Steven Spielberg.

LONDON, THURSDAY 22
Major resigns as Tory party leader

John Major announces his resignation in the rose garden of 10 Downing Street.

John Major stunned the British political world tonight by announcing his resignation as leader of the Conservative Party in order to submit himself for reelection. The move is designed to silence his right-wing critics and to end the damaging speculation about his leadership. Challenging his opponents to stand against him, he told them that it is now time "to put up or to shut up." Mr. Major continues as prime minister in the meantime. Talk of a leadership challenge this autumn has been rife for some time, although no candidate has appeared. Eurosceptics have been openly hostile to his policy on Europe. (→ June 26)

LONDON, TUESDAY 20
Shell abandons plan to sink oil rig Spar

The Brent Spar oil platform.

Shell UK has caved in in the face of massive objections from environmentalists and has announced that it will not, after all, dump the aging Brent Spar oil platform in the North Sea. Instead, it will seek to dismantle the platform on dry land.

The decision is being hailed as a victory by Greenpeace, which has occupied the platform while it was being towed toward the proposed dumping ground off Scotland, but it is an embarrassment for the British government, which had publicly supported Shell's plan. The main cause of the change of heart seems to have been "consumer power." There was a mass switch away from Shell products in Germany, Holland, and Scandinavia, and the company could not resist such pressure.

TOKYO, THURSDAY 22
Japanese police storm hijacked jet

At dawn this morning police stormed a hijacked airliner at the city of Hakodate, on the northern island of Hokkaido, freeing the 365 passengers and crew. The lone hijacker, who threatened the pilot with a bomb, is reported as belonging to the Aum Supreme Truth sect accused of the Tokyo subway gas attack, and is said to have demanded the release of the sect's leader. (→ July 4)

WASHINGTON DC, THURSDAY 22
Senate and Congress square their balanced budget proposals

Senate majority leader Bob Dole and Speaker of the House Newt Gingrich announced tonight joint proposals on taxation and spending. The deal will cut taxation by $245 billion over the next seven years, and will reduce expected spending by $1 trillion.

The principles of cutting have never been in doubt between Republicans in the two houses of Congress. Last month the Senate and the House of Representatives each approved proposals to balance the budget, but there were small differences between them. The new agreement irons out those differences. Newt Gingrich said of the proposals, "After decades of reckless spending, we are committed to making government leaner, more efficient, and cost effective." But Leon E. Panetta, the White House chief of staff, voiced the President's objections to the proposals, saying they were the wrong cuts, and that they entailed "cuts in Medicare and unwise cuts in education to pay for tax cuts to those who don't need them." Cuts are also likely to be made in roads and the environment.

Johannesburg, Saturday 24. Hosts South Africa win rugby's World Cup, uniting black and white across the nation.

MOSCOW, TUESDAY 20
Zhirinovsky in TV orange juice brawl

Russia's extreme nationalist politician Vladimir Zhirinovsky enhanced his reputation for emotional and aggressive behavior tonight by assaulting a fellow guest live on television. He was taking part in a talk show with an old adversary, Boris Nemtsov. The debate quickly degenerated into personal abuse, and when Mr. Nemtsov accused Mr. Zhirinovsky of having syphilis, Mr. Zhirinovsky stood up, swore at him, and threw the contents of a glass of orange juice in his face, followed by the glass.

Berlin, Thursday 22. A 24-year-old dream is realized as the artists Christo and his wife Jeanne-Claude supervise the completion of the wrapping of the Reichstag. It will be covered up for two weeks.

S	M	T	W	T	F	S
				1	2	3
4	5	6	7	8	9	10
11	12	13	14	15	16	17
18	19	20	21	22	23	24
25	26	27	28	29	30	

Sarajevo, 25
Bosnian Serb sniper-fire and shelling kills at least nine civilians in Sarajevo, including four children. (→ July 6)

West Bank, 25
Israeli soldiers kill two Arabs and injure more than 30 during a protest in Nablus calling for the release of 5,000 Palestinian prisoners. (→ July 4)

Bonn, 26
Germany resolves to send armed forces to the Balkans for the first time to support UN peacekeepers.

London, 26
Welsh Secretary John Redwood resigns his post to stand against John Major in the forthcoming leadership contest. (→ July 4)

Qatar, 27
The Crown Prince of Qatar, Hamad Bin Khalifa al-Thani, forces his father to leave the country in a bid to take control of the tiny Arab emirate.

California, 27
Orange County voters reject a half-cent increase in sales tax to bail their government out of bankruptcy.

Oregon, 27
British women Sally-Anne Croft and Susan Hagan, one-time followers of Bhagwan Rajneesh, go on trial for conspiracy to murder.

India, 28
Madhya Pradesh in central India is designated a "tiger state" to protect the animal from poachers and settlers.

Sri Lanka, 28
Tamil rebels kill 161 people.

Johannesburg, 28
Mandela sets up a Truth Commission to expose human rights abuses committed in the apartheid era.

Germany, 28
IRA member Donna Maguire is convicted of attempting to bomb a British Army barracks in Germany, but is freed because of having spent almost six years in jail on remand.

Moscow, 29
Yeltsin asks top ministers to resign after the botched hostage rescue operation in southern Russia.

Death
Former chief justice Warren E. Burger, at age 87, June 25.

SEOUL, THURSDAY 29
At least 63 killed as South Korean store collapses

The tangle of concrete and steel left by the collapse of a crowded department store in Seoul.

A five-story department store packed with shoppers in Seoul, South Korea, collapsed today, killing at least 63 people and injuring more than 850.

Injured people – some unconscious – were carried out of Seoul's Sampoong Department Store in a steady stream. Helicopters carried many to hospitals because evening rush-hour traffic slowed ambulances.

The disaster has left South Koreans anguished over yet another tragedy attributed to slipshod construction and poor government foresight. Two fatal gas explosions in the last six months killed 113, and a bridge collapse killed 32. The government has promised to do all it can to punish those responsible for the country's latest disaster. (→ July 9)

NEW YORK, FRIDAY 30
Serial bomber sends manifesto

An artist's impression of the Unabomber.

The serial mail bomber known as Unabomber, who last struck in April, has delivered a 35,000-word manifesto to *The New York Times* and *The Washington Post*. In it, he calls for revolution against a corrupt industrial-technological society. He says that if one of the papers publishes his script within three months, plus three annual follow-up messages, he will stop trying to kill people. (→ September 19)

HOUSTON, THURSDAY 29
US spacecraft docks smoothly with *Mir* space station

The American space shuttle *Atlantis* docked with the Russian *Mir* space station today. The operation was so flawless that officials hope it will aid the joint ambitions of the Russian and American space programs.

Ten astronauts greeted one another with hugs and handshakes, chattering in English and Russian while speeding around Earth at nearly five miles per second in the biggest craft ever assembled in space. The linkup, some 245 miles above central Asia, came after a tense orbital chase, in which the *Atlantis* slowly approached *Mir*, finally docking with a gentle kick from its engines after two hours of preparation.

Both the Russian and US spacecraft were once major weapons in the waging of the cold war. (→ July 4)

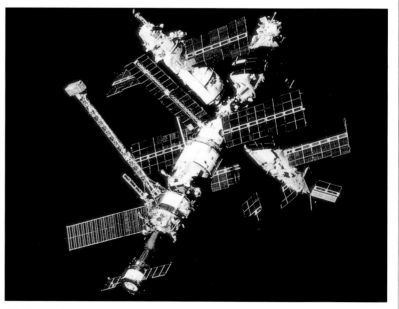

The historic linkup between the US space shuttle and Russia's Mir *space station.*

PORT-AU-PRINCE, HAITI, TUESDAY 27
Haitian elections flawed

Supporters of President Aristide take to the streets of Haiti's capital city.

Brushing aside complaints that irregularities at the polls and in the counting of ballots made Sunday's election in Haiti so flawed that it cannot be considered valid, President Jean-Bertrand Aristide today described the vote as "a major step toward democracy for my country." He said that its results would stand and that the second round of voting would take place on July 23 as scheduled.

Aristide spoke shortly after leaders of the Lavalas ticket, which he endorsed, held a news conference at which they claimed victory in the ballot, although the President declined to endorse their claim.

Opposition parties, including the National Front for Democracy and Change, under whose banner Aristide became president in 1990, denounced the election. Calls for its annulment came from the leftist Movement for National Reconstruction.

Aristide acknowledged that the vote, in which hundreds of polling places opened late or not at all and some candidates were left off ballot papers, had been beset by serious technical difficulties. "The technical aspect was not what we would wish," he said. He attributed most of the problems to Haiti's lack of experience with democracy. (→ July 5)

GENEVA, WEDNESDAY 28
US and Japan settle trade dispute

The US and Japan reached a broad but ambiguously worded accord on automotive trade today. The agreement ended a two-year dispute just hours before $5.9 billion in tariffs against Japanese luxury cars were due to go into effect.

The overall goal of the agreement is to reduce the US trade deficit in autos and auto parts, which stood at $36.1 billion in 1994. The accord sets out voluntary plans for Japanese companies to buy more US parts and build more cars in the US. Japan will also encourage its dealers to sell more US cars and take steps to open the market for repair parts.

Los Angeles, Tuesday 27. British actor Hugh Grant is arrested and charged with lewd conduct with a prostitute. (→ July 11)

WASHINGTON DC, WEDNESDAY 28
Affirmative-action plans under fire

Jesse Jackson: against the new guidelines.

Reacting to a recent Supreme Court ruling, the Clinton Administration today issued guidelines for evaluating Federal affirmative-action programs that may make many of them harder to justify legally. The guidelines say that these programs must now be justified by evidence of specific discrimination in a particular sector, rather than by a general assumption of widespread racism or sexism.

At the same time, Republicans in Congress are moving forward with plans to do away with all Federal efforts intended to give women and ethnic minorities extra help in employment and contracting.

California, Thursday 29. Lana Turner dies, aged 75. Famous as the "sweater girl", her films included *The Postman Always Rings Twice* **(1946).**

NEW YORK, MONDAY 26
United Healthcare to buy Metrahealth

The United Healthcare health maintenance corporation agreed today to buy Metrahealth, a more traditional health insurance company. The deal makes United the largest provider of healthcare plans in the US.

The $1.65 billion deal will mean that millions of people accustomed to the freedoms allowed by traditional health plans will now get their insurance from a company reputed to offer plans that restrict both the doctors to whom members can go and the treatment those doctors provide. However, its size means United should be able to offer lower prices.

CAIRO, MONDAY 26
Assassination attempt on Mubarak

Egypt's President Hosni Mubarak survived an assassination attempt without injury this morning when several gunmen carrying automatic weapons opened fire on the motorcade carrying him to the opening of an African summit meeting in the Ethiopian capital, Addis Ababa.

Mubarak was rushed back to Cairo, where he vowed that the attackers, believed to be Islamic fundamentalists, would "pay dearly for their actions." Two gunmen and two Ethiopian policemen were killed in the assault, but no bullets penetrated the armored car in which Mubarak was traveling. He has already been the target of two assassination plots.

A warm return to Cairo for Mubarak.

S	M	T	W	T	F	S
						1
2	3	4	5	6	7	8
9	10	11	12	13	14	15
16	17	18	19	20	21	22
23	24	25	26	27	28	29
30	31					

London, 1
Californian tennis player Jeff Tarango, yet to win a match at Wimbledon after seven tournaments, is disqualified after accusing an official of corruption. He is later fined a record £10,000.

Rome, 3
Antonio Di Pietro, formerly a leading Italian anticorruption magistrate, is accused of extortion and abuse of office.

Miami, 3
Lawyer Donald L. Ferguson pleads guilty to aiding Colombian drug traffickers.

Outer Space, 4
The space shuttle *Atlantis* and the Russian space station *Mir* separate after circling the Earth together for five days.

Jerusalem, 4
Israel and the PLO reach an outline agreement on withdrawal of Israeli troops from the West Bank, to be followed by Palestinian elections. (→ July 30)

Washington DC, 4
Congress prepares a budget allowing for even more military spending than was requested by the Pentagon, giving rise to accusations that the Republicans are reviving a cold-war mentality.

Trenton, 5
The New Jersey Board of Education announces that a management team will be sent in to manage the troubled Newark schools.

Port-au-Prince, 5
The second round of elections in Haiti are postponed after protests of widespread irregularities.

Los Angeles, 6
The prosecution rests in the O.J. Simpson case after 92 days. (→ July 13)

Bosnia, 6
Bosnian Serbs bombard the so-called UN "safe area" of Srebrenica. (→ July 8)

Death
Eva Gabor, the youngest of the three Hungarian-born actress sisters, in Los Angeles at age 74, July 4.

NEW YORK, THURSDAY 6
Don Nelson new coach of Knicks

Don Nelson faces the press after signing a three-year contract with the Knicks.

Don Nelson, who has been named National Basketball Association coach of the year three times, and who recently resigned from the Golden State Warriors, replaced Pat Riley as head coach of the New York Knicks. His basic salary for a three-year contract is almost $6 million.

As a player with Boston Celtic Nelson, 55, won five championships although as a coach he has yet to secure one, in spite of more than 88 victories. One of his aims, then, is to become the tenth man to win championships as both a player and coach.

Nelson, who left the Warriors after a well-publicized feud with rookie player Chris Webber, confirmed that to achieve a coaching title is a burning ambition, "the one thing I want."

Las Vegas, Monday 3. Pancho Gonzalez, tennis player, dies aged 67. In 1969, he and Charlie Pasarell played the longest match in Wimbledon history.

NEW DELHI, TUESDAY 4
Hostages taken by Kashmiri rebels

Two Britons and two Americans have been kidnapped by armed Kashmiri rebels while trekking through thick forest to the east of Srinagar.

The kidnappers belong to one of several Muslim groups fighting for Kashmiri independence from India. Kashmir has been under direct federal rule since its elected state government was deposed in 1990, shortly after separatists began their armed struggle. The kidnappings are believed to be part of a campaign to draw western attention – particularly that of the US – to the problems in Kashmir. (→ July 9)

ANCHORAGE, MONDAY 3
Bear kills two in Alaska park

An attack by a bear in Chugach State Park, 20 miles south of Anchorage, left a 77-year-old woman and her son dead. The victims were Marcie Trent and Larry Waldron. Mr. Waldron's 14-year-old nephew, Art Abel, survived the incident by climbing a tree.

Mr. Waldron, alerted to the danger by Art, ran back down the trail to help his mother. He was still alive when found by a hiker an hour later, confirming that a bear had attacked them, but he bled to death before help could arrive. Mrs. Trent died of massive head and chest injuries.

The park trail was closed while rangers searched for the killer bear.

SARAJEVO, SATURDAY 8
Serbs bombard Srebrenica

As Bosnian Serb artillery continues to bombard the Muslim enclave of Srebrenica, United Nations peacekeeping forces appear powerless to prevent the fall of this safe haven.

Several outposts held by Dutch UN troops were captured during heavy fighting on the outskirts of the town, and one Dutch soldier was killed. Bosnian President Izetbegovic has appealed to world leaders to protect the enclave. (→ July 11)

London, Saturday 8. Steffi Graf wins the Wimbledon ladies' singles. Meanwhile her father Peter, has mounting tax problems. (→ July 17)

CALIFORNIA, MONDAY 3

Unabomber contacts California professor

A professor of social psychology at the University of California, Tom R. Tyler, confirmed that he had received a letter, together with a copy of a manuscript already sent to *The New York Times* and *The Washington Post*, from the so-called Unabomber, the serial mail bomber who has teasingly eluded capture for 17 years.

"The letter is in response to comments I made about social malaise that appeared in May in the *San Francisco Chronicle*," explained the professor. This development is one of several in the last few days – there were, for example, rumors of a new photograph of a possible suspect, although this was denied by the FBI. It is believed, however, that federal agents have visited Californian scrap dealers who may have sold material to the bomber.

The Unabomber has offered to quit killing, but not necessarily property damage, if one of the newspapers he contacted agrees to publish a 35,000-word manifesto, calling for a revolution against the industrial and technological society. The papers are considering their response.(→ September 19)

ULSTER, MONDAY 3

Riots in Ulster after paratrooper Lee Clegg is released

Republican protests in Belfast against the release of Private Clegg.

Dozens of cars and vans were set ablaze on the streets of Belfast and Londonderry today in the worst disturbances since the start of the IRA cease-fire last year. Army bomb disposal experts were called in to deal with suspect vehicles and a cache of bombs was seized by police in the Ardoyne. Tonight, Crumlin Road in Belfast was blocked by about 100 demonstrators demanding the release of Republican prisoners. The violence was sparked by the release from Wakefield Prison of Private Lee Clegg, the British paratrooper who had been serving a life sentence after being convicted in 1993 of murdering 18-year-old Karen Reilly, who was traveling in a stolen car.

The car drove through an army checkpoint in Belfast in September 1990. Reilly, was killed by a bullet fired by Private Clegg after the car had passed. The Life Sentence Review Board freed him, deciding he had been sufficiently punished. (→ July 11)

LONDON, TUESDAY 4

Major wins leadership election

John Major emerges from No. 10 Downing Street after the result.

The gamble taken by Prime Minister John Major last month, when he resigned as Conservative leader and called an election, paid off handsomely today when he was reelected by a substantial majority. He defeated John Redwood by 218 votes to 89.

Mr. Major needed only 165 votes – half of those entitled to vote – so this result now gives him a clear mandate to continue unchallenged as prime minister until the general election.

Mr. Major called the leadership contest in order to clear the air after years of whispered discontent from the "Eurosceptic" right wing of the Conservative Party. After his victory the prime minister stressed that there would be "no recriminations." However, this will not extend to the reappointment of John Redwood in the expected cabinet reshuffle.

TOKYO, TUESDAY 4

Gas attacks cause panic in Japan

Security was tightened across Japan after a renewed spate of gas attacks on the country's rail system. The new wave began on Sunday when hundreds of commuters in Yokohama complained of sore throats and eyes; 50 were taken to the hospital but none was seriously injured.

Today two gas bombs containing sulphuric acid, sodium cyanide crystals, and timing devices were found in station lavatories in Tokyo. The first hit the evening rush hour at Kayabacho station, and six hours later a device was found at the world's busiest railroad station, Shinjuku. At two other Tokyo stations commuters complained of sore throats and eyes caused by fumes.

Police have no firm idea of who planted these devices. Nevertheless, despite repeated denials, suspicion continues to fall on the Aum Supreme Truth cult. Twelve Tokyo commuters were killed by sarin nerve gas in March.(→ October 4)

S	M	T	W	T	F	S
						1
2	3	4	5	6	7	8
9	10	11	12	13	14	15
16	17	18	19	20	21	22
23	24	25	26	27	28	29
30	31					

Sri Lanka, 9
The Sri Lankan government sends 10,000 troops to combat in a major offensive against Tamil Tiger guerrillas. (→ August 7)

New York, 9
The murder rate in New York has dropped to its lowest level since 1970.

New York, 9
Seventh Avenue is flooded when a water main is severed.

Union, South Carolina, 10
Susan Smith, accused of drowning her two sons, is passed competent to stand trial after controversy over her mental stability. (→ July 22)

Northern Ireland, 11
A march by Protestants ends in violence as police block their route through a nationalist area. (→ August 28)

Washington DC, 11
President Clinton announces that full diplomatic relations with Vietnam are to be restored after a 22-year break.

Ivory Coast, 12
Reports of secret trials and even of executions of the Nigerian military regime emerge. (→ October 31)

Washington DC, 11
Federal prosecutors are seeking the death penalty in the trial of Timothy J. McVeigh, accused of blowing up the Federal building in Oklahoma City. (→ August 10)

Beijing, 12
China insists that the US should reaffirm the "one China" policy that states Taiwan is part of China.

Washington DC, 12
President Clinton backs the right of parents to expect religion to have a place in American schools.

Los Angeles, 13
Judge Ito bars O.J. Simpson's lawyers from putting forward their theory that Nicole Simpson and Ronald L. Goldman were killed by drug dealers. (→ July 27)

CHICAGO, FRIDAY 14
Chicagoans die in heat wave

The Windy City sweltered under a blanket of heat yesterday as temperatures reached a record 106° F in the in downtown areas.

As the heat wave continued across the US, another 12 fatalities were reported, while many more victims of the stifling heat were taken to the hospital. Few sections of the country have managed to escape the effects of a heat wave that is also affecting the continent of Europe.

Humans were not the only victims of the weather. In the Midwest, farmers were devastated as thousands of cattle became victims of the freakish temperatures. (→ July 16)

KASHMIR, SUNDAY 9
American hostage escapes rebels

An American hostage, John Childs, made a daring escape from his Kashmiri captors during the weekend. But the lives of another American, Donald Hutchings, and two Britons, Keith Mangan and Paul Wells, were still hanging in the balance last night as the Kashmiri rebels who are holding them set a deadline for their demands. They want 22 imprisoned Muslim rebels to be released by the Indian government by Saturday.

London, Sunday 9. Pete Sampras celebrates his third consecutive Wimbledon title, after defeating the former champion Boris Becker in four sets.

SARAJEVO, TUESDAY 11
Serbs overrun Srebrenica

The struggle for Srebrenica is over. Bosnian Serbs took over the town yesterday. Srebrenica was taken over by the Bosnian Serbs yesterday. Srebrenica was one of six Muslim "safe areas" under NATO protection. It is the first safe area to fall to the Bosnian Serbs and its capitulation is a massive blow to the UN.

As the Bosnian Serbs increased the severity of their attacks on the town, NATO planes responded by destroying two of the tanks involved in the assault. However, when the Bosnian Serbs threatened to execute 32 peacekeepers held hostage, plans to continue the defense of the enclave were abandoned. Along with 20,000 refugees, 400 Dutch peacekeeping troops fled the area. Another "safe haven," Zepa, is thought to be the next to fall to Bosnian Serbs. (→ July 16)

An Israeli soldier mourns his murdered comrades after the suicide bombing.

RALEIGH, MONDAY 10
Terror bomb in North Carolina

A mail bomb that was addressed to a female employee at the BTI telephone company exploded, seriously injuring Tracy Bullis, 35, a manager at the company, when she opened the package shortly before noon. She was rushed to Waco medical center with head and torso injuries. The other woman injured, Judith Collins Harrison, 38, of Wake Forest, suffered hearing loss but was later released from the hospital.

The authorities initially ruled out any link with the Unabomber, but it has been noted that the FBI are among those investigating the case.

ROME, MONDAY 10
Pope apologizes to women

The Pope said sorry to women today, taking it upon himself to retract centuries in which women have been considered inferior to men by the Catholic church. "...for this I am truly sorry," he stated. The letter was an open letter to all women, and made a specific reference to equality in pay and equality in civil and political rights: "the recognition of everything that is part of the rights and duties of citizens in a democratic state." However, the letter does not open any path toward female ordination, and, most significantly, does not mention birth control.

LOS ANGELES, TUESDAY 11
Hugh Grant makes TV confession

Hugh Grant (left) looks sheepish during his televised interview with Jay Leno.

Actor Hugh Grant was fined $500 plus costs, put on probation, and instructed to participate in an AIDS education program as a Los Angeles court found him guilty of "lewd conduct" with a prostitute, Divine Brown.

Later, while discussing the matter on TV, Grant paid tribute to the support of his girlfriend, Elizabeth Hurley, and his father, and put on a performance that won over the studio audience on *The Tonight Show with Jay Leno*. "I've done an abominable thing, and she's been amazing about it," the Englishman said of Hurley. "And, contrary to what I read in the paper today, she's been very supportive and we're going to try to work it out."

The star of the hugely successful 1994 movie *Four Weddings and a Funeral* had been booked to appear on Leno's show prior to being arrested on Sunset Boulevard with Brown. His appearance was scheduled to publicize his latest film *Nine Months*.

Grant looked nervous as Leno asked him tough questions but by the end of the show his apparently genuine remorse had convinced members of the studio audience that he deserved to be shown understanding for his actions. (→ July 18)

AUCKLAND, SUNDAY 9
French seize *Rainbow Warrior II*

France defied world public opinion when its navy commandos seized the Greenpeace ship *Rainbow Warrior II*. The environmentalists had sailed into French waters off Mururoa Atoll in protest against continued French nuclear testing in the area. Tear gas was used and two dozen Greenpeace activists arrested as President Chirac showed the world that France will not flinch despite widespread condemnation of its nuclear policy. The New Zealand prime minister, Jim Bolger, commented that the French actions had been "over the top." (→ September 1)

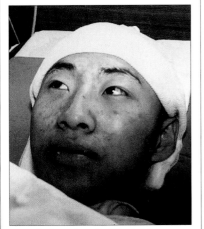

Seoul, Sunday 9. Choi Myong-Suk is pulled from the rubble of the collapsed Korean department store after surviving for nine days in a four-foot space.

MOSCOW, TUESDAY 11
President Yeltsin taken to hospital with heart condition

The Russian president, Boris Yeltsin, 64, was taken to the Moscow Central Clinic today with a recurrence of his serious heart trouble.

President Yeltsin has been plagued by health problems in recent months, and suspicions are growing both in Russia and abroad that he may no longer have the strength to continue as leader. Worries about his health are exacerbated by indications that the president also has a serious, long-standing drinking problem.

It is widely suspected inside Russia that Yeltsin has not been running the government for a while. He is regarded in some quarters as a figurehead, with day-to-day decisions being taken by Prime Minister Viktor Chernomyrdin.

Even when Yeltsin has been well, he has found himself at times upstaged by Chernomyrdin. While Yeltsin was meeting with world leaders at the Group of Seven summit in Canada in June, the Prime Minister was carrying out official duties that emphasized his increasingly important role as a statesman.

Chernomyrdin has also been the focus of commanding performances in the Russian parliament. Western observers and investors would have few fears if he were to replace Yeltsin, who has become unpopular with the Russian people. (→ July 24)

President Boris Yeltsin: back in hospital with heart trouble.

BOULDER, THURSDAY 13
Creation of super atom predicted by Einstein is announced

After 70 years, a theory that was first proposed by Albert Einstein and Indian physicist Satyendra Bose has finally been tested and a new "super atom" has been created.

This new type of matter is produced when thousands of atoms are cooled to a temperature just above absolute zero. Electrons, which orbit around the nucleus of every atom, then spread out, dissociate from the nucleus, and finally act like a single entity. The successful experiment, which used atoms of the metallic element rubidium, took place on June 5, and the results have just been published. Dr. Carl Wieman of the National Institute of Standards and Technology said of the "super atom" in the publication *Science*, "It really is a new state of matter. It has completely different properties from any other kind of [solid, gas, or liquid]."

Dr. Eric Cornell, his colleague, added, "The sample in our lab is the only chunk of this stuff in the universe, unless it is in a lab in some other solar system." The Colorado success ends a race in which more than a dozen laboratories in America and Europe sought to be the first to create the "super atom".

S	M	T	W	T	F	S
						1
2	3	4	5	6	7	8
9	10	11	12	13	14	15
16	17	18	19	20	21	22
23	24	25	26	27	28	29
30	31					

London, 16
A new book, *The Lodger,* by British author Stewart Evans, claims that Jack the Ripper was an American.

Bradford, England 16
Scientists have, for the first time, isolated the cells that regulate hair growth and are moving closer to discovering a cure for baldness.

Rio de Janeiro, 16
Up to 40 people are feared dead after several explosions at the Brazilian Navy's main weapons base.

Bonn, 17
Wimbledon tennis champion Steffi Graf is considering leaving Germany after raids by tax inspectors on her home. (→ August 2)

Brussels, 17
The European Union signs a far-reaching trade pact with Russia.

Chicago, 17
The last remaining American TV manufacturer, the Zenith Electronics Corporation, is to sell a controlling interest to a South Korean company.

Los Angeles, 18
Divine Brown, the prostitute arrested with actor Hugh Grant, pleads not guilty to a charge of lewd conduct and seeks a trial.

Washington DC, 18
President Clinton's reelection campaign raises more than $9.3 million in its first three months.

Kiev, 18
The funeral of Patriarch Volodymyr, leader of the Ukrainian Orthodox Church, erupts into violence.

Tallahassee, 18
Dr. Rolando Sanchez is suspended amid allegations that he cut off a patient's toe without her consent. In February he amputated the wrong leg from another patient.

New York, 20
Duke Snider and Willie McCovey, two of the greatest stars of baseball's golden age, plead guilty to charges of tax fraud.

Death
Sir Stephen Spender, British poet, essayist, and critic, at age 85, July 17.

US prepared to send helicopters to Gorazde

These US helicopters are currently under mothballs, but could quickly be brought into active service to transport French troops in Bosnia.

The US appears to be on the verge of taking drastic action to halt the advance of the Bosnian Serbs on the Muslim "safe areas." President Clinton is said to be considering using a fleet of US helicopters to transport 1,000 French troops to help defend the designated Muslim "safe area" of Gorazde. Such an action would almost certainly lead to the loss of American lives.

General John Shalikashvili, the chairman of the Joint chiefs of Staff, is discussing operational matters in London with Field Marshal Inge, chief of the British Defense Staff, and Admiral Lanxade, chief of the French Defense Staff.

The US secretary of state, Warren Christopher, said, "No decisions have been made…we operate in the context of the fact that President Clinton has decided, and I think the American people want to keep it that way, that we will not inject American troops into Bosnia, except to use them to withdraw allied forces." (→ July 17)

WASHINGTON, TUESDAY 18
FBI men attend racist "Roundup"

The Federal Bureau of Investigation stated that seven of its agents had been identified as having attended racist "Good Ol' Boys Roundups" in the past few years. The "Roundups," at which paraphernalia denigrating blacks is sold, are organized by Gene Rightmeyer, a former FBI agent.

Film of a recent gathering was made by the paramilitary group the Alabama Minutemen, who wish to humble the FBI because of the Bureau's handling of the 1993 Branch Davidian siege at Waco, Texas, and their shooting dead the wife and son of a white separatist at Ruby Ridge, Idaho, in 1992.

Johannesburg, Friday 21.
Winnie Mandela begins legal action against F. W. de Klerk, ex-South African President, over alleged police conspiracy.

CHICAGO, SUNDAY 16
Heat waves claim hundreds of lives

Temperatures of 106° F have filled the Cook County morgue in Chicago to capacity with heat fatalities, leaving around 300 bodies awaiting autopsies in funeral homes. Bodies brought to the morgue for which no room can be found have been stored in refrigerator trucks. Dr. Edmund Donoghue, the Cook County medical examiner, expects that the final fatality count from the heat will be over 400 in Chicago.

In New York, declining temperatures were greeted with relief after the heat had climbed above 100° F and had claimed 11 lives.

KEARNEY, MISSOURI, MONDAY 17
Remains of Jesse James exhumed

The body of Jesse James is dug up for examination over a century after its burial.

One of the Wild West's greatest legends, gunslinger Jesse James is to be unearthed by Prof. James Starrs of George Washington University. The body of James, the notorious nineteenth century bankrobber, has been exhumed for an autopsy that the professor hopes will finally determine the circumstances of his death.

James' body was no sooner in its grave than rumors began that the outlaw faked his own death. Prof. Starrs intends to prove that it was indeed Jesse James who was shot dead by Robert Ford in 1892. He also wishes to establish the caliber of bullet used in the killing and the angle and distance from which it was fired.

SARAJEVO, MONDAY 17
5,000 Muslims held in Srebrenica

There are reports that thousands of Muslim men were detained by the Serbs after they overran the town of Srebrenica last week. Many women in the flood of refugees that overwhelmed the aid agencies have reported that their husbands and sons were separated off and taken away for "questioning" by the Serbs. All of those so treated have disappeared, for the moment anyway. It is hoped that members of the Dutch UN contingent based in the town, 55 of whom were captured and then released yesterday, may be able to shed some light on this alarming story. (→ July 23)

St. Andrews, Scotland, Friday 21. Golfing great Arnold Palmer plays his last-ever round in the British Open amid emotional scenes.

BAGHDAD, SUNDAY 16
Two Americans released by Saddam

Two American citizens, sentenced to eight years in prison for entering Iraq illegally, have been freed. David Daliberti and William Barloon enjoyed an impromptu celebration with pizza and champagne in the Polish Embassy in Baghdad. Both had been working close to the Iraqi border in Kuwait and inadvertently strayed into Iraq.

The man behind their release was the Democratic congressman Bill Richardson, who has a history of intervening successfully in matters involving American citizens abroad. Mr. Richardson flew into Baghdad on Saturday for a meeting with Iraqi leader Saddam Hussein.

After the two Americans were sentenced President Clinton wrote to the Iraqi authorities asking for them to be released. However, Secretary of State Warren Christopher said that Congressman Richardson's visit to Iraq was "a private humanitarian mission" and that no deals had been done with Iraq in return for the release of the two Americans.

UNION, SOUTH CAROLINA, SATURDAY 22
Susan Smith found guilty

Susan Smith: guilty of murder.

The jury took two and a half hours of deliberation, but they gave the state prosecution service the result they wanted: Susan Smith was found guilty of murdering her two sons, Michael and Alex. The defense team had tried hard for a verdict of involuntary manslaughter, but the jury would have none of it.

The town of Union has found the publicity surrounding the case distasteful. And even with this verdict, public interest will not go away, since the same jury has to spend next week selecting a penalty, and may send Smith to the electric chair. The penalty phase of the trial promises to be as absorbing as the first. (→ July 29)

Buenos Aires, Monday 17. One of the greatest drivers in the history of car racing, Juan Manuel Fangio, has died at the age of 84. Fangio, who won five Formula One World Championships between 1951 and 1957, later became an international ambassador for the sport and president of Mercedes-Benz in Argentina.

	S	M	T	W	T	F	S
							1
	2	3	4	5	6	7	8
	9	10	11	12	13	14	15
	16	17	18	19	20	21	22
	23	24	25	26	27	28	29
	30	31					

Moscow, 24
President Boris Yeltsin leaves the hospital almost two weeks after being admitted with heart problems. (→ August 7)

Washington DC, 24
The Senate unanimously backs legislation to make compulsory the registration of lobbyists.

Boston, 24
Conrail Inc. is to pay a $2.5 million fine for letting oil flow into the Charles River over a 15-year period.

The Hague, 25
Radavan Karadjic and Ratko Mladic, leaders of the Bosnian Serbs, are formally charged with war crimes. (→ July 27)

Geneva, 27
Tadeusz Mazowiecki, the United Nations Human Rights Special Investigator, quits in disgust at the international community's failure to protect Muslims in eastern Bosnia. (→ July 30)

Johannesburg, 27
Footprints preserved in volcanic ash show that humans in Africa were walking upright 3.7 million years ago.

Washington DC, 27
Congressional Republicans, led by Senator Bob Dole, introduce legislation that would bar the Federal Government from granting benefits on the basis of race, ethnicity, or sex.

Tomislavgrad, 30
An escalation of the war in the former Yugoslavia looks certain with the increasing mobilization of Croatian and Bosnian Serb troops. (→ August 5)

Jerusalem, 30
The Israeli government is to seek the extradition of Mousa Mohamed Abu Marzook, a leading member of terrorist group Hamas, who has been detained in the US. (→ August 1)

Death
Charlie Rich, US country singer and composer of "Behind Closed Doors" and "The Most Beautiful Girl", in Hammond, Louisiana, on July 25, at age 62.

Cork, Ireland, Monday 24. The filming of *Rapture*, a movie set in Ireland and starring Marlon Brando (above, on set), has been suspended after its backers encountered financial problems.

UNION, SC, SATURDAY 29

Susan Smith gets life

The jury that found Susan Smith guilty of murder a week ago decided today that she should serve a life sentence with parole possible after 30 years. The jurors had the opportunity to send the convicted woman to the electric chair, but they were swayed by powerful arguments about her emotional state. During the trial itself, law officers said that they were convinced of her remorse when she prayed with them after confessing. During the penalty hearing itself, her stepfather, Beverly Russel, admitted sexually molesting her as a teenager and claimed that he shared the guilt for the murders.

WASHINGTON DC, THURSDAY 27

Three big US unions to merge

Three of the largest unions in the US are to join forces after suffering years of falling memberships and influence. The United Steelworkers of America, the United Automobile Workers, and the International Association of Machinists and Aerospace Workers have decided to pool their resources. The new combined membership will total approximately two million.

Leaders of the three unions admitted that the process of uniting their organizations, each of which is run by a massive administration, would take close to five years.

MOSCOW, SUNDAY 30

Russia signs accord with Chechens

Russia and Chechnya are at peace after representatives of the two states signed a joint agreement to end the war that has been raging in Chechnya since last December. Chechnya was occupied by 40,000 Russian troops seven months ago after it had threatened to break away from the new Russian federation. The pact was signed in Grozny and will lead to the gradual withdrawal of Russian troops from the area. (→ August 3)

PARIS, TUESDAY 25

Paris Metro bomb kills four

Emergency aid for the wounded after the bombing on the Paris Metro.

Four people were killed and 60 injured, ten severely, when a terrorist bomb ripped through a Metro train in central Paris. The explosion took place during the evening rush hour at St. Michel station, close to Notre Dame Cathedral, one of the French capital's most popular tourist sites.

Police investigators discovered evidence that the bomb had been hidden beneath a seat on the train. Paramedics set up emergency hospital facilities in a cafe close to the scene of the explosion while the most badly injured victims were transported to the hospital by helicopter.

"There was a blast and the train door blew out," said one survivor. "There was a deafening explosion. Everyone got down on the ground. There was not much panic," said another. Algerian extremists are suspected of having been behind the bombing. (→ August 17)

TEL AVIV, MONDAY 24

Suicide bomber kills five in Tel Aviv

At least five people were killed and 30 injured when a radical Arab blew himself up on a Tel Aviv bus during the morning rush hour. The Hamas group, an extreme organization opposed to the Israeli-Palestinian peace talks, immediately claimed full responsibility for the incident.

Israel's Prime Minister Yitzhak Rabin afterward expressed his commitment to the peace process when he told his colleagues in the Labor Party, "I saw the bus, it was a painful sight. It is difficult for all of us. But we cannot allow the acts of these crazed murderers who are enemies of peace to prevent us from continuing with the process to solve once and for all the Israeli-Palestinian conflict."

Talks on peace between Israeli representatives and Yasser Arafat's Palestinian Authority are being held on a 24-hour-a-day basis close to the Dead Sea. They are to cease temporarily, but only until the funerals of the victims on the bombed bus have been held.

The bombing is the latest in a series that has been carried out by Hamas sympathizers during the past year as the peace talks have gathered pace. The bombing was condemned internationally, and Palestinian leader Yasser Arafat said, "This is an attempt to sabotage the peace process." The bombing prompted Israeli opposition parties to again call for the peace talks to be suspended. (→ July 30)

LOS ANGELES, THURSDAY 27

O.J.'s lawyers argue that sock and glove were part of frame-up

Defense lawyers for O.J. Simpson have started putting forward their case: that the former football hero is the victim of a police conspiracy.

They claim that certain police officers tampered with forensic evidence in a bid to strengthen the case against Simpson. The three key pieces of evidence that the defense alleges were interfered with are a bloody sock, a bloody glove, and laboratory tests that were subsequently leaked to

members of the press. The defense also alleges that one officer in particular, Detective Mark Fuhrman, is a racist and that his bias led him to alter evidence in the Simpson case.

Mr. Herbert MacDonell, a member of the International Association of Blood Stain Pattern Analysts, gave evidence that threw doubt on the incriminatory nature of the bloody sock that was offered as evidence by the police. (→ August 15)

A glove found at the scene of Nicole Simpson's murder is shown to the jury.

LONDON, SUNDAY 23

1,200 UK troops bound for Sarajevo

British troops, who will be deployed in strengthening defenses around UN "safe areas."

A 1,200-strong force of British troops is heading for Sarajevo after a joint warning from British, French, and US government military officers that further Bosnian Serb aggression in the UN-designated "safe areas" would not be tolerated. The joint communiqué was delivered to the Bosnian Serb commander, Ratko Mladic, in Belgrade.

The troops' first task will be to make safe the only passage into

Sarajevo. Fifty British Warrior tanks are moving into position around the dirt track over Mount Ignam that provides that access. They are to respond with fire if the Serbs resume their bombardment of the track. The British will be joined by 500 French Foreign Legionnaires, who will be backed up by 12 light tanks and other armored vehicles. This is the first real deployment of the UN's Rapid Reaction Force. (→ July 25)

WASHINGTON DC, TUESDAY 25

Grand Jury to look at tobacco industry

Tobacco companies are under fire again. The Justice Department is convening a Grand Jury to investigate claims that the companies did not give correct information to federal regulators concerning the contents of their cigarettes or the likely ill effects of these contents. The heads of seven leading companies testified in 1994 to a Congressional committee that they did not think cigarettes were harmful or addictive, nor that they controlled the levels of nicotine in the cigarettes they produced. Internal company documents now appear to contradict that claim.

Seattle, Wednesday 26. Al Hendrix, father of rock star Jimi, who died in 1970, has won the rights to his son's music after years of legal battles.

August

Washington DC, 1
President Clinton attacks Congress, accusing it of being in the control of polluters and gun lobbyists.

Jerusalem, 1
The Israeli Government makes the first legal moves toward bringing the man it identifies as leader of Hamas from the US to stand trial in Israel.

Bonn, 1
The former East German head of the Stasi secret police, Erich Mielke, is released after having served four years in jail.

Beijing, 2
China announces that it has arrested two United States Air Force officers, accusing them of "sneaking into a number of restricted military zones."

Columbia, 2
Defense Minister Fernando Botero resigns after a scandal linking contributions by drug barons to President Ernesto Samper's election campaign.

Washington DC, 3
The Senate Whitewater panel seeks information regarding Hillary Clinton's role in handling files in the aftermath of White House lawyer Vincent W. Foster's suicide.

Moscow, 3
President Boris Yeltsin claims that a new agreement between Moscow and the rebel republic of Chechnya, involving Chechen disarmament and eventual Russian troop withdrawal, is a major step toward peace.

London, 4
Queen Elizabeth the Queen Mother celebrates her 95th birthday, greeting enthusiastic crowds outside her London residence, Clarence House, and riding on a golf buggy.

Teheran, 5
Leading members of the Islamic regime in Iran are put on trial accused of wholesale embezzlement from two of the country's banks.

Death
Ida Lupino, the British-born actress who once described herself as "the poor man's Bette Davis" and who turned to writing, directing, and producing in the 1950s, in California, at age 77, August 3.

JERUSALEM, WEDNESDAY 2
Israeli settlers clash with police on West Bank

There was tension in Israeli settlements on the West Bank tonight after a day of clashes and protests. The settlers bitterly oppose Premier Yitzhak Rabin's plan to hand the West Bank over to the Palestine Liberation Organization. Settlers occupied hills near the settlements of Beit El and Kidumin, as police kept a watchful eye, but at the hill of Al-Khader, to the south of Jerusalem, there was violence as soldiers forced settlers to disperse. There were also violent scenes in Jerusalem, when settlers gathered outside the police headquarters where Rabbi Shlomo Riskin, whom they regard as their spiritual leader, was being held. Riskin was released late today (→ August 13)

Soldiers try to remove settlers who are occupying hills in the West Bank region.

Michael D. Eisner of Disney and Thomas S. Murphy of ABC announcing their deal.

LOS ANGELES, TUESDAY 1
ABC and CBS are sold off

Big changes of ownership in the TV world are taking place. Walt Disney has bought ABC for $19 billion, while the Westinghouse Electric Corporation has agreed to pay $5.4 billion for CBS. The Walt Disney move is seen as a logical step, creating what will be a powerful world media player. The Westinghouse acquisition has puzzled some analysts, who believe that CBS needs more programming talent to make the most of its position. (→ August 14)

BONN, WEDNESDAY 2
Steffi Graf's father on tax charges

Peter Graf, the father of reigning Wimbledon champion Steffi Graf and her financial manager since the start of her tennis career, was arrested at his home in Brühl, near Bonn, and charged with tax evasion.

It has been confirmed that Miss Graf herself is also being investigated. Most high-earning German sports stars have emigrated for tax purposes, but Graf has chosen to remain in Germany. It was recently revealed in the German magazine *Der Spiegel* that the Grafs have not made any tax declarations for four years.

Fort Pierce, Florida, Wednesday 2. Hurricane Erin came ashore near Vero Beach in the early hours of the morning, bringing with it heavy rain and winds, before heading north-west toward Orlando. In Brevard County more than 10 in (25 cm) of rain were forecast.

As Croatian forces move on Serb-held Knin, a vast exodus of refugees begins.

BOSNIA, SATURDAY 5

Croats take Knin

In a bold offensive that could mark a turning point in the war in former Yugoslavia, the Croatians and Bosnian Muslim allies have inflicted a major defeat on the Serb militias.

After 30 hours of intense fighting Croatian forces took Knin, the capital of Serbian-held Krijina, while the Bosnian Muslims attacked the Krajina Serbs from the rear. To the east of Knin, further Serb-held towns of strategic significance were under Bosnian attack.

As the Croatians advanced on Knin, some 35,000 Krajina Serbs took to the roads leading out of the area in what UN officials termed the biggest single refugee movement of the war. Croatian sources claimed that corridors out of Serb territory had been left open to allow the escape of civillians, a growing tide predicted to reach 100,000.

On Friday, the Krajina Serb leader Milan Babic was in Belgrade, appealing for support from the Serbian army. But he secured only a promise of humanitarian aid.

Among the casualties of the Croatian advance on Knin were two Czech UN peace-keepers, killed in Gospic. Following the Croatian bombardment of the Serb capital, one UN official said that "almost the only people remaining in Knin were the dead and dying." (→ August 9)

ARGENTINA, TUESDAY 1

Jet and UFO in near miss

During the early hours of Tuesday morning the pilot of an Aerolineas Argentinas jet, Jorge Polanco, reported a UFO that flew into the path of the plane before proceeding to cruise alongside it.

His observations were confirmed by Air Force Major Jorge Oviedo and a number of other witnesses.

Simultaneously, there was a total power failure in the city of San Carlos de Bariloche, forcing pilot Polanco to abort his landing approach.

LOS ANGELES, WEDNESDAY 2

Thai "slaves" are released

From daybreak to midnight, working for $1.60 an hour and in fear of their lives, nearly 70 Thai workers have been stitching clothes in a grim factory in El Monte, east of Los Angeles. They have been struggling with impossible debts incurred during their initial journey to the US.

They were freed during a predawn raid by immigration officials, a result of which eight employees have been charged with abuse of the workers. Neighbors of the barbed-wire compound say that they had not suspected anything was wrong.

ANTARCTICA, THURSDAY 3

Ozone hole over Antarctica widens

The sea ice of the Antarctic begins to melt as the hole in the ozone layer above the continent deepens.

A study by the British Antarctic Survey, published ten years after its original revelation of a "hole" in the ozone layer above the ice, suggests that the danger continues to increase.

Ozone measurements at the Halley Research Station show values of less than 40 percent of those recorded in the 1960s. Writing in the science magazine *Nature*, team members Jonathan Shanklin and Dr. Anna Jones suggest that the fall in ozone levels, previously limited to the Antarctic spring, are now detected in summer as well.

Loss of ozone, which is essential for protection against the harmful effects of ultraviolet rays, is caused by increases in levels of chlorine and bromine in the atmosphere, brought about in turn by emissions of man-made chemicals, notably the CFCs that are used, for example, as aerosol propellants.

The recent Montreal agreement on the control of ozone-destroying chemicals suggests that the problem will eventually diminish, but Dr. Jones predicts that the hole in the ozone layer will nonetheless last for decades.

S	M	T	W	T	F	S
		1	2	3	4	5
6	7	8	9	10	11	12
13	14	15	16	17	18	19
20	21	22	23	24	25	26
27	28	29	30	31		

Hanoi, 6
Secretary of State Warren Christopher formally opens the new American Embassy in the capital of Vietnam during his tour of Asia.

Philadelphia, 7
Former Black Panther Mumia Abu-Jamal, who is on death row and was due to be executed on August 17 for the murder of a policeman, is granted a stay of execution.

Gothenburg, Sweden, 7
Britain's Jonathan Edwards set a new world record for the triple jump at the World Athletics Championships.

Moscow, 7
President Boris Yeltsin, 64, returns to work at the Kremlin four weeks after being admitted to hospital with acute heart trouble.

Colombo, Sri Lanka, 7
A suspected Tamil suicide bomber causes an explosion at a government building in the Sri Lankan capital, killing 22 people.(→ October 20)

Washington DC, 9
In a magazine interview Marianne Gingrich, wife of the Speaker of the House, says, "I don't want him to be president and I don't think he should be." In the same article British woman Anne Manning claims an adulterous affair with Gingrich during his previous marriage.

New York, 9
Airlines and airports throughout the country inaugurated heightened security measures following the arrests in New York City of Palestinians accused of terrorism.

New York, 11
The first Mickey Mouse film since 1953, a seven-minute short called *Runaway Brain*, opens as support to the Disney movie *A Kid in King Arthur's Court*.

Deaths
David Begelman, former president of MGM, was found dead of a gunshot wound in a Los Angeles hotel, at age 73, August 8.

Phil Harris, band leader, singer, comedian, and voice of Baloo in Disney's *The Jungle Book*, at age 91, August 11.

Hiroshima remembers the A-bomb

In the Peace Park at Hiroshima, 50 years to the minute since the atomic bomb fell on the city, a bell was struck, and a crowd of over 60,000 observed a minute's silence.

There were survivors present, many with the scars of half a century still visible, as the Peace Bell tolled. The centerpiece of the park is a memorial arch, beneath which a register of those who died is preserved inside a stone chest.

Hiroshima stands on the delta of the River Ota, which 50 years ago was spanned by a T-shaped bridge that provided a target for *Enola Gay*, the B-29 plane that carried the four-ton atomic bomb over the city. The bomb was released at 31,000 ft (10,500 m)

Floating candles commemorate those who died 50 years ago when the bomb was dropped.

With few exceptions, the buildings of Hiroshima were razed to the ground.

and fell for 43 seconds before exploding. At this point the temperature reached 5,400° F, and severe burning was suffered by people two-and-a-half miles away.

Hiroshima today is an industrial city of more than one million people. Its mayor, Takashi Hiraoka, in a historic speech, apologized for Japanese conduct during World War II, and warned that the horrors of Hiroshima and Nagasaki could be repeated as long as nuclear weapons still exist.

Wreaths were laid at the Peace Park memorial and 1,500 doves were released. After the ceremony the crowd dispersed to various smaller, more private, commemorations.

780,000-year-old European found

Reports in the journal *Science* suggest that human ancestors reached Europe from Africa at least 780,000 years ago, far earlier than was previously thought, based on analysis of fossils and tools found in caves near Burgos, Spain.

The material does not match any species already described – neither *Homo erectus* nor Heidelberg Man, at 500,000 years old who is thought to be among the earliest Europeans. The newly discovered humanoids could instead be primitive Neanderthals, who were eventually replaced by modern humans.

Saddam hit by family defections

Two of Saddam Hussein's daughters, together with their husbands, have fled Iraq and sought refuge in the neighboring country of Jordan.

Raghad, the Iraqi leader's eldest daughter, is married to General Hussein Kamel Hassan, who was in command of Iraq's military industrialization. Rana's husband, General Saddam Kamel, was a personal bodyguard and military adviser to the President.

The defections are regarded as a serious blow to President Saddam's attempts to retain a hold on power in a country weakened by sanctions.

California, Wednesday 9. The rock generation mourned the death of Jerry Garcia, leader of the Grateful Dead, who died at a drug treatment center.

COLOMBIA, SUNDAY 6

Leader of Cali drug cartel arrested in Colombia

Miguel Rodriguez Orejuela, one of the leaders of the Cali drug cartel, was arrested by police at an apartment in the town. Following his capture he was flown to police headquarters in Bogota and presented to the press.

Of the seven top men in the cartel, six have now been placed under arrest. The sequence began two months ago with the arrest of Gilberto Rodriguez Orejuela, Miguel's older brother, following which three more men, surrendered, and another was captured. In the opinion of Colombian police chief General Serrano, Miguel Rodriguez Orejuela is the number-one man in the cartel, identified by American law enforcement officers as being in charge of their drug trafficking and money-laundering operations.

The arrest comes at a convenient time for the Colombian government, beset as it is by accusations that ties between the country's political establishment and the cartel have allowed the latter to prosper.

Colombian President Ernesto Samper hailed the arrests as a decisive move in ending the trade in cocaine that has blighted his land. "This is the end of the Cali cartel and the beginning of a new era for the country," he said when the news of the arrest was announced.

Miguel Rodriguez Orejuela following his arrest in Cali.

OKLAHOMA CITY, THURSDAY 10

McVeigh and Nichols indicted by Grand Jury

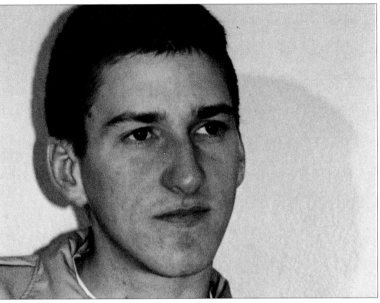

Timothy McVeigh, who is accused of causing the Oklahoma bomb blast.

Timothy McVeigh and Terry Nichols were indicted by a Federal Grand Jury on charges of causing the explosion at the Federal building in Oklahoma on April 19.

It is alleged that the two conspirators financed the crime by robbing an Arkansas gun dealer, raiding a Kansas quarry for dynamite and fuses and concocting an explosive mixture of fertilizer and diesel fuel. McVeigh is further charged with parking a truck containing the explosives in front of the Federal building and then setting off the bomb. At least 167 people lost their lives in the blast.

The two accused are former army buddies, and a third ex-soldier, Michael Fortier, pleaded guilty to a separate indictment concerning his knowledge of the intention to carry out the bombing. (→ August 15)

WASHINGTON DC, WEDNESDAY 9

Spy plane photos indicate mass graves at Srebrenica

Chilling evidence provided by photographs that were taken from satellites and U-2 planes over the Bosnian town of Srebrenica suggests that Bosnian Serbs have committed atrocities on a massive scale.

One photograph shows hundreds, possibly thousands, of Muslim men and boys being held in a field five miles north of the town, where thousands were rounded up by Bosnian Serbs last month. Another shows an extensive area of freshly-dug earth, consistent with the appearance of mass graves. David T. Johnson of the US State Department said, "We've got some evidence from sensitive sources that tend to corroborate accounts of atrocities against the Bosnian men and boys who were prevented from leaving Srebrenica." This evidence will be presented to the United Nations Security Council.

The International Red Cross reports that more than 6,000 people are still missing following the fall of the town to the Bosnian Serbs, and there are grave fears for their safety. The last massacre is on the scale of that in 1991 when the Serbs overran the town of Vukovar. Thousands of people remain unaccounted for. (→ August 30)

Los Angeles, Thursday 10. Hollywood madam Heidi Fleiss is found guilty of using a bank account for tax evasion and money-laundering operations.

LOS ANGELES, MONDAY 7

NBC to broadcast the Olympics

NBC broke with the tradition of bidding between rival networks for the television rights to the Olympic Games, when it announced that it had already agreed to pay $1.27 billion for the Summer Olympics 2000 in Sydney and the Winter event in Salt Lake City in 2002.

The move frustrates Rupert Murdoch's News Corporation, owner of the Fox Network; the Walt Disney Company, who agreed to buy Capital Cities/ABC last week and are looking to break into sports TV; and CBS, who have shown the last three winter games.

S	M	T	W	T	F	S
		1	2	3	4	5
6	7	8	9	10	11	12
13	14	15	16	17	18	19
20	21	22	23	24	25	26
27	28	29	30	31		

Srinagar, 13
Kashmiri separatists kill a kidnapped Norwegian tourist and threaten to kill other hostages unless India frees 15 militants.

Bogotá, 13
Bands of armed men kill at least 38 people in a series of raids in northwestern Colombia.

New York, 14
A mayoral advisory panel recommends that New York City abolish its municipal hospital system.

Bermuda, 14
In a referendum disrupted by Hurricane Felix, 74% of people vote against independence from Britain.

Los Angeles, 15
O.J. Simpson trial judge Lance Ito faces demands to withdraw from the case so that his wife Margaret York, the highest-ranking woman in the LAPD, can give evidence about racist tapes. (→ August 31)

Washington DC, 15
The dollar soars to its highest level in six months after concerted buying by the US, Germany, and Japan.

Oklahoma City, 15
Timothy J. McVeigh and Terry L. Nichols plead not guilty to charges of planting the bomb that killed 167 people in the Oklahoma City Federal building.

Boston, 16
A long-term study shows that the drug AZT does not help fight off the development of full-blown AIDS.

Moscow, 16
Wealthy Russians demonstrate outside former KGB headquarters against the large number of murders in the business community.

Washington DC, 17
The Pentagon orders military equipment into the Persian Gulf after warnings that Iraq may be planning attacks on Kuwait or Saudi Arabia.

Deaths
On August 17, Howard Koch, Hollywood screenwriter and co-writer of *Casablanca*, in Kingston, New York, at age 93.

LOS ANGELES, MONDAY 14
Michael Ovitz becomes president of Disney corporation

Michael Ovitz with his wife, Jody.

In a surprise move, the Walt Disney Company announced today that its new president will be top Hollywood talent agent Michael Ovitz.

The appointment shocked an industry still reeling from the news, announced only two weeks ago, that Disney was to acquire ABC for $19.2 billion, which will make it the world's largest entertainment company.

Ovitz will now work closely with Disney chairman Michael D. Eisner. Eisner had previously been criticized for failing to appoint a strong deputy after the death 16 months ago of his trusted lieutenant Frank Wells. Some commentators had expected the high-profile Disney studio chief Jeffrey Katzenberg to take over, but acrimonious disputes with Eisner led to his departure from the company.

TOKYO, TUESDAY 15
Japanese premier apologizes on 50th anniversary of VJ Day

While veterans' associations across the nation observed ceremonies commemorating the end of World War II, Japanese Premier Tomiichi Murayama delivered an apology for the atrocities Japanese forces committed during the conflict. Mr. Murayama's Socialist Party has always been willing to admit war guilt, but the official Japanese attitude has previously been that Japan was not necessarily the aggressor in 1941. This speech, which included the phrases "heartfelt apology" and "deep remorse" will be welcomed by many survivors and their families.

Mexico City, Thursday 17. Research by US scientist F. Sherwood Rowland suggests that the veil of corrosive brown smog that hangs perpetually over Mexico City is not caused primarily by motor exhaust, as officials have long believed, but by leaks from millions of steel tanks containing bottled gas used for cooking and heating.

Dallas, Sunday 13. Mickey Mantle, New York Yankees star of the 1950s and 60s, died at 63 from recently diagnosed cancer of the liver. The most powerful switch-hitter in baseball history, Mantle retired from the game in 1969.

JERUSALEM, SUNDAY 13
Palestinian shot by Israeli settlers

A Palestinian man was killed when Israeli settlers opened fire on protesters who had wrecked an encampment near Beit El on the Israeli-occupied West Bank. The dead man was identified as Kheir Abdel Hafid Qassem, 24. The shooting reawakens concerns about how peace between rival factions will be maintained when the Israeli army withdraws from parts of the West Bank in the preliminary to the forthcoming Palestinian elections. (→ August 18)

JERUSALEM, FRIDAY 18
Hamas activists arrested in Gaza

Palestinian police have captured a militant Muslim after an intelligence tip-off, and handed him over to the Israelis. Wael Nasser, 23, and another member of the Hamas movement gave themselves up after a three-hour siege in Gaza City.

Israeli officials were quick to praise the role of the Palestinian police in the arrests, saying that their actions augured well for future security cooperation between the two Middle East communities. In the meantime, however, the border between Israel and the West Bank remains closed. (→August 21)

Storm over Tyson's comeback victory

On his return to the ring after two years in prison, former undisputed World Heavyweight boxing champion Mike Tyson won his comeback fight easily, beating Peter McNeeley after only 1 minute 29 seconds of the first round.

The bout ended in controversial circumstances. Tyson landed two lefts and a right in quick succession. McNeeley fell backwards, and while referee Mills Lane was ushering Tyson to a neutral corner, Vinny Vecchione, McNeeley's manager, climbed into the ring and effectively disqualified his fighter.

The outcome provoked storms of protest from fight fans at the ringside who had paid up to $1,500 a ticket to attend. Disappointment and anger were also expressed by members of the pay-per-view television audience, over a million of whom had paid an average of $40.

The fight cost a total of $70 million to stage, and $25 million of that went to Tyson himself.

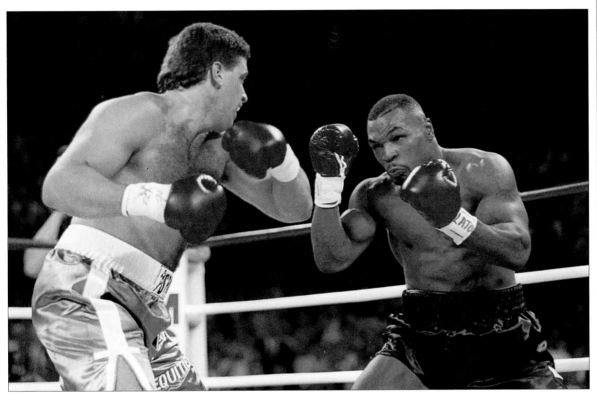

Peter McNeeley (left) and Mike Tyson during their 89-second confrontation.

Paris nail bomb injures 16

A bomb exploded in a trash can near the Arc de Triomphe just after 5 p.m. today, injuring 16 people, three of them seriously.

The device, a canister of camping gas stuffed with nails and bolts, was placed at the Avenue de Friedland entrance to the Charles de Gaulle-Etoile metro station.

The bombing is the latest in a series of terrorist attacks in Paris, which have occurred through the year. No group has claimed responsibility, but the attacks are believed to be the work of the Algerian Armed Islamic Group. (→ October 17)

Clinton associates charged with fraud

A Federal grand jury today indicted Arkansas governor Jim Guy Tucker and two business partners of Bill and Hillary Clinton on 21 counts of fraud, conspiracy, and making false statements in obtaining millions of dollars of federally backed loans.

The indictment relates to a series of fraudulently concocted loans from Madison Guaranty Savings and Loan, an Arkansas savings association at the center of the investigation into the Whitewater land venture.

$3.1 million paid to family of white separatist in Idaho siege

The US government has agreed to pay $3.1 million to the family of a white separatist whose wife and teenage son were killed when federal agents laid siege to their Idaho home in August 1992.

Although the government did not admit wrongdoing, lawyers involved in negotiations said that the size of today's settlement could be seen as a tacit acknowledgment that officials feared a worse result if the case had gone before a jury in Idaho. Separatist Randall C. Weaver and his three surviving daughters had originally filed claims for $200 million with the Justice Department. They accused the FBI of violating the family's constitutional rights by firing on them near their home at Ruby Ridge and killing Mrs. Vicki Weaver and her son Samuel, aged 14.

The decision to compensate the Weavers represents a significant climbdown by federal prosecutors: two years previously they had tried to have Mr. Weaver convicted of killing US marshall William Degan and sought the death penalty. The case was subsequently abandoned because of doubts over the identities of those involved, and who fired first.

Charleston, South Carolina, Monday 14. After a two-and-a-half-year battle to become the first female cadet in the 152-year history of The Citadel, Shannon Faulkner (above, center), 20, was unable to take the oath on her first day of training. She was overcome by the 100° F (38° C) heat and taken to the infirmary.

S	M	T	W	T	F	S
		1	2	3	4	5
6	7	8	9	10	11	12
13	14	15	16	17	18	19
20	21	22	23	24	25	26
27	28	29	30	31		

Iowa, 20
In a straw poll conducted by the Iowa Republican Party, Senator Phil Gramm receives as many votes for his Presidential candidature as does Senator Bob Dole.

Carrollton, Georgia, 21
Three people, including the pilot credited with limiting the scale of the disaster, die when a commuter plane crashes on a flight from Atlanta to Gulfport, Mississippi. There are 26 survivors.

Munich, 22
Germany's highest court has ruled that the Bavarian law requiring a crucifix to be hung in every classroom is unconstitutional, following a ten-year challenge by parent, Ernst Seler.

New York, 22
State education officials reject a request by the New York City Board of Education to shorten elementary schooling by up to two periods a week, one possible way of making necessary budgetary cuts.

Taiwan, 23
President Lee Teng-hui announces his intention to run in the island's first democratic presidential election.

Georgetown, Guyana, 24
A cyanide spill into the Essequibo River, caused when a "holding pond" at a nearby goldmine cracked, is staunched when the crack is sealed. President Jagan declares a 50-mile stretch of the river a disaster zone.

Alstead, New Hampshire, 24
A retired Episcopal Bishop, Walter C. Righter, 71, is accused of heresy and faces church trial for ordaining a gay deacon, Barry L. Stopfel, in 1990.

Sheffield, England, 25
The Reverend Chris Brain, a New Age priest who held controversial "rave" services, is admitted to psychiatric hospital. He has been barred by the Archbishop of York from preaching.

Death
Adele Simpson, the fashion designer who gave postwar America its own couture identity, at her home in Connecticut, at 91, August 23.

China convicts Harry Wu of spying

Harry Wu has been sentenced to 15 years for spying but is to be expelled from China.

The Chinese authorities announced that the American human rights activist Harry Wu, 58, had been convicted of spying and sentenced to 15 years imprisonment. However, the statement also confirmed that Mr. Wu would be expelled from China.

When Mr. Wu, who has run afoul of the authorities by documenting abuses in the Chinese prison system, attempted to enter the country on June 19, he was arrested, rather than being turned back at the border. China stated that Mr. Wu had been convicted of "spying, illegally obtaining, buying and providing state secrets to overseas institutes, organizations and people, and of passing himself off as a government worker for deceptive activities."

America has confirmed that Mr. Wu's release is a prerequisite of any improvement in the strained relations between the US and China.

Zaire troops expel Rwandan refugees

About 750,000 Rwandans, almost all Hutus fleeing the Tutsi-led rebel government, have been living in camps at Goma, on the border between Zaire and Rwanda. Now Zairean soldiers have begun to expel the refugees forcibly, setting fire to huts and looting the camps.

This action began on Saturday but has increased daily, to the point where an estimated 10,000 were expelled in one day. A further 60,000 Rwandans, fearful of being murdered if they are forced to return home, have fled to the hills in an attempt to escape the soldiers.

3,000-year-old Siberian in ice

A 3,000-year-old tattooed man has been found, preserved in permafrost, in a Scythian burial mound in Siberia, near the borders with China and Mongolia.

The tattoo, covering his back and chest, is of an elk. The man had long, red, braided hair and was dressed in embroidered trousers, fur coat, and boots. His horse was buried nearby.

The corpse has been moved to the Mausoleum Institute in Moscow, which looks after Lenin's body.

Bus bombing in Jerusalem

Another suicide bomber struck at the heart of the Israeli state when he killed himself and four passengers, including a woman from Connecticut, by detonating an explosive device aboard a Jerusalem bus. The toll of injured was put at 100.

The incident provoked protests against the government's negotiations with the Palestine Liberation Organization, whose leader Yasser Arafat said on television, "I condemn the attack completely."

The Islamic resistance movement, Hamas, has claimed responsibility for the bombing. (> August 29)

Washington, Thursday 24. Workers at Bothell, preparing for the midnight launch of Microsoft Windows 95. It will be the computer industry's most expensive launch ever, costing an estimated $300 million. Microsoft have paid the Rolling Stones $10 million to use one of their songs, *Start Me Up*, for the launch.

FIROZABAD, NORTHEAST INDIA, MONDAY 21
Death toll could reach 500 in Indian train crash

Rescue workers anticipate finding more bodies as they cut their way into the wreckage.

The death toll of 350, following the collision of two passenger trains, both bound for New Delhi, was expected to rise as teams equipped with cranes and oxyacetylene cutters worked on the crumpled cars. The list of injured totals 500.

One of the express trains, between them carrying around 2,200 passengers, was stalled on the line after hitting a cow. Police are now seeking the signalman who fled after he gave a green light to the following train to continue on the same track. It hit the stationary train at about 60 mph, throwing cars into the air.

A makeshift morgue is being established at nearby Firozabad, but in the meantime, hundreds of bodies lie in the fields alongside the track, awaiting identification.

Victims of the disaster included laborers, a team of athletes and their coaches, and about 60 soldiers.

TORONTO, SUNDAY 20
Monica Seles begins her comeback with a commanding victory

Monica Seles marked her return to competitive tennis, following the serious injury inflicted on her by a fanatic in April, 1993, with a commanding victory at the du Maurier Ltd. Open.

In winning her thirty-third title, 21-year-old Seles brushed aside the unseeded South African Amanda Coetzer, ranked 27th in the world, 6-0, 6-1, "I wasn't sure I'd ever be back to play tennis again," said Seles, who won all five rounds of the tournament in straight and very one-sided sets, confirming that it was the mental scars resulting from the terrible assault, rather than the stab wound itself, that took the longest to heal.

Monica Seles proves unstoppable on her comeback, winning every set in Toronto

Massachusetts, Wednesday 23. Alfred Eisenstaedt, one of the top names in photo-journalism and most famous for his work in *Life* magazine, died at 96.

WASHINGTON DC, SATURDAY 26
Russia prepared to supply Iran with nuclear reactors

A new diplomatic row seems certain to blow up between Washington and Moscow following the news that Russia is apparently prepared to supply Iran with two more atomic reactors. This flies in the face of the international initiative designed to prevent Teheran from being able to develop atomic weapons.

Russia has already supplied Iran with reactors, and in May, President Clinton was in Moscow attempting to persuade the Russians to stop the trade. It is now said that a new deal was agreed this month, during a visit to Moscow by an Iranian delegation that included Reza Amrollahi, Iran's atomic energy chief.

The two 400-megawatt reactors are intended for the Neka nuclear research complex, part of Iran's concerted drive to develop nuclear technology. Pakistan and China have also shown themselves to be willing to deal with the Iranian regime.

One diplomatic source was quoted as saying, "If the Russians are prepared to sell Iran this kind of equipment it is only a matter of time before Teheran develops its own nuclear warhead." Meanwhile, Moscow remains defiant.

California, Saturday 26. The former *Dallas* actor Larry Hagman was recovering in hospital today after having undergone a liver transplant.

S	M	T	W	T	F	S
		1	2	3	4	5
6	7	8	9	10	11	12
13	14	15	16	17	18	19
20	21	22	23	24	25	26
27	28	29	30	31		

Beijing, 27
Following two days of talks a Sino-American summit meeting is confirmed for October.

Colorado, 27
A bus taking gamblers to a casino north-west of Denver collides with a van, killing two.

Belfast, 28
James Molyneaux, leader of the fiercely loyalist Ulster Unionist Party, announces his retirement. (→ September 8)

Washington, 28
Governor Jim Guy Tucker of Arkansas pleads not guilty to fraud and conspiracy charges relating to the Whitewater investigations.

Gaza, 29
Palestinian police arrest dozens of suspected Muslim militants in the Gaza Strip, as part of a crackdown on opponents of the peace talks between Israel and the Palestine Liberation Organization. (→ September 28)

Copenhagen, 29
American neo-Nazi Gary Lauck applies for political asylum in Denmark to avoid extradition to Germany, where he faces charges of Nazi propaganda activities. Lauck runs a neo-Nazi publishing concern in Nebraska.

Freetown, Sierra Leone, 29
Starvation is widespread as thousands flee the civil war in the south of Sierra Leone.

North Korea, 30
The government of North Korea seeks aid from the UN in Geneva for the first time, saying that serious flooding has affected five million people and caused billions of dollars' worth of damage.

Monrovia, Liberia, 31
People throng the streets of the West African country to celebrate peace after six years of civil war.

Death
Frank Perry, the film director whose successes included *David and Lisa*, *Diary of a Mad Housewife* and *Mommie Dearest*, in Manhattan, at age 65, August 29. Given a year to live five years ago, he made the film *On the Bridge* about his fight against cancer.

LOS ANGELES, THURSDAY 31

Judge rules on Fuhrman tapes in O.J. trial

Detective Mark Fuhrman (left), whose racist comments on tape are vital to the defense.

In a dramatic development in the trial of O.J. Simpson, Judge Lance Ito ruled that the jury should hear only two of 41 instances on tape where Detective Mark Fuhrman refers to blacks as "niggers." Just 15 seconds of tape will be played to them, culled from more than 14 hours displaying Fuhrman's racial bigotry and boastful disregard of the law.

The tapes, made over a period of years by screenwriter Laura Hart McKinny, who was seeking background material on police procedures, were considered a trump card for the defense, allegedly proving that Fuhrman is so racist that he could, for example, have "planted" the bloodstained glove on Mr. Simpson's property. Lead defense lawyer Johnnie L. Cochran said, "To say we are outraged and livid by this ruling would be a master understatement." (→ September 6)

New York City, Monday 28. Governor Pete Wilson of California opens his campaign for the Republican nomination in New York.

ALBANY, TUESDAY 29

86 Colombians deported

A group of 86 illegal immigrants from Colombia were flown home from Kennedy International Airport in New York's largest-ever single deportation of what are officially known as "criminal aliens."

Governor George E. Pataki said that the move was intended to save money and free up prison space, and that more such moves would follow, predicting that New York would "deport these illegal aliens...and take them off the backs of taxpayers."

NEW YORK, MONDAY 28

Chemical and Chase to merge

The agreement between the Chase Manhattan Corporation and the Chemical Banking Corporation to merge, in a deal valued at $10 billion, will create a bank with combined assets of $297 billion. This will make the merged organization America's biggest bank, ahead of Citibank.

Although Chemical is the bigger company, the new organization will retain the identity of the better-known banking name, Chase.

LOS ANGELES, WEDNESDAY 30

Time Warner and Ted Turner in negotiations

Time Warner Inc. has offered $8.5 billion to take over the cable television network Turner Broadcasting Inc., according to insiders, although neither party has given official confirmation. Ted Turner was said to be considering the deal, and rumors suggested that he was enthusiastic about the deal and about playing a leading role within Time Warner.

The proposition is that the latter company would acquire the 81 percent of Turner that it does not already hold, with Ted Turner continuing to run his part of the business. This would form the biggest media company in the world, larger even than that resulting from the marriage of Disney and Capital Cities/ABC, announced on July 31. (→ September 22)

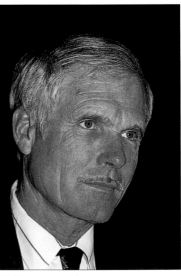

Ted Turner, considering a merger.

New York airports shut down because of bomb threat

The air traffic control center on Long Island was put out of operation for more than an hour, freezing all traffic movement in and out of La Guardia, JFK and Newark. There was an inevitable domino effect throughout the country.

The reason for the disruption was a bomb threat, awkwardly exposing the fact that one malicious telephone call can have a devastating influence on the nation's air traffic movements. The emergency came only ten days after La Guardia was evacuated following another bomb threat, and two weeks after fears of terrorist action prompted increased security measures throughout the country.

The anonymous call was made at 4:35 p.m. to an unlisted number at Long Island's New York Tracon (terminal radar approach control), threatening an explosion at 6:00 p.m. By 7:00 p.m. it was concluded that the call was a hoax, but nevertheless many passengers were delayed for hours.

First anniversary of cease-fire in Northern Ireland

Belfast citizens celebrate a year of peace after a quarter of a century of violence.

A year ago the Irish Republican Army announced a cessation of their violent campaign against British occupation of Northern Ireland, a gesture that was followed in October by a cease-fire by Protestant "loyalist" paramilitaries as well.

After 25 years, during which violent, politically motivated death was almost a daily occurrence, there has been just one such murder in a year, when an IRA gang shot a post office worker while carrying out a robbery.

Self-appointed vigilante groups on both sides have continued to mete out punishments.

Progress towards all-party peace talks has proved slow, however. The British demand for the decommissioning of weapons before negotiations has been one sticking point, while hardline loyalists cannot envisage talking to those whose goal is a united Ireland. Meanwhile, ordinary people enjoy the peace, however uneasy it may be. (→ September 8)

NATO bombs Serbs

NATO's rapid reaction force scores a direct hit on an armaments dump.

As a direct response to the shelling of the Sarajevo market from Bosnian Serb positions around the city on Monday, when dozens of civilians died, NATO warplanes carried out a retaliatory action early this morning.

The attacks were concentrated on positions to the south and east of the city, in the direction of the Bosnian Serb headquarters at Pale.

An estimated 100 NATO aircraft were involved in the action, drawn from the forces of the United States, Britain, France, Spain, and the Netherlands. No NATO casualties were reported. In Washington DC a Defense Department official said that 24 military targets had been hit.

These were identified as surface-to-air missile sites, artillery batteries, ammunition depots, and control centers. The spokesman confirmed that, if the Serbs respond violently, NATO action will intensify. (→ September 1)

Shevardnadze survives car-bomb assassination attempt

The Georgian leader Eduard A. Shevardnadze sustained superficial injuries when a car bomb exploded near his vehicle as he was on his way to sign a new constitution for Georgia. He had just departed from the parliament building in Tbilisi.

Several other people were injured but there were no fatalities. Mr. Shevardnadze appeared on television, dazed and with cuts on his face.

His press secretary, Ramaz Sakvarelidze said, "It's clear that Shevardnadze's enemies tried to assassinate the head of our state to stop the signing ceremony."

Mr. Shevardnadze has confirmed that he will run for the post of president, which is to be restored under the new constitution. (→ November 5)

Eduard Shevardnadze, target for bombers.

S	M	T	W	T	F	S
					1	2
3	4	5	6	7	8	9
10	11	12	13	14	15	16
17	18	19	20	21	22	23
24	25	26	27	28	29	30

Sarajevo, 1
NATO air strikes against the Bosnian Serbs are suspended for 24 hours in an attempt to accelerate peace talks in Belgrade. (→ September 5)

Johannesburg, 1
One man is killed and more than 20 injured during a clash between blacks and whites in Kuruman in South Africa's northern Cape.

Tahiti, 1
On the eve of a scheduled nuclear test, French commandos board two Greenpeace ships and tow them toward their base at Mururoa. (→ September 5)

Paris, 1
Riot police break up Greenpeace protest against France's resumption of nuclear tests in the Pacific. (→ September 5)

Beijing, 1
Chinese authorities attempt to curb free discussion by delegates at the World Conference on Women. (→ September 15)

London, 2
British boxer Frank Bruno beats American Oliver McCall to take the WBC World Heavyweight title and is now looking to fight Mike Tyson.

Johannesburg, 3
The African National Congress angers whites with a proposal to drop the white national anthem and keep the black one.

Beijing, 5
First Lady Hillary Clinton addresses the World Conference on Women.

Belgrade, 5
NATO resumes bombing Bosnian Serbs after four days of negotiations fail to end in Serbs withdrawing guns from around Sarajevo. (→ September 6)

Washington DC, 6
NATO intends to intensify and expand its bombing campaign against Serbian targets. (→ September 11)

Deaths
Sterling Morrison, at the age of 53, former Velvet Underground guitarist, September 3.

William Kunstler, radical lawyer, , September 4, at age 76, September 4.

Detective in O.J. case pleads the Fifth Amendment

Courting controversy in the O.J. trial: Detective Mark Fuhrman (left) and Judge Ito.

The detective at the heart of the O.J. Simpson case, Mark Fuhrman, invoked the Fifth Amendment when he took the witness stand today, refusing to answer possibly incriminating questions. Simpson's chief lawyer, Johnnie L. Cochran Jr., whose case rests on the allegation that Fuhrman falsified evidence against Simpson, said, "What more does anyone need out there?"

Detective Fuhrman, who is alleged to have boasted of his racism, was asked questions such as, "Have you ever falsified a police report?" and "Did you plant or manufacture any evidence in this case?" After each question was put to him, the detective would look to his lawyer before saying, "I wish to assert my Fifth Amendment privilege." (→ September 22)

Colin Powell remains undecided over whether to run in presidential elections

Colin Powell meets the public in San Bernardino, California.

Colin Powell, chairman of the Joint Chiefs of Staff during the Gulf War, will wait until November to decide whether he is going to stand as a candidate in the next presidential election. Speculation has been growing for much of the year that the 58-year-old retired general will run as a Republican. But he has carefully avoided answering direct questions from reporters on either that subject or on his political views.

He is about to embark on a tour of the US that will take him to 23 cities to promote his autobiography, *My American Journey*. The publicity generated will be enormous. Television and magazine interviews as well as book signing sessions will guarantee he stays firmly in the public eye during the forthcoming weeks. The interest has been generated by his potential candidature and his book's revelations on the Gulf War. (→ November 8)

Senate opens Ruby Ridge siege inquiry

Suspicions that the FBI acted irresponsibly in the Ruby Ridge siege will be investigated in a Senate inquiry starting today. During the siege in Idaho, which was begun to apprehend white separatist Randy Weaver, his 14-year-old son, and his wife were shot dead.

US marshals first approached Weaver's log cabin with the intention of arresting him on charges of selling two sawn-off shotguns to federal firearms agents. However, as they crept toward his home, a dog belonging to Weaver's son Samuel sensed their presence. In the shooting that followed, the boy was shot dead along with a marshal. At that point, the FBI's Hostage Rescue Team was alerted, and heavily armed agents were rushed to the scene by air.

During the flight to Idaho, the commander of the Hostage Rescue team, Richard Rogers, made the decision that any armed adult in the vicinity of the cabin could be shot on sight without warning. Rogers claims that he discussed that decision fully with Larry Potts, the then FBI Assistant Director. As a consequence, Weaver was shot and his wife was killed as she held her ten-month-old baby at the cabin door. Weaver and his family have been awarded $3.1 billion compensation. (→ October 3)

St. Maarten, Thursday 7. The 140-mph hurricane Luis devastates the Dutch/French Caribbean island of St. Maarten.

TAHITI, TUESDAY 5

France carries out underground nuclear test at Mururoa Atoll

One of the French commandos who stormed the Greenpeace vessel Rainbow Warrior.

A demonstrator shows her feelings.

Tahitians rioting in protest at the French program of nuclear testing in the Pacific.

France exploded a nuclear bomb at 12:30 p.m. local time today in defiance of international protests. The device was buried deep below the coral-ringed Mururoa Atoll, about 750 miles (1,200 km) southeast of the Pacific island of Tahiti.

Until now, the French themselves have released few details about the exact weaponry being tested, but today the country's defense ministry announced that the explosion was the equivalent of less than 20,000 tons of TNT. (For the purposes of comparison, the nuclear bomb exploded at Hiroshima in 1945 had a force of 15,000 tons of TNT.) This is

the first in a series of tests which the French plan to carry out between now and May 1996. They have promised to renounce nuclear testing for ever after that, and sign a comprehensive global test ban treaty.

The tests were originally ordered by the French president, Jacques Chirac, shortly after he took office in the spring. He insists that the tests are essential to confirm the accuracy of the latest generation of nuclear warheads and to perfect computer simulation techniques that would eliminate the need for further explosions. The French also maintain that the testing is safe because the basalt rock

around the bomb prevents radioactivity from leaking into the sea.

Protests against French policy continued throughout the build-up to today's explosion. Tens of thousands of people have taken part in demonstrations in Australia, New Zealand, and Japan. French goods are widely boycotted in the South Pacific.

The environmental group Greenpeace called the explosion "an outrage." New Zealand and Australia have now withdrawn their ambassadors to France. For its part, the US expressed regret and hoped that France would join the moratorium on further tests.(→ September 10)

WASHINGTON DC, THURSDAY 7

Senator Packwood to resign due to misconduct

A massive collection of evidence gathered by the Senate Ethics Committee has forced Senator Bob Packwood to announce his resignation. A ten-volume, 10,145-page indictment, much of it taken from Mr. Packwood's diaries, found he had been guilty of sexual harassment of female employees, exerted pressure on lobbyists to give his wife financial favors, and corruptly handled campaign funds. Mr. Packwood also tampered with his diaries before handing them over to the Ethics Committee.

Mr. Packwood, who had been the junior senator for Oregon for 27 years, was an extremely capable individual who had a spectacular grasp of taxation issues. His departure from the Senate will be a massive blow to Republican presidential candidate Bob Dole, who was visibly shaken by Packwood's resignation.

BELFAST, FRIDAY 8

Ulster Unionist leader poses new threat to Major

David Trimble was elected leader of the Ulster Unionists in succession to James Molyneaux, who stepped down earlier this year. Trimble, the 50-year-old MP for Upper Bann, is a hardliner who may be less biddable than his predecessor in the Northern Ireland peace pro-cess, which is now at a delicate stage of negotiation.

The new leader has been particularly uncompromising on the decommissioning of IRA weapons, and he will not take the Unionists into all-party talks until he is convinced of the IRA's commitment to exclusively peaceful means. He is particularly sceptical about "symbolic gestures" such as the surrender of token quantities of weaponry and Semtex explosives.

British Prime Minister John Major needs the Ulster Unionists' support to advance the peace talks and to maintain his slim majority in the House of Commons. (→ September 21)

September

Moscow, 10
Vladimir Zhirinovsky, the far-right nationalist, assaults a female MP by pulling her hair during a disturbance in the Russian Parliament.

Tokyo, 11
Mitsubishi is planning to withdraw its $2 billion stake in the Rockefeller Center in Manhattan.

Moscow, 11
Russian defense minister Pavel Grachev criticizes NATO's bombing of Serb targets.(→ September 14)

Washington DC, 11
Figures released by the Census Bureau show that fewer Americans are moving home than at any time since 1950.

New York, 11
The match between Russian Gary Kasparov and Indian Viswanathan Anand for the Professional Chess Association's world title begins in Manhattan.

New York, 12
Waneta Hoyt, 48, is sentenced to 75 years in jail for killing five of her six children between 1965 and 1971. Their deaths had been attributed to sudden infant death syndrome.

Paris, 12
The French army is guarding the Channel Tunnel entrance as part of the French government's anti-terrorist measures.

Moscow, 13
A rocket grenade, launched from a moving car, is fired into a side wall of the US Embassy.

New Orleans, 13
A police officer, Antoinette Frank, 24, is sentenced to death for the murders of a colleague and two other citizens during a failed robbery.

Belarus, 13
Two American balloonists competing in the Gordon Bennett race are shot down and killed by Belorussian armed forces.

Cameroon, 14
At the beginning of a six-day tour of African countries, the Pope voices his concerns about human rights and government corruption.

PARIS, SUNDAY 10
French nuclear tests will continue

President Chirac refuses to allow world opinion to stop French nuclear tests in the Pacific.

France will continue nuclear testing in its territory in the Pacific – that is the new defiant message from French President Jacques Chirac. He suggested that political motives rather than worries about the environmental effects of the testing were what motivated antipodean antipathy toward France's program of nuclear testing in the Pacific.

In an interview on French TV, Chirac said that objections to the tests from Australia and New Zealand are "not really anti-nuclear." Instead, he added, critics in those countries are "motivated by their wish to see us out of the Pacific." The President insisted that he would not allow French defense policy to be swayed by agitators, opinion polls, or international condemnation.

At Mururoa Atoll, where the tests are being held, eight protesting MPs, from Sweden, Luxembourg, Japan, Italy, and Australia were arrested by French commandos. (→ October 1)

New York, Sunday 10. Pete Sampras took four sets to beat Andre Agassi and win the US Open Championship for the third time in five years.

WASHINGTON DC, WEDNESDAY 13
The Senate votes to cut Federal welfare budget

Under majority leader Bob Dole, the Senate took yet another step toward fulfilling the "contract with America" here as it voted to cut the federal welfare budget. This move reflects right-wing impatience with groups such as single mothers. A Democratic amendment designed to provide $11 billion for child care for single mothers (who will be required to work under the Republican plan) was rejected. Senator Edward Kennedy described the bill as a "Home Alone" plan that could have tragic consequences.

Southeast Asia, Wednesday 13. The World Wide Fund for Nature says one tiger in southeast Asia is killed every week and that they now face extinction.

PARIS, TUESDAY 12
Alfred Dreyfus officially absolved

The French army has finally given Captain Alfred Dreyfus an official pardon for crimes on which he was convicted more than a century ago.

General Jean-Louis Mourrut, chief historian of the French army, said the charge of high treason on which Dreyfus was convicted was "a judicial error and a military conspiracy." Dreyfus was Jewish, and the case exacerbated anti-Semitic feeling prior to World War I. A civil court reversed the ruling in Dreyfus's lifetime, and he was reinstated in the army. Until now, however, the army had not commented on the case.

Alfred Dreyfus, the wronged soldier.

BELGRADE, THURSDAY 14

NATO halts Serb bombing in new peace hopes

Communications have been devastated in Serb-held areas of Bosnia.

NATO's bombing of the Bosnian Serbs was halted yesterday. The tactic appeared to have had its desired effect with the imminent withdrawal of the Serbs from around Sarajevo. On Wednesday, US peace envoy Richard Holbrooke had a meeting with Serbian leaders Radovan Karadzic, General Ratko Mladic, and President Milosevic in Belgrade. It was agreed that the Bosnian Serbs would withdraw their weapons from around the besieged city. The order to cease bombing the Bosnian Serbs was then given by NATO's secretary general, Willy Claes.

With the Bosnian Serbs in retreat and suffering severely from NATO's bombing, worries have arisen that the conflict could be exacerbated by Bosnian Muslims attacking their weakened enemy. "It is no secret that I made interventions to parties urging them not to exploit the situation," said Claes. (→ September 18)

Pasadena, California, Sunday 10. Actress Candice Bergen has won a fifth Emmy for her role in the comedy *Murphy Brown*.

BEIJING, FRIDAY 15

UN women demand change

Sexual freedom and an end to violence against women were the two main resolutions adopted by the United Nations' Fourth World Conference on Women, which ended today. In particular, the 5,000 delegates condemned trafficking in women and genital mutilation of girls. However, some of the views that were upheld by the conference, such as its implicit recognition of homosexual relationships, were rejected by representatives of Islamic countries and by the Vatican.

WASHINGTON DC, THURSDAY 14

FBI arrests 12 on Internet porn

The Federal Bureau of Investigation has initiated a clampdown on pornography that is transmitted on the Internet. In the first stage of the bureau's all-out war on individuals who peddle porn on the system, a dozen individuals were yesterday arrested on child pornography charges. Approximately 125 domestic residences and office buildings were raided as part of the operation that is dedicated to fully examining the activities of America Online, the largest computer network. It has been alleged that the network is used to entice minors into sex.

The Internet is used extensively internationally by pedophiles and pornographers. It has been estimated that close to 50 percent of those who used the worldwide computer service for leisure purposes do so to send or receive pornographic material. Governments are just becoming aware of the extent of the harmful material being transmitted across national boundaries, but controlling the Internet is very difficult.

CAMBRIDGE, ENGLAND, TUESDAY 12

Pigs' hearts to be used in transplants

Scientists hope to use pigs' hearts for transplants within a year.

Hearts, lungs, and kidneys from specially bred pigs could be transplanted to humans in a major breakthrough announced by British research scientists. The first operation is planned for spring 1996 provided that research progresses at its current rate. The organs could be in widespread use by the end of the century.

Dr David White, the founder of Imutran, the company that conducted the research, said, "This will give hope to hundreds of thousands of patients around the world who would otherwise die waiting for a heart, lung, or kidney." In the US, approximately 30,000 patients are waiting for transplants but only half that number will receive an organ.

Specialized pig breeders have collaborated with the researchers to develop a unique herd of 300 transgenic pigs, each of which is given a human gene by the scientists at birth.

S	M	T	W	T	F	S
					1	2
3	4	5	6	7	8	9
10	11	12	13	14	15	16
17	18	19	20	21	22	23
24	25	26	27	28	29	30

Sarajevo, 18
The UN Secretary General, Boutros Boutros Ghali, says that UN troops should make a withdrawal from Bosnia, ending their less-than-successful three-year peacekeeping mission there.(→ October 5)

Hong Kong, 18
The first fully democratic election in the British colony gives victory to anti-Beijing parties, making a smooth transition to Communist rule unlikely. China and plans to scrap the colony's governing body when it takes over in 1997.(→ September 24)

Glasgow, 18
A 32-year-old man posed as a 17-year-old boy, hoping to get better grades at school second time around.

Washington DC, 19
The House speaker Newt Gingrich's $4.5 million book advance from Rupert Murdoch is to be investigated by the ethics committee. The committee wants to know if any chicanery was involved in the deal.

Los Angeles, 19
Police Chief Willie Williams files a lawsuit against the city and the Police Commission to end a "smear campaign" aimed at him.

Yorkshire, England, 19
The water chief of the drought-stricken county says he has not had a bath for three months and urges others to follow his example.

Rome, 20
Diplomats, statesmen, terrorists, and jailed mafiosi say they will testify for former Italian Prime Minister Giulio Andreotti, who is charged with aiding the Mafia throughout his 50-year political career. (→ September 26)

Washington DC, 20
Ethnic divisions hit the newsroom at the Washington Post. Blacks claim racism, while whites claim blacks are being promoted beyond their ability.

Calais, 20
A cross-Channel ferry from England to France is beached, trapping 245 passengers. After 24 hours it is set afloat. Salvage cost $4 million.

Los Angeles, 22
O.J. Simpson tells the jury he will not testify in his own defense.
(→ September 27)

WASHINGON DC, TUESDAY 19

Unabomber has manifesto published

The *Washington Post* published a special supplement carrying the manifesto of the Unabomber, a lone terrorist who has eluded the FBI since the late 1970s. So far he has killed three people and injured 23 in 16 bombings. *The New York Times* backed the publication.

The Unabomber's manifesto, called *Industrial Society and Its Future*, was mailed to the *Post*, *The New York Times* and *Penthouse* magazine after his last attack on April 24, when lumber industry lobbyist Gilbert Murray was killed by a skillfully constructed bomb. Murray had campaigned for logging in a habitat of the threatened spotted owl. In a joint statement, the *Times* and the *Post* said that they were troubled by the decision to print the manifesto, but had made it on the advice of Attorney General Janet Reno and FBI Chief Louis Freeh, who urged publication for "public safety reasons." The Unabomber promised to stop his mail-bomb campaign if his

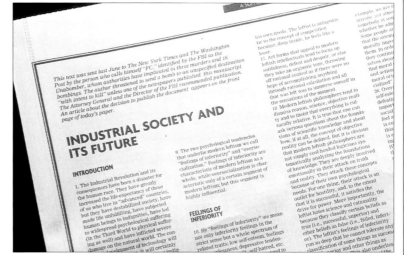

The Unabomber's manifesto in the Washington Post.

manifesto was published by at least one major newspaper next Sunday. The *Washington Post* decided to publish because it had the capacity to print a weekend supplement. Extracts of the manifesto had already been

published by both the *Times* and the *Post* for journalistic reasons in August. The Unabomber still reserves the right to attack property and demands more space in the papers over the next three years.

NEW DELHI, THURSDAY 21

Hindu idols around the world in milk-drinking "miracles"

Worshipers get in line with milk for Hindu god Ganesh.

Rumors that statues of the Hindu god Ganesh were drinking milk spread around the world today. They began in New Delhi where thousands of believers got in line with offerings. Milk prices soared. The story quickly spread to other temples in India. Soon hundreds of people

were lining up to feed milk to statues of Ganesh in places as far away as London and New York, after receiving telephone calls from relatives and friends. "When we tried feeding spoonfuls of milk to the gods, the milk disappeared," said one. Sceptics say that the stone is absorbent.

NEW YORK, FRIDAY 22

Time Warner Inc. and Turner Broadcasting agree on merger

After five weeks of negotiations, Ted Turner has agreed to merge his Turner Broadcasting System with Time Warner Inc. In a deal worth roughly $7.5 million, Turner, who founded Cable News Network (CNN), will renounce executive power over his company to become vice chairman of Time Warner.

The merged group will have annual revenues of $19.8 billion, leapfrogging Disney's $16.4 billion. It will own everything from *Time* magazine and CNN to Warner Bros. and the Cartoon Channel. Mr. Turner and his wife Jane Fonda, will continue to base themselves in Atlanta, Georgia, home of CNN.

Turner gave up control of his cable company after years of trying to buy a TV network. "I'm tired of being little for the whole of my life," he said. "This is a chance to see the world from a different perspective."

TOKYO, THURSDAY 21

US agrees to review troop rights in Japan in wake of rape protests

The American ambassador to Tokyo, Walter Mondale, has promised that the US will review the special rights afforded US servicemen accused of crimes in Japan. This follows a popular outcry against two Marines and a sailor accused of raping a 12-year-old girl on the island of Okinawa.

Under the current arrangements, the three men are held, not in police cells, but on the US Marine base, until formally indicted. Japanese detectives are allowed to question them at length – but only if a military lawyer is present. If they were in police custody, they could be held for 23 days without charge. Japanese police allow suspects little contact with their lawyers and attempt to wring confessions out of prisoners by depriving them of sleep. US authorities are eager to prevent American personnel from suffering such treatment, but fear new calls to have US troops withdrawn from Okinawa,

Okinawans in an anti-American protest.

which America has occupied since 1945. World War II ended 50 years ago, and there are increasing calls for US troops to be removed from Japan. The Japanese also claim that the special arrangements given to US troops hamper criminal investigations. Ambassador Mondale says that he will conduct a "fact-finding" study into their effects.

Johannesburg, Sunday 17. The Pope began a six-day visit to Africa by celebrating his first papal mass in South Africa. A crowd of 80,000, including President Mandela (above right, with the Pope) and the man he succeeded, F.W. de Klerk, were present.

ALASKA, FRIDAY 22

US Air Force surveillance crashes

A USAF plane of the type that has crashed in Alaska.

A US Air Force Airborne Warning and Command System (AWACS) aircraft with a crew of 22 Americans and two Canadians crashed shortly after takeoff from Elmendorf Air Force Base in Alaska.

Witnesses said one of its four engines caught fire as it roared down the runway. The pilot still tried to take off, but did not have enough power to get properly airborne. The plane crashed into a forest two miles northeast of the airstrip and burst into a fireball. No one survived. The crash occurred at the beginning of a seven-hour training mission. There are 68 AWACS aircraft in service, half of them with the USAF. They have flown more than 100,000 missions since they were introduced in 1977.

BELFAST, THURSDAY 21

Peace process doomed, says Adams

Sinn Fein president Gerry Adams has warned that the Anglo-Irish peace plan – which has brought peace to the troubled province for a year – will be near to collapse if Britain continues to insist that the IRA lay down its arms before all-party talks can begin. This comes on the eve of talks between British Prime Minister John Major and Irish Prime Minister John Bruton at the European summit, the first since the recent postponement of a top-level meeting at Chequers, the British Prime Minister's country home.

The problem remains that the IRA sees any handing over of arms as symbolic surrender. Bruton believes that the IRA will not tolerate this. Major insists he is sympathetic to Adams's difficulties. "I am not looking for people coming out, throwing their weapons at the feet of the British," the prime minister said.(→ September 29)

ANKARA, WEDNESDAY 20

Turkish PM resigns

In a surprise move, Turkey's first woman prime minister, Tansu Ciller, has resigned. She faced calling a general election a year early after her coalition partner, the Social Democrats, withdrew their support.

The dispute between the coalition partners is over Istanbul's police chief, who enjoys the support of Ciller's conservative True Path Party. The Social Democrats have called for his resignation after he accused the Social Democrats' Human Rights Minister of encouraging Kurdish separatism. Around 150,000 government employees who support the Social Democrats are on strike for higher pay. The leader of the Motherland Party is prepared to form a coalition with Ciller, provided elections follow soon.

London, Friday 22. McDonald's pays over $1,000 in damages to a customer who is burned by an apple pie. Lawyers claimed he might be scarred for life.

September

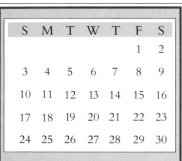

S	M	T	W	T	F	S
					1	2
3	4	5	6	7	8	9
10	11	12	13	14	15	16
17	18	19	20	21	22	23
24	25	26	27	28	29	30

Washington DC, 24
Former US Secretary of State, James Baker, reveals that Iraq planned to invade Saudi Arabia after taking over Kuwait at the start of the Gulf War.

Athens, 24
Greek newspapers print pictures of Prime Minister Andreas Papandreou's wife in the nude.

Hong Kong, 24
Governor Chris Patten's demand that the colony's 3.5 million passport holders be allowed into Britain, after China's takeover, is rejected by UK Home Secretary Michael Howard.

Freetown, 25
Aid agencies warn that the threat of mass starvation looms in the west African country Sierra Leone.

London, 26
Humphrey, the British Prime Minister's cat who went missing for three months and was presumed dead, returns to Number 10. It is thought he climbed on a mail van and was taken to the Royal Army Medical College nearby.

Oak Hill, New York, 24
The European golf team wins the Ryder Cup against a much favored American Team. This is the first European victory in the US since 1987.

Los Angeles, 27
The voice of O.J. Simpson's dead wife, Nicole Brown Simpson, is heard in court. Assistant Prosecutor Christopher Darden plays the tape recording of her 911 call, pleading for help. O.J.'s voice, shouting and cursing, could be heard in the background. (→ September 29)

London, 28
England's rugby captain Will Carling splits from his wife after rumors he is having an affair with Princess Di.

Belfast, 29
The IRA refuses to hand over their weapons. They call British demands for decommissioning arms before talks "ludicrous."(→ November 10)

Paris, 29
France places its forces on alert after a call from the Comoros Island government asking for help in suppressing a coup d'état.(→ October 4)

LONDON, TUESDAY 26
Sting accuses accountant of theft

Rock star Sting claims that his accountant stole £6 million ($9 million) from him. Keith Moore, 51, who was paid more than $1.2 million a year by the lead singer of rock band the Police, denies 15 theft charges. The prosecution maintains that Moore diverted Sting's money into his own property. The musician had hired a private detective to trick Moore into a taped confession.

Sting accuses his accountant of fraud.

LOS ANGELES, FRIDAY 29
Final summing up in O.J. case

The longest-sequestered jury in American legal history soon face the prospect of freedom as the summing up in the O.J. Simpson trial begins. But first they have to make one momentous decision – should O.J. regain his freedom too?

There were originally 12 alternates plus 12 jurors but that has now dwindled to 12 jurors with just two alternates. At one time, a mistrial seemed inevitable. The jury has heard testimony from 126 witnesses – 72 for the prosecution and 54 for the defense. They saw 857 exhibits and sat through testimony that filled more than 200 volumes.

The trial has been televized and has been compulsive viewing for a huge section of the American people. The lawyers for the prosecution and defense – Marcia Clark, Johnnie Cochran, F. Lee Bailey, and Robert Shapiro – as well as the judge, Lance Ito, are household names.

The defense successfully shifted the central issue of the trial on to race, painting key police witness Mark Fuhrman as a racist.(→ October 3)

WASHINGTON, MONDAY 25
Nancy Reagan talks to the press about husband Ronald's Alzheimer's

Former first lady Nancy Reagan has told *Newsweek* magazine that her husband, Ronald Reagan, is suffering from Alzheimer's, a disease that results in progressive memory loss. She characterized his deterioration as the "long goodbye." Ronald Reagan, who was US president between 1981 and 1989, first revealed that he was suffering from Alzheimer's in November 1994. One positive aspect to her husband's disease, said Mrs. Reagan, was that it had brought her family closer together.

Nancy Reagan.

STRASBOURG, WEDNESDAY 27
European Court of Human Rights rules against Britain over "Death on the Rock" shootings of IRA members

The European Court of Human Rights condemned the British government over the killing of three IRA members in Gibraltar in 1988. Sean Savage, Daniel McCann, and Mairead Farrell were shot dead by undercover SAS men who thought they were about to detonate a car bomb. They were unarmed, and their car did not contain a bomb. But another car rented by Farrell and left in Spain did contain a Semtex bomb.

The Court ruled that the British government had breached the European Human Rights Convention, which guarantees the right to life. British Prime Minister John Major was "appalled" by the Court's ruling.

Provence, Sunday 24. A teenage boy slays his parents and brother, then randomly shoots people in the next village. Eight more people die before Eric Borel, 16, turns the gun on himself. "It was like he was hunting birds," said a witness in Cuers.

WASHINGTON, WEDNESDAY 27
Senator Dole video dwells on his war wounds

Presidential hopeful Bob Dole has released a video called *Bob Dole, an American Hero*, portraying him as a war hero in a pre-emptive strike against Republican rival General Colin Powell. Dole, 72, was severely injured seizing a German machine-gun nest in Italy in 1945. It left him with a withered arm.

American hero Bob Dole.

WASHINGTON DC, THURSDAY 28
Israel and PLO reach accord in West Bank deal signed at White House

A historic agreement giving the Palestinians self-determination on the West Bank of Jordan was signed at the White House today. The so-called occupied West Bank will no longer be occupied. Israeli troops will begin to withdraw within ten days, and the pull out should be complete in six months.

The agreement was signed by Israeli prime minister, Yitzhak Rabin, and the PLO's Yasser Arafat, whose name, until two years ago, was synonymous with terrorism. But although peace has been reached on paper, militant Palestinian groups and Jewish settlers denounce the accord. Both see their leaders as traitors to the cause. But Americans see the president basking in another foreign policy triumph. (→ October 25)

Israel's Yitzhak Rabin and the PLO's Yasser Arafat sign the historic accord.

HOLLYWOOD, TUESDAY 26
Macaulay Culkin fires father

Macaulay Culkin.

Home Alone star Macaulay Culkin and his brother, wannabe child star Kieran, have split from their manager father. Kit Culkin, who has proved to be one of Hollywood's toughest negotiators, can now only see his children with a judge's permission. Kit had pulled Kieran off a movie set without warning, and Macaulay and his brother fled to find sanctuary with their mother. Patricia Culkin fears "If Kit deliberately botches this deal, no one in Hollywood will want to work with our children again."

CALIFORNIA, TUESDAY 26
Ross Perot's supporters plan to put third party back on the ballot

Followers of Ross Perot are hard at work in California collecting the 900,000 signatures needed to establish the billionaire's Independence Party, ready for the Presidential elections next year. Despite a bungled campaign in 1992, which saw the candidate withdraw then return, Perot took a creditable 19 percent of the vote. This time Perot is not putting himself forward as a candidate – at least, not right away. He said on CNN's *Larry King Live*: "This is not about me running for president.

The last thing I want is for this to be about me." General Colin Powell, Perot said, had the "stature and quality" needed for a presidential candidate. However, Perot would not rule out that he would be a candidate himself. Some believe that Perot is trying to co-opt Powell, who has reservations about the Republican ticket. But if Powell ran as a Republican, Perot could benefit as a third party candidate from Republican defections. It is now up to Powell to make his move. (→ November 8)

LANGLEY, VIRGINIA, WEDNESDAY 27
CIA disciplines officers for stifling reports of human rights abuses in Guatemala

The Central Intelligence Agency are disciplining a dozen officers, including the former chief of covert operations in Latin America, for concealing human rights abuses in Guatemala. The agency had longstanding ties to Guatemalan army officers involved in the torture and murder of civilians.

The station chief also failed to tell the US Ambassador that a suspect in the murder of US citizen Michael DeVine was a CIA agent.

The case raises questions of accountability and control within the agency where involvement in "dirty wars" is concerned.

SICILY, TUESDAY 26
Andreotti trial opens

Giulio Andreotti in court.

Former Italian Prime Minster Giulio Andreotti went on trial in a bunkered Palermo courtroom today, accused of aiding the Mafia. He faces 22 years in jail. Lined up against him are 401 prosecution witness. The defense has 126. Andreotti has dominated Italian politics for 50 years and has been prime minister seven times. The accusations are based on the evidence of former mafioso Eduardo Ascari, who turned state's evidence. Andreotti's defense attorney says Ascari's evidence is full of contradictions.

Lisbon, 2
The center-left party sweeps to power in Portuguese elections, on a platform of educational reform and a clampdown on crime.

Gary, Indiana, 2
State troopers are sent in to help police cope with the city's rampant crime wave.

London, 3
The trial of Rosemary West, accused of murdering ten young women with her husband Frederick, starts in the ancient English city of Winchester. Frederick West committed suicide in January 1995. (→ November 22)

Skopje, 3
The president of the Balkan republic of Macedonia is injured when a car bomb explodes as his car passes it.

Comoros Islands, 4
Bob Denard, leader of a coup in the Comoros seven days ago, surrenders to French forces in this former French colony.

Tokyo, 4
Japan's public television channel announces that Shoko Asahara, the leader of the Aum Supreme Truth cult, has confessed to the Tokyo gas attack.

Florida, 4
Hurricane Opal hits the Florida Panhandle, devastating homes and property along the coast.

Washington DC, 5
President Clinton tells *Good Housekeeping* in an interview how his political career was shaped by an unhappy childhood.

Paris, 6
The public prosecutor's office confirms that it is to launch an investigation into corruption charges against Alain Juppé, the French prime minister, over his rental of a city-owned apartment in Paris.
(→ October 11)

Washington DC, 6
President Clinton says he may send US troops to Bosnia, and appeals against the growing strength of isolationism. (→ October 13)

French explode second atomic test

Japanese protesting the tests.

Despite condemnation by Australia and New Zealand, and the rioting in Tahiti that followed the first test, France tonight carried out the second of its series of nuclear bomb tests. The explosion, on Fangataufa atoll, was five times more powerful than the first test. Greenpeace said that the test was outrageous and an affront to the people of the Pacific area, while the Japanese Prime Minister said that it was "extremely regrettable." In the face of this international censure, the French government continues to argue that the tests are essential to maintaining a viable nuclear defense.

Stockholm, Thursday 5. Seamus Heaney, the 57-year-old Irish poet, wins the Nobel Prize for Literature.

American diplomacy opens possibility of Bosnian peace

American diplomacy has succeeded where the Europeans have failed, in obtaining a ceasefire in Bosnia that has a real chance of turning into a lasting peace. President Clinton announced today that after weeks shuttling around the Balkans, Richard C. Holbrooke, assistant secretary of state, has returned from Sarajevo with signatures to a lasting truce from representatives of all three warring parties. After the ceasefire has taken effect, delegations from Bosnia, Serbia, and Croatia, led by their presidents, will come to the United States for negotiations on a lasting peace. These will take the form of "proximity" talks, in which the different parties meet at the same location but do not necessarily argue face to face in the same room. The truce guarantees the restoration of gas and electricity to Sarajevo, and will not come into effect until supplies are reconnected by the deadline of next Tuesday morning. The agreement also involves an end of the Serb blockade of the enclave of Gorazde so that the United Nations can move in relief supplies. (→ October 6)

Sixty-eight killed in earthquake in western Turkey

A survivor among the rubble of Dinar in southwestern Turkey after today's earthquake.

An earthquake measuring 6.0 on the Richter scale has hit the town of Dinar in western Turkey, 200 miles southwest of the capital Ankara. The death toll is at least 68 people, and 200 have been injured, but according to a government spokesman the fatalities could well rise to 100. Rescuers have been pulling people from the rubble still alive.

Sunday's quake lasted 30 seconds and was followed by 43 aftershocks. It followed a tremor on Wednesday that did not take lives but did damage homes. Many people in the town are furious with the government for telling them that it was safe to return to their homes. However, many of the town's population of 100,000 had been sleeping in the open since Wednesday and that may have reduced today's death toll.

LOS ANGELES, TUESDAY 3

Jury declares O. J. Simpson not guilty

The relief shows — O. J. Simpson with his chief defense counsel, Johnnie Cochran, to his right, after the verdict was announced.

The "trial of the century" came to its conclusion this morning, but the controversy continues. The jury of ten women and two men returned to the Los Angeles courtroom to give their verdict on the charge that O.J. Simpson had murdered his wife and her friend: America's most famous ex-football star was not guilty.

The trial lasted nine months, all of it under the full glare of national and international publicity, but the verdict was astonishingly swift. After retiring for less than four hours, the jury announced yesterday to Judge Ito that they had reached their decision. The judge chose to wait until today to hear that verdict. As it was announced, O.J. visibly relaxed and smiled calmly.

The popular verdict, however, remains split. Questioned in the hours after the verdict, most whites, persuaded by his record of wife-beating and the prosecution accusations of jealousy, still thought that O.J. did commit the murders. Blacks, on the other hand, welcomed his release, accepting that he was set up by the LAPD, whose chief witness, detective Mark Fuhrman, they believe was revealed in the trial as a bigot and a racist. (→ October 11)

(→ October 11)

WASHINGTON DC, MONDAY 2

Terrorism bill now off course

Conservative Republicans and Democrats interested in civil liberties have combined to put a brake on new counter-terrorist legislation that looked likely to come into force with only minimal opposition from Congress. In the aftermath of the Oklahoma bombing, the public mood was such that the legislation swiftly went through the Senate and the House Judiciary Committee. It would give Federal agencies more power on wire taps, enable the military to be brought into play in certain cases, and institute Federal powers to deport illegal aliens who were suspected of terrorism.

The atmosphere regarding terrorism has changed greatly in recent months, however, principally because both the Ruby Ridge and Waco hearings have given many Congressmen pause for thought about the problems of wide Federal powers. Lobbying against the measures has come from groups as various as civil libertarians, explosives manufacturers, and the gun lobby. The result is that Luis J. Freeh, director of the FBI, is unlikely to get the measures that he says he needs.

NEW YORK, SUNDAY 1

Blind sheik found guilty of terrorism

An eight-month trial ended today with guilty verdicts against a blind Islamic cleric and nine followers on the charge of conspiracy to commit terrorist acts. Sheik Omar Abdel Rahman, a 57-year-old Egyptian who came here in 1990, had plotted with his accomplices to explode five bombs in New York in a single day, with the aim of destroying the United Nations building, the main government buildings in the city, the Lincoln and Holland tunnels, and the George Washington Bridge. The ten were not charged with the World Trade Center bombing, but according to the prosecutors they have close links with those who were involved in this incident.

Sheik Rahman and accomplices.

LONDON, MONDAY 2

Salt proved as cause of hypertension

A study published in today's *Nature* journal establishes that salt definitely causes high blood pressure. Although suspected for some time by scientists, some researchers and food manufacturers have claimed that no link has been positively established. But an Australian experiment with chimpanzees in the Gabon discovered that those given a diet high in salt showed markedly higher hypertension than others in the same group who had little salt. Additionally, members of South American Indian societies with a low salt diet do not suffer increasing blood pressure with age.

New York, Wednesday 4. The Pope arrived in New York today, flying into Newark for the start of a five-day tour.

O.J. Simpson and American race relations on trial

Judge Lance Ito, who heard the case.

The trial of former football star O.J. Simpson was one of the most controversial events America has seen this century. Simpson had been "every white man's favorite black man." His celebrity and the racial tensions exacerbated by the case made for gripping TV in the US and abroad.

Simpson was accused of murdering his former wife Nicole Brown Simpson and her friend Ronald Goldman on June 12, 1994. A glove found at the scene of the crime linked him to the murder. He agreed to appear at an arraignment to face the charges but instead fled with police in pursuit. When he gave himself up, he had with him a false beard, a passport, and $10,000.

After 1,000 jurors were vetted, the trial began in central LA. It had been moved there from Brentwood, where the crime was committed, because Brentwood is a white area and the jury would have been white. For political reasons, District Attorney Gil Garcetti switched venue.

The trial opened on January 24 this year with the statement of Marcia Clark, chief prosecutor. The court heard that DNA testing confirmed that blood belonging to Nicole was found on a pair of socks discovered in Simpson's home. Detective Mark Fuhrman had also allegedly found a bloody glove linking Simpson to the crime in the ex-footballer's garden.

The defense team, led by Johnnie Cochran, played the race card, and they were presented with a golden opportunity to come up trumps when it was revealed that Fuhrman was a virulent racist.

After that, the prosecution, despite strong forensic evidence, was fighting a losing battle. On October 3, the jury of eight blacks, three whites, and one Hispanic, found O.J. Simpson not guilty of murder. One juror gave a black-power salute after the verdict was announced. Simpson was free but the US was more anxious than ever about racial problems. (→ October 11)

The not-guilty verdict is announced and O.J. Simpson (center) visibly relaxes.

Chief Prosecutor Marcia Clark.

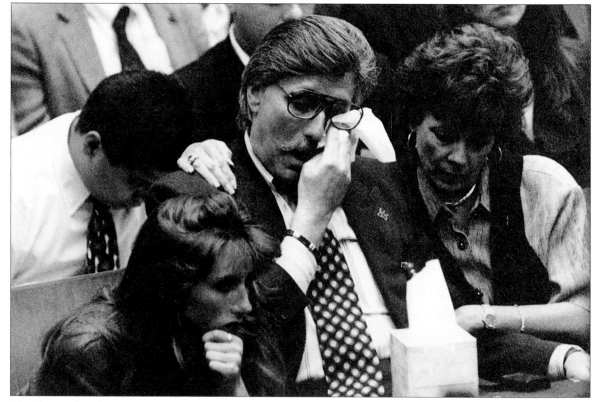

The relatives of murder victim Ronald L. Goldman were distraught as they listened to the evidence.

Housekeeper Rosa Lopez gives evidence.

Margaret York, wife of Judge Ito.

Controversial detective Mark Fuhrman.

Murder victim Ronald Goldman.

O.J. and Nicole Simpson before their separation.

O.J. Simpson's attorneys, Johnnie Cochran (left) and Robert Shapiro leave the courtroom on the second day of the trial.

Key evidence, key moments

Scene of the crime: the steps at Nicole's house.

Simpson flees on the free-way, filmed live on TV.

The body of Nicole Simpson is taken away.

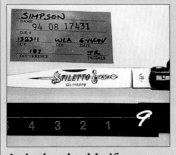

The gloves that appeared to link O.J. Simpson to murder.

A single-edged knife was used to kill both victims.

S	M	T	W	T	F	S
1	2	3	4	5	6	7
8	9	10	11	12	13	14
15	16	17	18	19	20	21
22	23	24	25	26	27	28
29	30	31				

Baltimore, 8
The Pope ends his brief US tour by celebrating mass in a sports stadium.

Atlanta, 9
Senator Sam Nunn of Georgia, 57, a leading southern Democrat, announces that he will not seek reelection next year.

Moscow, 9
Officals announce that Russia's grain harvest will be the worst in 30 years due to the summer's drought and poor management.

New York, 10
Microsoft boss Bill Gates buys the huge and highly prestigious Bettmann Archive of photographs.

Paris, 10
Five million public service workers go on strike across France, protesting at a government pay freeze and job cuts.

New York, 11
A UN report to the Security Council says that Saddam Hussein has enough chemical and biological weapons to destroy the population of the world several times over.

Paris, 11
Court finds Prime Minister Juppé guilty of corrupt practices for occupying a city-owned apartment, but imposes no punishment provided he vacates it.

New York, 11
Prosecution tells court that boxing promoter Don King made huge fraudulent insurance claims.

Stockholm, 11
Two Americans and a Dutchman are awarded the Nobel Prize in Chemistry for their work on the ozone layer.

Rome, 14
A judge orders Silvio Berlusconi to stand trial on corruption charges.

Deaths
John Cairncross, the "fifth man" in Russia's postwar UK spy ring, at the age of 82 in the west of England, October 9.

Lord Home, British prime minister 1963-4 as Sir Alec Douglas-Home, and twice foreign secretary, in Scotland, at age 92, October 9.

MEXICO CITY, MONDAY 9
More than 60 die in Mexican earthquake

Rescuers hunt through the rubble for victims near the port of Manzanillo.

More than 60 people are believed to have died when an earthquake rocked west central Mexico today. The worst-hit area is the Pacific coast, the epicenter being located off the coastal port of Manzanillo. The devastated area includes several resort towns, and in Manzanillo itself nine people are believed to have died when the eight-story Hotel Costa Real collapsed. President Ernesto Zedillo has declared Manzanillo a disaster area.

The greatest fatalities are almost certainly in Cihuatlan, where 26 people were killed. The school, bank, church, and jail all collapsed. Tremors were felt as far away as Mexico City, 524 miles east of Manzanillo, but no damage occurred.

BEIJING, SATURDAY 14
China snubs US by agreeing nuclear deal with Iran

China has resisted US pressure and has signed a deal with Iran to supply a nuclear plant that will enable the Iranians to produce nuclear weapons. The move comes only weeks after the Chinese foreign finister, Qian Qichen, responded to US requests and agreed to abandon the planned delivery of two 300-megawatt nuclear reactors ordered by the Teheran government. The Clinton administration assumed then that China was sensitive to the nuclear threat posed by Iran and had recognized that they should not assist that country.

Relations between the US and China have deteriorated in recent months over the issues of human rights in China and the status of Taiwan. White House officials then announced yesterday that American companies were unlikely to get financial support to win work on China's proposed Three Gorges dam.

China has now agreed to sell Iran a uranium hexafluoride plant, to be built in the north of the country. An expert from the Carnegie Endowment for International Peace, Leonard Spector, commented, "It is hard to imagine why Iran would have the peaceful need for such a plant. The reason you want a uranium hexafluoride plant is to do uranium enrichment, and it would suggest this is a step toward acquiring nuclear arms." Given Iran's oil reserves, the country has little apparent need to develop domestic nuclear energy.

LOS ANGELES, TUESDAY 10
Retrial of Menendez brothers opens in Los Angeles

Erik (left) and Lyle Menendez.

The opening statements were made today in the second trial of two brothers for the murder of their parents in Beverly Hills six years ago. Although two juries were impaneled to hear the evidence, last year's ruling was declared a mistrial after neither jury could reach a verdict. This time, only one jury has been appointed.

The two brothers, Erik, 24, and Lyle, 27, do not dispute that they killed their parents. They say that they shot them dead in self-defense after years of sexual and emotional abuse. Their plea briefly made them popular heroes among some groups of American young people last year. The prosecution maintains that the killings were carried out because the brothers were frightened of being disinherited by their parents who left a $15 million estate. Deputy District Attorney David Conn said, "They shot their parents in the arms, legs, torso, and heads. Hundreds of shotgun pellets tore into the bodies of Jose and Kitty Menendez." He claimed the boys then shot their parents in the knees to make it look like a Mafia killing.

Judge Stanley Weisberg has barred TV coverage of the trial, which had a massive impact on the first trial. It is also thought that he has taken note of the effects of TV coverage on the O.J. Simpson case.

PHOENIX, MONDAY 9

Arizona train crash blamed on terrorists

The derailed Amtrak train that was hit by what appears to have been a terrorist attack.

An Amtrak train carrying 248 people spun from the track in the Arizona desert at 1:40 a.m. today and crashed into a ravine. One of the crew was killed and over 100 people were injured, some of them seriously. Police are sure that the crash was caused by sabotage. Investigators have found that a bar connecting the rails had been removed, and the electric current at either end of it reconnected so that the signals would remain green. "Someone obviously intended to have the train drop off the ravine without any precautions," said Thomas M. Downs, the president and chairman of Amtrak. "They could easily have killed a large number of passengers." Right-wing ter-

rorists are strongly suspected because a note has been found at the scene of the derailment. Written by an unknown group calling itself Sons of Gestapo, the note contains a poem about the women killed in the siege of the Branch Davidian sect at Waco, Texas. It also criticized, among others, the Bureau of Alcohol, Tobacco and Firearms, However, no motive was given for sabotage.

The train, the Sunset Limited, was traveling from Miami to Los Angeles. Four of its 12 cars turned over and another three were skewed off the tracks. Because of the remoteness of the area, rescuers have had to reach the wreck in a posse of helicopters and all-terrain vehicles.

Stokholm, Friday 13. The Nobel Peace prize is awarded to Joseph Rotblat, scientist and anti-nuclear campaigner.

NEW YORK, WEDNESDAY 11

O.J. pulls out of TV interview

Six hours before he was due to go on the air, O.J. Simpson pulled out of what was to be his first television interview since his acquittal last week. Lawyers advised him against being questioned on *Dateline NBC* due to some of the questions his interviewers were going to ask. O.J. still faces civil suits from the families of his former wife and Ron Goldman, the other victim, and lawyers felt that he should avoid putting himself in a situation that might jeopardize his defense. (→ November 2)

BOSNIA, FRIDAY 13

Muslims and Croats besiege Banja Luka

Refugees have crowded into makeshift accommodation in Banja Luka.

Despite the recently announced cease-fire, fighting is still going on in Bosnia around the Serb stronghold of Banja Luka. Muslim and Croat forces are close to capturing the nearby town of Prijedor, from where more than 40,000 people fled this afternoon.

The joint forces have made considerable advances into the area over the last three days. It is thought that the Muslims want to squeeze Banja Luka, which has largely escaped

direct action during the war, and is considered to be the cradle of the Serbian ethnic cleansing policy. In answer to criticisms for continuing to fight after the cease-fire, one Muslim commander said, "The international community does not understand the Serbs. Serbs only listen to military action and we cannot stop now."

UN observers have reported that fighting has all but ceased throughout the rest of Bosnia. (→ November 1)

Baghdad, Saturday 14. It is reported that Saddam Hussein has burned the cars of his errant son Uday (center, bearded, at back).

S	M	T	W	T	F	S
1	2	3	4	5	6	7
8	9	10	11	12	13	14
15	16	17	18	19	20	21
22	23	24	25	26	27	28
29	30	31				

Baghdad, 15
Saddam Hussein is reelected as president of Iraq with nearly 100 % of the vote.

Tel Aviv, 15
Six Israeli soldiers are killed in an ambush by Hezbollah guerillas. (→ October 25)

Ankara, 15
Turkish prime minister, Tansu Ciller, resigns after the Turkish parliament passes a vote of no confidence in her government.

Paris, 17
A Frenchwoman, Jeanne Calment, reaches the age of 120 years and 238 days to become the longest-living human on record.

Tripoli, 18
Libya announces that it intends to deport more than one million people

Moscow, 19
President Yeltsin gives a speech denouncing NATO and the US.

Moscow, 19
The Pushkin Museum unveils art treasures removed from Germany by Soviet troops at the end of World War II.

Lisbon, 19
An official report states that almost 37 % of the Portuguese population is illiterate.

Paris, 19
France puts 2,500 more troops on its streets after a spate of terrorist bombings.

Washington, 19
Fidel Castro's daughter Alina is to travel to New York to protest about his visit there.

Colombo, Sri Lanka, 20
At least 25 people are killed when two oil-storage sites are bombed by Tamil Tiger guerrillas. (→ October 22)

Cape Canaveral, 20
Space shuttle *Columbia* blasts off, carrying scientists who will perform groundbreaking scientific tests.

Okinawa, 21
Thousands of Japanese protest about the alleged gang rape of a 12-year-old girl by US servicemen.

PARIS, TUESDAY 17
Bomb on Paris metro

A bomb injured 26 early-morning commuters when it ripped through a subway. Some victims were said to have had their feet blown off, and a man had his leg amputated by a doctor at the scene of the explosion. The bomb was planted beneath a seat on the train. Algerian terrorists are suspected of the bombing.

New York, Tuesday 17. Superman actor Christopher Reeve appeared in public for the first time since becoming paralyzed in the spring.

LAS VEGAS, FRIDAY 20
Student wins $10.9 million jackpot

A $10,918,881 jackpot gave a history student a place in the annals of American gambling legends when he struck it rich at a Las Vegas slot machine. The 29-year-old, who has requested that he not be identified, won the sum with a single pull of the arm of a slot machine at the Gold Coast Hotel and Casino in Las Vegas on Wednesday. He was unaware he had won until someone pointed it out to him. It is the highest jackpot to ever have been won on a slot machine. The previous record, said International Game Technology, the manufacturers of the machine on which the prize was won, had been $9.3 million. The Megabucks dollar progressive machine, on which the lucky gambler made the move that has changed his life, is part of a sophisticated and lucrative jackpot system that joins it to 725 other machines in 137 casinos in Nevada.

TOKYO, MONDAY 16
Japanese fury over CIA spying

Japanese government officials are seeking clarification about alleged US spying on their trade representatives. A report in *The New York Times* on Sunday stated that the Central Intelligence Agency had conducted a spying operation before trade talks in June, and it alleged that the CIA used electronic devices to listen in on Japanese preparations for the talks before they met with American trade representatives. In Washington, a prominent official from the Japanese Embassy met with Thomas Hubbard of the State Department to discuss the matter. However, Japanese officials, including trade minister Ryutaro Hashimoto, insisted that the spying could not have had any effect on the trade talks.

NEW YORK, TUESDAY 17
Crackdown on New York's Fulton Fish Market, in fight against Mafia

Trade was virtually nonexistent at the Fulton Fish Market yesterday, and it was the traders themselves who put a stop to business. They blockaded the stands where they usually earn a living as a direct response to a determined attempt by Mayor Rudolph Giuliani to rid their workplace of extortion by the Mafia. City authorities have used their powers to ban companies with Mafia links from trading, and to install new, "clean" workers. The traders' action led Mayor Giuliani to threaten to close the market on a temporary basis.

Traders at the Fulton Fish Market.

NEW YORK, FRIDAY 20
Castro gets mixed reception

Both President Bill Clinton and Rudolph Giuliani, Mayor of New York, will snub Fidel Castro this weekend. The Cuban leader, who is in New York for the celebrations marking the fiftieth anniversary of the United Nations, will be the only one of the world's leaders in attendance whom the US president will make a point of avoiding. President Castro has, however, been inundated with invitations to attend receptions by American businessmen, many of whom oppose the US trade ban on Cuba.

Cubans in New York protest Fidel Castro's visit to the city.

Belgian MPs send the head of NATO to trial

Willy Claes, the secretary general of NATO, has resigned after his fellow countrymen in the Belgian parliament decided that he should be put on trial. Claes will face allegations of corruption with regard to massive irregular payments made to the Flemish Socialist Party by Italian and French defense contractors anxious to secure deals. Although it is unlikely that Mr. Claes will be summoned to appear in court in the near future, the threat of court action hanging over him will probably tarnish his reputation in the eyes of many.

He was said to have told NATO ambassadors at a lunch on Tuesday that if the Belgian parliament voted to bring proceedings against him he would resign to save NATO from embarrassment. Four other high-ranking Belgian ministers who have been implicated in the scandal have also been forced to resign, while the Belgian air force's chief of staff committed suicide. Mr. Claes had been NATO secretary general since September 1994. He commented: "I have fallen into a dark hole."

Louis Farrakhan leads 400,000 black men on march on Washington DC

Crowds pack the Mall in Washington DC to listen to black Muslim separatist Louis Farrakhan.

New York, Wednesday 18. Mary Tyler Moore has revealed in her autobiography that she assisted her brother John in a failed suicide attempt when he had terminal kidney cancer.

The "Million Man March" on Washington that Louis Farrakhan organized was not as well supported as had been expected. Around 600,000 fewer marchers than he had promised showed up. That still made it the biggest march by black people in the history of the US, and one that mobilized approximately 150,000 more than Martin Luther King's civil rights march on Washington in 1963.

Farrakhan, the leader of a controversial group, the Nation of Islam, showed that he has the power to captivate on an awesome scale. The man who had been denounced in some quarters as a purveyor of racism directed against Jews and whites gave a speech that called on black men to scrutinize their own behavior.

During his 150-minute speech, Farrakhan demanded of those in attendance that they desist from violence unless it was in self-defense, that they do everything in their power to

Representatives of Louis Farrakhan's Nation of Islam in Washington for the march.

show respect toward black women and that they also denounce rape and drugs. It was an inward-looking message that was directed at the black community, a plea for self-reformation through self-respect and self-discipline. Although most speakers at the event emphasized these

ideas, Mr. Farrakhan also used the occasion to launch virulent verbal attacks on the white founding fathers of the US, on Abraham Lincoln, President Clinton, and modern white America. The atmosphere among the black men who thronged the Mall was orderly and attentive.

New York, 23
Mayor Giuliani asks Yasser Arafat to leave a concert for assembled world leaders at the Lincoln Center, explaining that the Palestinian leader was a terrorist.

Riohacha, Colombia, 25
An epidemic of Venezuelan equine encephalitis, a virus spread by mosquitoes and dubbed the "mad plague," spreads through Colombia.

West Bank, 25
Palestinian police officers arrive in Jenin at the start of the process to end 27 years of Israeli military rule in most of the mainly Palestinian West Bank. (→ November 4)

Moscow, 26
President Yeltsin is rushed to hospital suffering from heart problems, for the second time in three months, and almost immediately after returning from the UN celebrations in the US. (→ November 3)

Fort Bragg, North Carolina, 27
A sniper kills one and wounds 18 when he opens fire on hundreds of soldiers assembled at an army base for a four-mile run.

Dayton, Ohio, 31
The three presidents at the center of the Bosnian conflict, Alija Izetbegovic of Bosnia, Slobodan Milosevic of Serbia and Franjo Tudjman of Croatia, arrive at Dayton, Ohio, for talks aimed at ending four years of war. (→ November 1)

Washington DC, 31
The CIA admits that it knowingly supplied the White House and the Pentagon with information on the Soviet Union from agents it knew, or suspected, were controlled from Moscow. This "tainted" information, passed on to protect sources, could have affected decisions on billions of dollars of arms expenditure.

Deaths
Bobby Riggs, Wimbledon tennis champion and the world's top player in 1939, in San Diego, California, at age 77, October 25.

Gavin Ewart, one of Britain's funniest poets, at age 79, October 23.

Clinton and Yeltsin make little progress on Bosnia

President Clinton enjoys Boris Yeltsin's joke at the expense of the press.

Presidents Clinton and Yeltsin held a four-hour meeting at Hyde Park, seeking a formula whereby Russian troops could be integrated into the peacekeeping efforts in Bosnia. They admitted to having made little progress, while confirming that both were committed to finding a solution.

The main gain from the session was the obvious warmth between the two leaders, and it concluded with the Russian's accusation that the press was predicting failure. "You're a disaster," he told the assembled journalists, to the surprised delight of President Clinton. (→ October 31)

New York attacks the sex shops and topless bars

New York's City Council announced a package of new regulations designed to reduce the number of sex-industry premises, including those in such world-famous red light districts as Times Square, and to relocate the concentration away from residential neighborhoods.

Unless successfully challenged in the courts, the council will give a year's notice to those sex industries affected, requiring them to change the nature of their business, close down, or move to designated areas. These will be largely in industrial environments. The plan faces opposition from civil libertarians, who claim that the measures will violate the First Amendment, which safeguards freedom of expression.

The face of Times Square could be changed in a sex industry crackdown.

Massacres by Tamil Tigers

Sri Lanka took military action against the rebel Tamil Tigers in the north of the island, and as they began to make inroads, the Tigers responded with sabotage and mass murder.

Last week they attacked the main oil depots. On the weekend, 68 Sinhalese who had settled in villages in the traditional Tamil territory were slaughtered by rebels using machetes and pickaxes. Colombo is now under curfew, and there have been instances of anti-Tamil reprisals there. (→ November 10)

London, Sunday 22. Sir Kingsley Amis, one of Britain's most celebrated authors, died at age 73. He came to fame in 1954 with his first novel, *Lucky Jim*.

Spielberg sues former backer

Film director Steven Spielberg has issued a lawsuit against Denis Hoffman, who invested a few thousand dollars in Spielberg's first film *Amblin*. Mr. Hoffman has claimed that he is now owed many times this amount by the phenomenally successful director, who, he says, shut him out of all future projects.

Mr. Spielberg has filed his suit to end what he describes as "financial harassment," and says that his obligations to Mr. Hoffman have been met.

NEW YORK, SUNDAY 22

200 heads of state at UN's birthday party

World leaders assemble at the United Nations for the organization's fiftieth birthday celebrations.

A mood for change was evident at the unprecedented gathering of world leaders in New York, celebrating the United Nations' fiftieth birthday.

President Clinton, the first to address the assembly, spoke of the need to join in the fight against international terrorism, organized crime, drug smuggling, and the spread of nuclear and other massively destructive weapons. President Frederick Chiluba of Zambia warned that the major powers should not become "high priests to the rest of the globe".

President Boris Yeltsin of Russia suggested that in one of the most pressing of current concerns, the future of Bosnia, the UN Security Council was being bypassed by NATO. The session was opened by the president of the General Assembly, Diego Freitas do Amaral of Portugal. The speakers included Cuba's President Fidel Castro, who replaced his more customary battle fatigues with a formal suit in honor of the occasion.

NIGERIA, TUESDAY 31

Ken Saro-Wiwa sentenced to death

Nigerian writer Ken Saro-Wiwa

A court tribunal in Port Harcourt, Nigeria, sentenced to death one of the country's most distinguished writers, political activist Ken Saro-Wiwa, together with three others. Five more activists were condemned on Monday. The charges arose from the deaths of four leaders of the Ogoni people, killed during a protest rally. Mr. Saro-Wiwa, 54, has been convicted of murder, even though it is conceded that he did not kill the men himself.

Mr. Saro-Wiwa has been at the forefront of protests by the Ogonis that their land has been polluted by the oil companies operating there. Nigeria is ruled by the military regime of General Sani Abacha, and human rights groups say that murders are carried out by troops to intimidate the people.(→ November 11)

MONTREAL, MONDAY 30

In close poll Quebec votes to stay in Canada

The people of Quebec have voted to maintain union with the rest of Canada, but only by the narrowest of margins, so leaving the long-term future of the province unresolved. With 50.6 percent voting against secession, little more than 50,000 votes divided the sides.

The referendum in Quebec was held at the instigation of the hardline separatist Parti Québecois, which has governed the province since winning elections last year. Quebec's prime minister, Jacques Parizeau, blamed "money and the ethnic vote" for the defeat of his bid to make Quebec an independent state.

Under Canadian law, the referendum cannot be repeated during the current provincial government's term of office. Canadian prime minister, Jean Chretien, must now seek ways of mollifying the disaffected half of Quebec's electorate.

HOUSTON, TUESDAY 24

Fan convicted of killing singer

Fans mourn the death of their idol, Selena Quintanilla Perez.

A row over money is believed to be behind the murder of singer Selena, 23, shot in a motel room in her home town, Corpus Christi, Texas.

Yolanda Saldivar, 35, the founder and former president of Selena's fan club, faces life imprisonment after being found guilty of the murder. The defence claimed that the gun had gone off accidentally, and that Saldivar meant to commit suicide, while the prosecution asserted that the shooting occurred after Selena accused Saldivar of stealing money from her business account.

Selena Quintanilla Perez was a Grammy-winning singer of Tejano, a modern mixture of Mexican- and European-influenced musical styles, and was the music's biggest star.

Hyannis, Massachusetts, Sunday 22. Maxene Andrews, the "one on the left" in the Andrews Sisters, died at age 79.

S	M	T	W	T	F	S
			1	2	3	4
5	6	7	8	9	10	11
12	13	14	15	16	17	18
19	20	21	22	23	24	25
26	27	28	29	30		

Washington, 1
The House of Representatives votes to ban a particular, specialized method of abortion, in the first limit on abortions since they were legalized in 1973.

Tokyo, 1
Defense secretary William J. Perry apologizes for the alleged rape of a Japanese girl by three Marines.

Washington DC, 1
Conservative author, Ben Wattenberg, reports that he has had a telephone conversation with Mr. Clinton during which the President admitted that in his first two years of office he had "lost the language" of centrism that had gotten him elected.

Lille, 1
French police find a terrorist bomb factory, shortly after arresting an Arab on suspicion of organizing the bombing campaign.

New York, 2
The Daiwa Bank of Japan is ordered to close its American operations after a Federal grand jury accuses it of covering up $1.1 billion of trading losses in New York.

Buenos Aires, 2
The Argentinian Supreme Court orders the extradition of a former SS captain to Italy to stand trial for a World War II massacre.

Los Angeles, 2
Atmospheric tests show that, every year, Los Angeles' smog is clearing.

Washington DC, 3
Relatives of the victims of the Lockerbie bombing of Pan Am flight 103 boycott a memorial service in protest at what they see as government inaction over the case.

Moscow, 3
President Yeltsin appears on Russian television for the first time since being hospitalized ten days ago.

Deaths
Florence Greenberg, producer of records by the Shirelles and other black pop singers, at age 82 in Hackensack, New Jersey, November 2.

Brian Lenihan, Irish former foreign minister, at age 64, November 1.

Washington, Friday 3. Pictures of the Eagle Nebula from the Hubble Telescope show, for the first time, stars being created.

DAYTON, OHIO, WEDNESDAY 1
Bosnia talks begin in Dayton, Ohio

Presidents Slobodan Milosevic of Serbia, Alija Izetbegovic of Bosnia, and Franjo Tudjman of Croatia met today for the first time in four years at the US military air base at Dayton, Ohio, to start talks aimed at ending the four-year civil war. The US government, coordinator of the talks, plans to keep the contents secret for the moment. (→ November 21)

MIAMI, THURSDAY 2
Ordeal of disabled children ends as bus hijacker is shot by police

Catalino Sang, shot dead by police.

A slow chase through Miami ended at 9:45 this morning at Miami Beach when police shot dead a man who had hijacked a school bus. The bus was carrying 13 disabled children, some of whom have severe learning disabilities, and some of whom are nonverbal. None of the children was hurt, apart from minor injuries to one from shattered glass. The man was attacked by a special hostage rescue team that, coincidentally, had recently practiced a scenario of rescuing hijacked bus passengers.

The hijacker told the driver that he had a bomb, but after the police had shot him they found that he had nothing more lethal than part of a child's respirator. It is not clear what his motives were, but the man, 42-year-old Catalino Sang, was reported to have financial problems. He had the driver take the bus to a restaurant where he had worked for seven years until quitting on Wednesday.

NEW YORK, THURSDAY 2
Paula Barbieri calls it off

Paula Barbieri and O.J. Simpson.

Despite having waited for him throughout the trial, O.J. Simpson's girlfriend has told viewers of *Prime Time Live* that their relationship is over. Model Paula Barbieri had been expected to marry O.J. once he was cleared of the murder charges, and when the couple were seen in the Dominican Republic just after the trial, speculation was rife that they had gone there for a quick wedding. Citing her reasons, she said, "It was a realization for me that he was going back to that lifestyle he used to have...I just want to work. I want to have children. I want to love."

SAN ANTONIO, FRIDAY 3
Scientists fnds a single gene is linked to nearly all breast cancers

Scientists from the University of Texas at San Antonio have announced a major breakthrough in their understanding of breast cancer. They have isolated a gene that seems to play a role in the formation of nearly all breast cancers.

The gene, called BRCA-1, was first implicated in breast cancers a year ago, but at the time it was thought responsible for only rare forms of the cancer that run in families. However, the latest research, which is published in today's *Science* journal, has found that the same gene also seems to be behind the more common forms of breast cancer. It has also been identified in some cases of ovarian cancer.

The gene triggers the manufacture of a particular protein, the BRCA-1 protein. In healthy people this protein works at the center of cells where genetic material is stored. In the cases of familial cancer the BRCA-1 protein is defective. Now the researchers have found that in other forms of breast cancer, where the protein is not defective, it is found in the wrong part of the cell. The discovery does not have any practical implications for women already suffering from breast cancer, but will help doctors in forecasting the onset of the disease and hence in treating it.

Geneva, Wednesday 1. The Aga Khan starts legal action to prevent his ex-wife from selling her jewelry, citing an agreement that the jewels stay in his family.

JERUSALEM, SATURDAY 4

Rabin assassinated after call for peace

Israeli Prime Minister Yitzhak Rabin was shot dead tonight minutes after leaving a peace rally in Tel Aviv. A student has been arrested. He is believed to have acted alone.

Mr. Rabin had been addressing a rally, "Peace Yes Violence No," that had been called to counter a rising right-wing tide of resentment at the concessions made to Palestinians over self-rule. The organizers had called the rally to show that most Israelis were in favor of the peace accord, under which Palestinians have already been given control of Gaza and Jericho and are shortly to take over more towns in the West Bank. More than 100,000 people attended the rally.

Mr. Rabin was killed at 9:50 p.m. as he was leaving the speakers' platform in the Kings of Israel Square for his car. The gunman pushed easily through the security men surrounding the Prime Minister and shot him twice from close range. Mr. Rabin was rushed to Ichilov Hospital for emergency surgery, but an hour later it was announced that he was dead.

The security forces seized the killer within seconds of the shooting. He was identified as Yigal Amir, a 25-year-old law student at a religious college. He had previously taken part in right-wing protests against the peace accord, including setting up illegal Jewish settlements in the West Bank. Amir told the police, "I acted alone on God's orders and I have no regrets." He had intended to kill foreign minister Shimon Peres at the same time, but was thwarted when the two politicians left the rally separately. Amir said that he had been planning to kill Mr. Rabin for almost a year, and twice before had gone to sites where Mr. Rabin was due to appear. Mr. Peres has taken over as interim prime minister.

Yitzhak Rabin, who was a hero of the 1967 war, was killed for the cause with which he is most associated. It is largely his conviction, and his ability to persuade the Israeli people that their security is not threatened by the concessions that have to be made to the Palestinians, that have kept the peace process afloat, despite some fierce opposition and the bloody Arab extremist bombings. His last words spoken in public, at the end of his speech, were: "This rally must broadcast to the Israeli public and to many in the Western and outside world, that the people of Israel genuinely want peace, support peace. Thank you." (→ November 6)

Yitzhak Rabin.

Yigal Amir is hustled away by police.

Songs for peace at the rally. The spirit of forgiveness that characterized the gathering was soon shattered by gunfire.

DURBAN, THURSDAY 2

Malan arrested for massacre

Malan, charged with apartheid murders.

South Africa's former defense minister General Magnus Malan and ten retired military officers have been arrested by police investigating violence and civil unrest in Natal province during the last years of whites-only rule. They have been charged with the massacre of a priest, five women, and seven children in a Natal township in January 1987. It is thought that the men may have been responsible for a conspiracy to boost the Zulu-based Inkatha movement at a time when its support was waning and thus provide opposition to Nelson Mandela's ANC. The whites-only government set up a training camp for Inkatha members who allegedly formed hit squads that targeted the ANC. The courtroom was packed with former police and military officials supporting the accused.

NEW YORK, THURSDAY 2

UN calls on US to end Cuba ban

The General Assembly of the United Nations today called on the US to lift its 30-year-old embargo on Cuba. The voting was 117 to 3, with only Israel and Uzbekistan siding with the US. Many European countries voted for the motion; Britain and Germany abstained. It is the fourth year in a row that the United Nations has voted that the US should end the ban, which in recent years has been made more stringent.

November

Poland, 5
Voting in the Polish presidential election puts the current president, Lech Walesa, neck and neck with the former Communist Aleksander Kwasniewski. (→ November 22))

Kazakhstan, 5
At least 28 people die in a gas explosion in a residential building.

Tokyo, 6
The Japanese government offers $24,000 to each of the 8,000 victims of a mass mercury poisoning that happened 40 years ago.

Bangladesh, 6
Thousands of anti-government protesters enforce a blockade of rail, road, and waterways.

Athens, 9
Greek police posing as a television crew overpower an Ethiopian hijacker while he is holding an air stewardess hostage at knifepoint.

Geneva, 10
The United Nations accuses Croatian troops of atrocities during the recapture of Krajina in August.

Brussels, 10
US officials bar the former Dutch prime minister Ruud Lubbers from becoming head of NATO.

Budapest, 10
Hungary braces itself for a wave of strikes by civil service unions opposed to austerity measures.

Ireland, 10
Irish police find a bomb containing more than 1,000 lb (454 kg) of home-made explosives in a stolen van.

Sri Lanka, 10
The Tamil Tigers resume public executions of alleged Tamil traitors.

London, 10
Siamese twin boys joined from the breastbone to the navel are born to a Kuwaiti at a London hospital.

Madrid, 10
Two Spanish bankers try to blackmail King Juan Carlos in an attempt to have their fraud charges dropped.

Death
Detective Eddie Egan, who inspired the film *The French Connection*, dies of cancer at age 65.

LAGOS, SATURDAY 11
Nigeria executes Ken Saro-Wiwa

Ken Wiwa denounces his father's execution.

Nigeria's military dictatorship defied international appeals for clemency yesterday and went ahead with the execution of the dissident writer Ken Saro-Wiwa and eight other environmental campaigners. The nine had been convicted of murder at a special military tribunal.

The hangings prompted an outcry from Commonwealth leaders meeting in New Zealand, who are now likely to vote for Nigeria to be expelled from the group. British prime minister John Major said: "I don't see how Nigeria can stay in the Commonwealth without a return to democratic government."

Saro-Wiwa headed a group that fought the exploitation of his native Ogoniland's oil. (→ December 8)

Paris, Monday 6. The trial begins of Christian Didier, alleged assassin of Vichy police chief René Bousquet who sent 12,000 Jews to their deaths.

TBILISI, SUNDAY 5
Shevardnadze land-slide in Georgia

Shevardnadze at the polls.

Eduard A. Shevardnadze, 67, the former Soviet foreign minister who returned to his native Georgia to become its leader three years ago, has won today's presidential election.

Shevardnadze, who was widely credited with helping to end the Cold War, ran as a moderate, a patriot, and a crimefighter. Incomplete official results show he already has about 70 per cent of the vote. His center-right Citizens Union Party also led in elections for the 250-seat parliament. His government will strengthen its fight against mafia-style crime and continue on a Western economic course.

JERUSALEM, MONDAY 6
World leaders mourn Rabin

Yitzhak Rabin was buried today before the greatest assembly of foreign leaders ever gathered in Israel. Among the 5,000 mourners of the 73-year-old Israeli Prime Minister were the Arab leaders King Hussein of Jordan, President Mubarak of Egypt, and representatives from Oman, Qatar, and Morocco.

King Hussein moved mourners by calling his former enemy "a brother, a colleague, and a friend," and tears flowed freely when Rabin's 17-year-old granddaughter recalled her warm and loving grandfather.

President Clinton and other leaders paid tribute to Rabin, and highlighted the threat his assassination posed to the peace talks. "Your Prime Minister was a martyr for peace, but he was a victim of hate," said Clinton. "If people cannot let go of the hatred of their enemies, they risk sowing the seed of hatred among themselves."

Scores of world leaders, including Jordan's King Hussein, at the funeral.

VIRGINIA, WEDNESDAY 8

Powell will not run for president in 1996

General Colin A. Powell, retired chairman of the Joint Chiefs of Staff and hero of the Gulf War, announced today at a packed news conference that he would not be competing in the 1996 presidential election.

He explained that he had made his decision after looking deep into his soul, concluding that he lacked the kind of passionate commitment to politics that had sustained his bond of trust with the public through 35 years of army service. He said: "For me to pretend otherwise would not be honest to myself, it would not be honest to the American people, and I would break that bond of trust."

He ruled out any second thoughts as the campaign proceeds, and said he would not consider serving as a candidate for vice president. However, he left future candidacy open to speculation, saying: "The future is the future." He added that he believed he could "help the party of Lincoln move once again close to the spirit of Lincoln," in a clear reference to the issues of race, opportunity, and social welfare that set him at odds with conservative Republican ideologues, who had threatened to put up fierce resistance to his candidacy.

Powell's decision has come as a great disappointment to the public, but it will be met with relief both by the Republican front-runner Bob Dole and by President Clinton.

Powell cites his lack of calling as his reason for not entering the presidential race.

WENATCHEE, FRIDAY 10

Washington child sex ring furore

More than 3,000 people have signed a petition calling for a Justice Department investigation into the police allegation of a child sex ring that has bitterly divided the central Washington town of Wenatchee.

Prosecutors claim that dozens of children in the town, recently named the fourth-best little city in America, were raped and molested over a seven-year period by up to 80 adults, including the local pastor and his wife. In the past year, 28 adults have been charged with child rape and sex abuse. The Reverend Robert Robertson, pastor of the Pentecostal Church of God House of Prayer, and his wife Connie, face 39 charges of child molestation and rape.

According to affidavits from children and statements from adults, Robertson, 50, used sermons to whip his congregation into sexual frenzies and once had sex with a teenage girl at the altar, telling them that he was driving out the devil.

However, critics accuse both Detective Bob Perez, who is in charge of the investigation, and social workers, of creating a climate of sexual hysteria in which children were coaxed into making accusations and parents were bullied into confessions. Their petition accompanies a 250-page document purporting to show civil rights violations during the case.

Egypt, Sunday 5. The tomb of Queen Nefertari, the favorite wife of the Pharaoh Rameses II, is opened to visitors for the first time since its discovery in 1904. Experts fear the opening could damage the fragile paintings which decorate the tomb at Luxor.

SINGAPORE, FRIDAY 10

Death sentence for serial killer

John Martin Scripps, 35, the British prison fugitive and convicted drug smuggler, was sentenced to hang in Singapore today, for murdering and dismembering a South African tourist. Scripps was convicted of murdering Gerard Lowe, 32. Parts of Lowe's body were found floating in bin liners in Singapore harbor.

He is already linked to three other killings. Thai police have charged him with murdering a Canadian mother and son, and he is the main suspect in the disappearance of a British tourist in Mexico. Scripps befriended his victims, then killed them for money.

London, Tuesday 7. Author Pat Barker wins the prestigious Booker Prize for her novel *The Ghost Road*.

S	M	T	W	T	F	S
			1	2	3	4
5	6	7	8	9	10	11
12	13	14	15	16	17	18
19	20	21	22	23	24	25
26	27	28	29	30		

Nepal, 12
At least 43 people died during the weekend while trekking near Mount Everest, when Nepal's worst recorded avalanches, were caused by violent winds and snowstorms.

Oklahoma City, 12
Three people are arrested by the FBI on charges of plotting to build a bomb in Vernon, 90 miles east of the city where the Federal building was bombed on April 19.

Riyadh, Saudi Arabia, 13
Five Americans are among those killed in two explosions in Saudi Arabia's capital, at an American-run military training establishment.

Jersey City, 13
"Operation Boneyard" is announced to have been solved. It appears that police have impounded stolen cars, sent letters informing the owners to wrong addresses, and sold the cars at rigged auctions.

Seattle, 14
The aircraft manufacturer Boeing gets a $12.7 billion order from Singapore Airlines.

Baku, Azerbaijan, 14
International observers report that elections in this former Soviet republic have been openly rigged by government officials.

Exeter, England, 15
The Black Baron, real name Christopher Pile, 26, becomes the first Briton to be convicted and jailed for creating and planting computer viruses.

Paris, 16
Beaujolais Nouveau is in the shops, but sales are likely to be affected by the French decision to resume nuclear tests. Quebec's orders, however, were up 50 % from 1994.

Montreal, 18
Former Canadian prime minister, Brian Mulroney, denies receiving kickbacks over the 1988 sale of Swiss aircraft to Canada.

Death
Sir Robert Stephens, British actor, in London at age 64, November 12.

JERUSALEM, WEDNESDAY 15
Peres appointed prime minister

Shimon Peres (right) shakes hands with President Ezer Weizman.

Following his nomination by the Israeli president, Ezer Weizman, Shimon Peres received official confirmation today of his appointment as successor to assassinated prime minister, Yitzhak Rabin. Peres had been chosen as the new leader of the ruling Labor Party on Monday.

A potential stumbling block was removed when the Likud opposition party announced that it would not obstruct the formation of a new Labor-led government, as to do so would mean that a murderer could affect political change. After two days of consultation with the various political parties, the president said formally to Mr. Peres: "I am giving you full backing for the continuation of the peace process."

Mr. Peres said that he accepted his new role "with a heavy heart." He told Israelis that he would "make every effort to boost understanding and peace with our neighbors, and among ourselves." He is expected to form a cabinet within a few days.

In the meantime, the arrest of Margalit Harshefi brought to eight the number of people held in suspicion of being involved in the assassination plot.

ALGIERS, THURSDAY 16
Algerians defy threats and cast their votes

Algerian women voted in huge numbers.

In spite of threats by Islamic fundamentalists to kill anyone who voted in the Algerian presidential election, there was an estimated 75 percent turnout. President Liamine Zeroual was reelected by a landslide majority.

Zeroual defeated three opponents. Said Sadi stood as a strong opponent of fundamentalism, while Mahfoud Nahnah and the less popular Noureddine Boukrouh advocated a more moderate approach. All four had pledged to bring an end to the civil war that has claimed up to 50,000 lives since it began in 1992, when elections were canceled with an Islamic fundamentalist party seemingly poised for victory.

NEW YORK, WEDNESDAY 15
The new 007 takes a bow

Pierce Brosnan with Izabella Scorupco.

The world premiere of James Bond's latest adventure, *GoldenEye,* with Pierce Brosnan in the lead role, took place at Radio City Music Hall yesterday evening.

Although the producers of the series long ago exhausted the supply of Ian Fleming stories, a link is maintained in that GoldenEye was the name of the author's Jamaican estate.

WASHINGTON DC, SATURDAY 18
US admiral forced to resign

The White House was quick to disassociate itself from remarks made by Admiral Richard Macke, commander of American military operations in the Pacific, concerning three US soldiers accused of abducting and raping a 12-year-old Japanese girl on the island of Okinawa. "For the price they paid to rent the car," he said, "they could have had a girl."

The Admiral was said to be taking early retirement. President Clinton issued an apology to Japan.

Careless talker Admiral Richard Macke.

WASHINGTON DC, WEDNESDAY 15

Deadlock over Federal budget

The operations of the US government were partially shut down today as the financial feud between the Republican Congress and the White House reached a crisis. With neither side ready to give ground to resolve the budget deadlock, President Clinton had attempted to extend the Federal debt limit to keep the government running. But Republican riders, prompted by their budget-cutting impulses, caused an impasse.

As the money dried up, all "non-essential" government workers were sent home, including 67 percent of those in the Commerce Department, 89 percent of Housing and Urban Development, and all but a skeleton 1 percent in the Education Department.

There was some comfort for the beleaguered President in the results of a national survey indicating that 48 percent of Americans blamed the Republican Congress for the situation, as opposed to 27 percent who blamed the President.

Mr. Clinton accused Congress of pursuing "an explicit strategy" to force through cost-cutting policies. Repub-

licans replied that cuts were both possible and necessary.

Republican Senator Phil Gramm said the confrontation was like root canal treatment, with the nation as the patient. If, during the treatment, the patient was asked if he'd like it to stop, he would say yes. But when the operation was over, he would "thank the dentist." (→ November 19)

Speaker of the House Newt Gingrich.

President Bill Clinton takes a stand against the Republicans in Congress.

PARIS, WEDNESDAY 15

EuroDisney shows first profit

In contrast to last year's losses of around $350 million, and following massive financial reorganization, EuroDisney (now known as Disneyland Paris) announced a small operating profit over the past 12 months.

This has prompted the troubled venture to announce plans to develop a second site near Paris, a project that had been shelved following fears over the original EuroDisney's survival.

The improvement in performance, with attendances up by two million, has been attributed to a lowering of prices, staff reductions, the opening of the fortieth and most spectacular ride, Space Mountain, and to the availability of wine and beer in some of the restaurants, breaking with Disney's "dry" tradition.

Six percent of Europeans have visited the park, and more than a quarter of admissions are repeat visits. The key to the park's survival, in the face of $4.5 billion in debts to the banks, was the involvement of a Saudi prince, Waleed, over the last two years. He agreed to buy 24 percent of EuroDisney's shares and to provide funds for expansion. As a result of this new confidence the banks agreed to delay interest payments.

Running counter to the optimistic move, however, are some new problems including international reaction to France's resumption of nuclear tests.

Moscow, Wednesday 15. The Russian enthusiasm for their national alcoholic drink, vodka, has long been a cause for concern. A conference on alcoholism is told that, on average, Russian men each drink the equivalent of 170 half-liter bottles of vodka a year.

IOWA, THURSDAY 16

New evidence of man's migration

Professor Russell Ciochon of the University of Iowa, coauthor of a paper in the journal *Nature*, says that primitive humans were living in China two million years ago, and that therefore far more of human evolution has taken place outside Africa than was previously thought.

It is now believed that there were three waves of migration out of Africa. The newly described movement was the earliest, followed by that of a more advanced species one million years ago, and finally the first modern humans, *Homo sapiens*, who moved north into Europe 150,000 years ago.

Sun City, South Africa, Saturday 18. Miss Venezuela, Jacqueline Aguilera Marcano, 19, is crowned Miss World.

Johannesburg, 20
Britain and Holland oppose a plan for a European Union oil embargo on Nigeria following the execution of writer Ken Saro-Wiwa and eight other environmental activists.

Argentina, 20
Erich Priebke, 82, an ex-SS captain, is extradicted to Italy to face trial for taking part in the massacre of 335 civilians at the Ardeatine Caves on March 24, 1944.

Beijing, 21
China's leading dissident, Wei Jingsheng, faces a long prison term after being charged with attempting to overthrow the government.

Paris, 22
Florencio Campomanes, president of the World Chess Federation, is forced to stand down after a vote of no confidence following his failure to organize the World Championship match between Anatoly Karpov and the American Gata Kamsky.

New Haven, 22
Genetic studies suggest that there was an ancestral "Adam" about 188,000 years ago to accompany the previously discovered "Eve."

Dublin, 22
The Republic of Ireland voted in favor of legalizing divorce. The majority in favor was just 9,114, about 6% of those voting.

Dar es Salaam, 23
Benjamin Mkapa is sworn in as President of Tanzania following the country's first multiparty elections.

Moscow, 23
A radioactive substance planted by Chechen rebels is discovered in the city's Izmailovsky Park.

Cairo, 23
An Egyptian military court jails 54 members of the fundamentalist Muslim Brotherhood and closes its offices in a pre-election purge

Rome, 24
Former Italian premier, Silvio Berlusconi, and four others are to stand trial for alleged embezzlement and fraudulant accounting over the 1988 purchase of an Italian film company.

LONDON, MONDAY 20
Attacks and admissions from Princess Di on TV

Diana, the Princess of Wales, gave a devastatingly candid interview on British television tonight. So frank were her confessions and so pointed her attacks that she may not only have brought divorce from the Prince of Wales closer, but she may also have driven a nail into the coffin of the British monarchy itself.

The interview had been reported beforehand: news of it had been leaked, seemingly to coincide with the birthday of her estranged husband, Charles, the previous week. The Princess covered a number of subjects including many areas that normally would have been strictly out of bounds to journalists. She was asked about extramarital love affairs, for example, and, said of her former friend, army officer James Hewitt: "Yes, I adored him. Yes, I was in love with him." She confessed she had been very hurt by Hewitt's book about their affair.

It was, however, her comments on the British constitution and the Prince of Wales's entourage that may cause the most damage. Obviously

Princess Diana during her interview with Martin Bashir of the BBC.

wishing to settle old scores, she responded to a question as to whether her husband Charles would eventually become king with: "I don't think any of us know the answer to that." She made no secret of the fact that she believed the advisors surrounding him were "the enemy" who were trying to keep her out of public life, because they resented her strong and forthright personality. Princess Diana also said she believed she would never be queen of Britain, but that she "would like to be queen of people's hearts."

WARSAW, SUNDAY 19
Ex-communist new Polish president

Kwasniewski casts his vote in the Polish presidential elections, which he won narrowly.

Aleksander Kwasniewski, a former communist, became Poland's new president by a narrow majority today. With 51.7 percent of the vote in the decisive second round of the presidential elections he defeated the incumbent president, Lech Walesa, whose program of free-market economics had become very unpopular in Poland. Kwasniewski joined the Communist Party at age 23, and under the communist regime ran a government-backed newspaper that urged Poles to reject Walesa's Solidarity. However, he has vowed there will be no return to the past.

WASHINGTON DC, SUNDAY 19
Compromise on Federal budget

Federal workers can return to their jobs this week, after a compromise was reached by the President and Congress on the Federal budget deficit. The Republican majority in Congress feels it has won a major victory, by forcing President Clinton to accept the principle that the budget must be balanced by the year 2002. The President had wanted to aim for 2005. A further victory for Congress was the acceptance that the Congressional Budget Office, rather than the Federal Office for Management and Budget, will provide the economic data plans are based on.

President Clinton may have had to make major concessions to Congress, but the scathing battle over the past two weeks has not been good for the Republican public image. Newt Gingrich, in particular, has lost popularity, and has been widely described as a "cry baby" becauses of his criticisms of the president.

DAYTON, OHIO, TUESDAY 21

US brokers Bosnian peace plan

From left: presidents Milosevic, Izetbegovic, and Tudjman applaud their agreement. The question is, will it last?

US negotiator Richard Holbrooke scored a victory here today, when the three main leaders involved in the Bosnian conflict accepted a peace plan that may end the fighting in the troubled nation. Slobadon Milosevic of Serbia, Franjo Tudjman of Croatia, and Alija Izetbegovic of Bosnia eventually consented to a formula that ostensibly creates a unified Bosnia, but in fact divided the country along racial lines.

To make the agreement work, 60,000 NATO troops will be sent into Bosnia before Christmas. Twenty thousand of the troops will be from the US and 13,000 will be from Britain.

There are four main points to the plan. The first is that there is to be a nation called the Union of Bosnia-Herzegovina. This Union is to consist of two self-governing parts: a Muslim-Croat federation and a Bosnian Serb republic. The presidency of the Union will rotate between the Muslim, Croat, and Serb groups. And a single parliamentary authority will handle foreign affairs.

International monitors will oversee the first elections; refugees will be allowed to return home; human rights are guaranteed and will be monitored; and war criminals will not be allowed to hold office. (→ November 29)

New York, Tuesday 21. *The Beatles Anthology* **sold 450,000 copies, a record in itself, on its first day of release. The group is as successful as ever.**

LONDON, THURSDAY 23

UK and Ireland fail to agree

The prospects for a meaningful agreement between the UK and Ireland were receding tonight. There was a third telephone conversation between the British prime minister, John Major, and the Irish premier, John Bruton, but nothing was decided about the conditions under which an international commission could oversee disarming paramilitary groups in Northern Ireland. The disagreement centers on John Major's insistence that the IRA give up some weapons before the commission starts work. It was hoped that there could be an agreement between the two governments before President Clinton's visit to the area next week, but this now looks unlikely. (→ November 30)

London, Tuesday 21. Dancer Rudolf Nureyev's possessions raised $2.7 million at auction.

LOS ANGELES, THURSDAY 23

Judge overturns Proposition 187

In a controversial ruling, Judge Mariana Pfaelzer has decided that California's "Proposition 187" is invalid since it deals with immigration, a subject over which the Federal government is the sole arbiter. Proposition 187 was given a massive mandate by California's voters last year. It denies illegal immigrants health care, education, and social services, and requires state officials to report illegal immigrants. California's governor, Pete Wilson, a strong supporter of the proposition, claimed that the judge's ruling "thwarts the will of the people."

LISBON, FRIDAY 24

Ancient carvings to cost millions

The Portuguese government today claimed that the cost of saving some paleolithic rock carvings will be $150 million. The paintings have been discovered in the Coa River valley in the north of Portugal, in an area that has been earmarked as the sight of a new dam that will produce hydroelectric power for the region. The carvings are, however, considered to be one of the greatest prehistoric collections in Europe. Upon taking office earlier this month, the new socialist government ordered work on the dam to be stopped and set up a group to study the carvings.

Beverly Hills, Thursday 23. Louis Malle, French film director, died today at age 63.

BOSNIA, NOVEMBER

Europe's worst conflict since World War II

General Mladic addresses Bosnian Serbs.

After four years of the worst fighting in Europe for half a century, the war in former Yugoslavia appeared over on November 21. The US-brokered cease-fire followed three weeks of negotiations at the Wright Patterson Air Force Base in Dayton, Ohio. A formal peace agreement is to be signed in Paris in December.

For over four years, Yugoslavia has been sliced apart by war. Around 200,000 people have lost their lives as tensions that had been simmering for decades boiled over into a vicious struggle for territorial domination.

Until 1990 the multinational state of Yugoslavia was held together by its communist rulers. But after democratic elections were held in the country's six constituent republics – Serbia, Croatia, Macedonia, Slovenia, Montenegro, and Bosnia – nationalism tore the country apart. In 1991, Slovenia declared its independence, as did Croatia. When Serb areas in eastern Croatia refused to become part of the new state, fighting began.

Bosnia has a mixed population of Muslims, Serbs, and Croats. In 1992, the Bosnian Muslims and Croats voted together to make Bosnia independent. The Bosnian Serbs rejected this decision and began to shell the Bosnian capital, Sarajevo. Despite the presence of UN peacekeepers, a war of blockade and atrocities followed.

The conflict has been marked on all sides by "ethnic cleansing" – the forcible removal or even massacre of local populations to create ethnically unified zones. The Bosnian Serbs are regarded as the worst offenders. Both their political leader, Radovan Karadzic, and their military chief, General Mladic, are wanted to stand trial as war criminals by an International War Crimes Tribunal.

Under the cease-fire agreement, all armed groups in Bosnia are to disband, except authorized police. A NATO force will take action against any that do not comply.

Sarajevo, the Bosnian capital, was devastated by Bosnian Serbs who besieged the city.

From the hills around Sarajevo, shells and mortars rained down on the population.

UN peacekeepers endured harsh conditions.

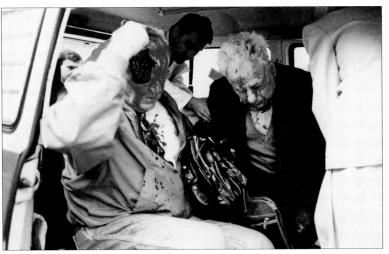

Victims of a Serb attack on the Croatian capital Zagreb.

Hundreds of thousands fled their homes, like these Serbian refugees in August 1995.

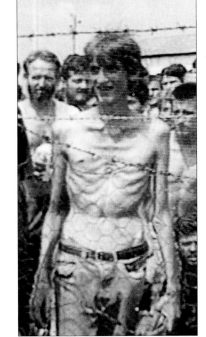

Starving Bosnian prisoners.

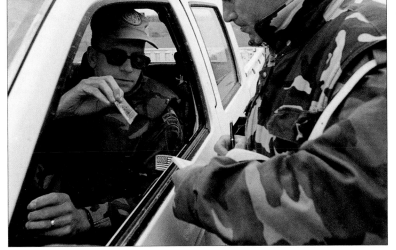

The first military personnel arrive to prepare for NATO's presence in Bosnia.

The war leaders

Slobodan Milosevic, president of Serbia.

Alija Izetbegovic, the Bosnian Muslim president.

Radovan Karadzic, the Bosnian Serb leader.

President Franjo Tudjman, leader of Croatia.

S	M	T	W	T	F	S
			1	2	3	4
5	6	7	8	9	10	11
12	13	14	15	16	17	18
19	20	21	22	23	24	25
26	27	28	29	30		

Sarajevo, 26
Bosnian Serb leader Radovan Karadzic warns that the peace agreement could turn Sarajevo into a "new Beirut." (→ November 29)

Jerusalem, 26
Police question two rabbis on suspicion that they had issued religious decrees condemning to death assassinated premier Yitzhak Rabin.

Moscow, 27
Boris Yeltsin leaves hospital after treatment for his heart condition and then immediately leaves on a rest cure. (→ December 17)

Beijing, 27
Chinese scientists announce that one of the country's spy satellites will crash to earth, making it a potential danger to life unless it hits the sea.

London 28
The British and Irish governments end a 12-week stalemate on Northern Ireland, opening the way to further talks. (→ November 30)

Maryland, 28
Warner-Lambert, one of the US's largest drug companies, pleads guilty to hiding faulty manufacturing processes from the FDA and agrees to pay a $10 million fine.

London, 28
The UK government reverses a 100-year tradition by reducing the tax on a bottle of whisky in the nation's annual budget changes.

Washington DC, 29
Congress passes a bill to regulate lobbying, requiring lobbyists to disclose who pays them. The vote in the House is 421 to 0, following a 98-to-0 vote in the Senate.

Mexico, 29
The police in the department of Baja California Sur are implicated in the landing of a jet full of cocaine, and the whole department is transferred.

Beijing, 30
Fidel Castro starts his first official visit to China.

Washington DC, 30
Nearly 500,000 Cadillacs are recalled following claims that carbon dioxide emissions exceed legal limits.

LOS ANGELES, SUNDAY 26
Model was killed "accidentally"

Charles Rathbun being taken to court.

Police who were yesterday led to a shallow grave in the Angeles National Forest, on the edge of the Mojave Desert, have today cast doubt on the story of the man who took them there. Photographer Charles Rathbun told members of the Los Angeles County Sheriff's Department that he had accidentally struck and killed 27-year-old model Linda Sobek when demonstrating a maneuver with his vehicle while they were on a photographic session. He said that when he realized she was dead, he panicked and buried her body.

However, the coroner's office said today that the autopsy revealed injuries to the body that do not appear to have been caused by an automobile accident.

Bucharest, Monday 27. Seventies' tennis star Ilie Nastase has entered Romanian politics, joining the national council of the Social Democracy Party.

PARIS, TUESDAY 28
Rail chaos in France

Most of France ground to a halt again today as railway workers already on strike were joined for a day by other public service unions. All are protesting proposed changes in the social security system, and the rail workers are further incensed by a new contract that they are being offered. No trains ran in Paris and most of the Metro was at a standstill. (→ December 7)

SARAJEVO, WEDNESDAY 29
Serbs protest peace plan

Several thousand people turned out in a rally today in a Serb-held suburb of Sarajevo to protest the peace plan, initialed on their behalf in Dayton, Ohio, last week by Serbian president Slobodan Milosevic. The Serbs are protesting at the prospect of having to live side by side with Muslims once again. They swear that they will never give up the city. The organizers of the rally, members of the Bosnian Serb government, said that they were determined to win, but would use only peaceful means to pursue their case. About 40,000 Serbs live in Serb-held areas of Sarajevo.

NEW YORK, MONDAY 27
Subway fire attack blamed on film

Yesterday's attack on a subway token booth in Brooklyn in which a clerk was badly injured has been blamed on a movie, *Money Train*. Early on Sunday morning two men threw a flammable liquid into the booth and then set fire to it with a match. In two similar scenes in the film a pyromaniac douses the inside of token booths with a flammable liquid and then sets them alight. The scenes were shot in the New York subway.

In the Senate today, Republican senator Bob Dole claimed that the film, which opened less than a week ago, inspired the attacks, and called on Americans to boycott it in protest. "The American people have a right to voice their outrage, and they can do so not through calls for government censorship, but by derailing *Money Train* at the box office." Columbia executives deplored the incident but denied there was any connection.

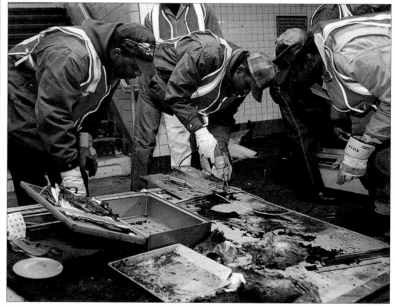
Subway workers dismantle the burned-out token booth in Brooklyn.

BELFAST, THURSDAY 30

Ulster visit triumph for Clinton

President Clinton turned on the Christmas lights in Belfast tonight. It was a gesture heavy in symbolism, appropriate to a historic day-long visit to Northern Ireland that seems to have brought more light to the Province than at any time since the peace process began 15 months ago.

Mr. Clinton is the first American president to visit Northern Ireland. He flew in shortly after 9 a.m. to begin a day that included a walk-about in the Protestant Shankhill Road, and then the nationalist Falls Road, where he met and shook hands with Sinn Fein leader, Gerry Adams. He visited a factory on the peace line, where he gave a carefully balanced speech that reiterated his support for the twin-track peace process and made it clear that he

thought terrorism had no role to play. Later he went to the town of Londonderry, and after his return to Belfast he had a 25-minute conversation with Protestant leader, Ian Paisley. He ended the day at a concert given by Van Morrison. He has been greeted everywhere by good-natured and cheering crowds from both sides of the political divide.

The huge success of the visit in

rekindling hope in the peace process was symbolized by two children presented to the President. One of them, Catherine Hamill, a nine-year-old whose father died in the violence, read Mr. Clinton a letter she had written him, which summed up the day's feelings: "Now it is nice and peaceful... My Christmas wish is that we have peace and love and that it will last in Ireland forever."

Catherine Hamill, aged 9, reads her letter.

President Clinton turns on the Christmas lights in Belfast during his visit.

Newt Gingrich not to run

Newt Gingrich, speaker of the House of Representatives, has ended a year of speculation by announcing that he will not seek the Republican nomination for president next year. This decision leaves the road clearer for Senator Bob Dole, whom Mr. Gingrich agreed was obviously the front runner.

Mr. Gingrich's candidacy seemed almost certain earlier in the year when he was buoyed on the tide of the Contract with America reforms, but of late his popularity has slumped to the point where a recent CBS News poll gave him an approval rating of only 27 percent. He denied that the poll influenced his decision, citing instead the need to concentrate on budget negotiations with the President. Speaking from the Atlanta suburb of Marietta, the Georgian congressman refused to endorse any other candidate as he hopes to become chairman of the Republican National Convention in August, and therefore needs to maintain his neutrality. However, as well as acknowledging the claims of Senator Dole, he said that Phil Gramm of Texas and Lamar Alexander of Tennessee were strong contenders for the nomination. He also noted that there could be three serious independent candidates in the final polling, making this the widest field for many years.

Athens, Wednesday 29. Andreas Papandreou, the Greek prime minister, seen here with his controversial wife and chief of staff, Dimitra, was today put on a kidney dialysis machine and a respirator. Mr. Papandreou is 76.

WASHINGTON DC, WEDNESDAY 29

Psychic "spies" used by Pentagon

It has emerged that the Pentagon employed psychics for 20 years in intelligence-gathering operations. Six psychics were regularly asked to perform such tasks as identifying the exact whereabouts of Colonel Qaddafi, locating North Korean plutonium, and providing the layout of a building in Iran where American hostages were held. The use of psychics came to light when the CIA was asked to take over managing them in the summer. One CIA advisor has commented that it is doubtful that the psychics contributed anything of use, although they have claimed successes.

New York, Wednesday 29. Ivana Trump, former wife of property billionaire Donald Trump, marries an Italian businessman.

December

Oregon, 1
Two British women jailed for five years for plotting, while members of the Bhagwan Shree Rajneesh cult, to kill a lawyer acting for the state of Oregon.

Dublin, 1
President Clinton finishes his trip to Ireland with a day in Dublin.

Moscow, 3
The USA wins tennis's Davis Cup, defeating Russia in the final.

Anchorage, 4
Alaska reports a fall heatwave, with only the thinnest dusting of snow, and temperatures reaching record seasonal highs in the 40s.

Los Angeles, 4
Police are starting a hunt for a person who placed death threats against actress Jodie Foster on the Internet.

Colombo, 5
Sri Lankan government forces recapture Jaffna, the rebel Tamil Tigers' capital for five years.

New York, 6
Jewelry belonging to the Duchess of York, reported missing 24 hours previously, is found in a garden shed in Queens. A teenage baggage-handler at JFK airport is arrested.

Washington DC, 6
Republicans bow to Democrat pressure and agree to an investigation into alleged funding improprieties by Newt Gingrich.

New York, 7
The *New York Times* refuses an advertisement placed by a right-wing Japanese group seeking to rewrite Japan's war record.

New York, 7
Michael Jackson collapses while rehearsing a television program with mime artist Marcel Marceau.

Los Angeles, 9
The Grateful Dead announce they are disbanding, after the death this summer of founder Jerry Garcia.

Death
Robertson Davies, Canadian novelist, aged 82, from a stroke, on December 2 in Toronto.

Spaniard to be new secretary-general of NATO

Six weeks after the resignation of Willy Claes, facing corruption charges in his native Belgium, a new secretary-general of NATO was announced today. He is Javier Solana, the foreign minister of Spain.

The appointment was greeted with some dismay in Britain by Conservative Euro-sceptics, who pointed out that, as a socialist, Señor Solana campaigned in 1982 for Spain to withdraw from the alliance. He also has a record of opposing nuclear weapons. However, the same Socialist Party of which he is a member reversed its policy when in power three years later, and called on the country to vote in a referendum in favor of staying in NATO. Solana is seen as a compromise candidate.

Britain was in favor of appointing the European Commissioner Sir Leon Brittan, but did not press his case when soundings indicated little support from other countries. Ruud Lubbers of Holland looked the likely nominee until the US made it clear that it did not consider him suitably charismatic to handle the PR element of the job. The former Danish foreign minister Uffe Ellemann-Jensen fell foul of the French for having publicly criticized their nuclear testing program.

It is believed that Germany was the main proponent of Señor Solana: he is reported to be a good friend of the US Secretary of State Warren Christopher. His appointment will be made official on Tuesday.

Javier Solana, NATO's new leader.

Close encounter with Jupiter

The first-ever close examination of Jupiter took place today when the Galileo space probe launched a capsule into the planet's atmosphere. Traveling at 106,000 mph (170,000 kmph) until slowed down by its parachutes, the capsule transmitted data for what is expected to prove to be 75 minutes. It was then burned up by the tremendous heat and crushed by the massive gravity of this planet 1,400 times larger than Earth. It registered details of Jupiter's chemistry, temperature and density. Galileo itself, which was launched in 1989, is expected to orbit Jupiter for two years, sending back further information about the planet and its moons.

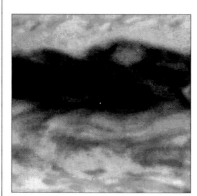

The probe's target area on Jupiter.

Chun Doo Hwan, former president of South Korea, arrested

Chun Doo Hwan, on television yesterday.

Chun Doo Hwan, president of South Korea from 1980 to 1988, was arrested today for organizing the coup that brought him to power in 1979. Under current South Korean law, if found guilty he would be sentenced to death, but the talk on the streets of the capital Seoul is that such a penalty would be instantly commuted. He is also expected to be charged with murder for the massacre of pro-democracy protesters in the city of Kwangju in 1980.

The current democratic government in South Korea is very different from Mr. Chung's, and is eager to get to grips with the political crimes of the past. Mr. Chung, 64, a retired general, presided over a police state during his rule. According to official figures, 200 demonstrators were killed in Kwangju, though some observers put the figure nearer 2,000. His arrest comes in the wake of the detention 19 days ago of his successor in office, Roh Tae Woo, on corruption charges. Mr. Roh led the 1979 coup with Mr. Chun, and is believed to have given evidence against him.

Mr. Chung is denying all the charges. Yesterday he appeared on television from outside his home and dismissed the clampdown on the pro-democracy demonstrations of his rule as being in the past. In the same television broadcast he was deeply critical of the current president Kim Young Sam, accusing him of opportunism and of "leftism." These public comments, followed by Mr Chun's leaving Seoul accompanied by a motorcade for his native village, where he is still regarded as a hero, were seen as an act of defiance against the government, and almost certainly hastened his arrest.

PARIS, THURSDAY 7

French strikes spread and bite

Comparisons are being made with the civil disturbances of 1968 in Paris as the protests against the government's economic policies spread. Today, as the national rail strike entered its fourteenth day, the Eurostar train service through the Channel Tunnel became a victim of strike action for the first time. Parisians have been walking to work, or else have been sitting in their cars in vast traffic lines, the subway and bus services being at a standstill. Schools have now closed as teachers joined the strike, and striking mail workers have prevented all but a trickle of letters being delivered. Public servants, electricity and telecommunications workers have all downed tools. Even employees of the Bank of France walked out today. Paris has also seen vandalism and rioting. On Tuesday a huge march of strikers, students and disaffected workers trailed through the capital to call for the resignation of Prime Minister Alain Juppé.

Talks to end the rail strike collapsed today. However, the government can take some comfort from the fact that the protest is not for revolution, but against proposed social security changes. (→ December 15)

London, Sunday 3. Britain is trying to stop crowns of kings George I and George IV being bought by an American.

Union banners of railway, Metro, and telecommunications workers at the start of Thursday's demonstration in Paris.

SINGAPORE, SATURDAY 2

Leeson gets six and a half years

Nick Leeson is reported to be shocked by the severity of the sentences handed down to him in court today. The 28-year-old British bond trader held responsible for the collapse of Barings Bank was given six and a half years in jail on two charges of fraud. The whole trial was over in a flash. Leeson faced 11 charges in total, but nine fraud and forgery charges were dropped as he pleaded guilty yesterday to the other two. Sentencing followed today. His term is nearly the longest permitted for the offences, and he had clearly been hoping for less after the prosecution said that they were not looking for an example to be made of him. With remission he should be free in 1999.

Germany, Saturday 2. After his visit to Ireland, President Clinton today visited Germany where he spent time with American troops bound for the peace-keeping mission in Bosnia. Altogether 20,000 American troops have been committed to the troubled area.

NEW YORK, WEDNESDAY 6

Nature could hold key to AIDS cure

Two papers published simultaneously today, one in *Science* and the other in the British scientific journal *Nature*, report that scientists have found chemicals occurring naturally in the human body that could halt the disease AIDS. The papers say that in laboratory experiments the HIV virus was prevented from replicating by one or other of a group of little-known chemicals produced by white blood cells. The chemicals themselves may not be suitable as a treatment, but the findings open up new possibilities, and are giving researchers genuine hope.

Hollywood, Tuesday 5. Michael P. Schulhof, head of Sony's US operations, resigns as the company continues to falter.

S	M	T	W	T	F	S
					1	2
3	4	5	6	7	8	9
10	11	12	13	14	15	16
17	18	19	20	21	22	23
24	25	26	27	28	29	30
31						

Madrid, 11
A car bomb kills six people and wounds 18. The attack is attributed to ETA, the Basque separatist group.

Paris, 11
French prime minister Alain Juppé is to hold talks next week with trade union leaders, following 19 days of strikes and disruption.

Nairobi, Kenya 11
Rwanda expels 38 foreign aid agencies for political reasons.

Washington DC, 12
The Senate rejects by just three votes an amendment that would have outlawed desecration of the US flag.

Nablus, 12
Israel hands over Nablus, the most important town on the West Bank, to the Palestinians. (→ December 21)

New York, 13
Christmas trees in Grand Central Station are taken down because they might have offended Muslims.

London, 13
Two people who threatened to release mice in Harrods food hall during the busy Christmas period are charged with blackmail.

Verona, Italy, 13
Forty-one passengers and five crew are killed when a Romanian charter aircraft crashes after take-off.

Beijing, 13
China sentences Wei Jingsheng, a pro-democracy activist, to 14 years in jail for "attempting to overthrow the government." He has previously served 14 years on similar charges.

New York, 14
Jewelry, furniture, and other personal effects from the estate of former First Lady Jacqueline Kennedy Onassis are to be auctioned at Sotheby's in 1996.

Athens, 14
Greece's socialists are to elect a new leader in place of Prime Minister Andreas Papandreou, who has been critically ill for a month.

Madrid, 15
European Community leaders decide on "Euro" as the name for their new single currency.

PARIS, TUESDAY 12
French pilots released by Bosnian Serbs

President Jacques Chirac welcomes home the freed French airmen.

Two French pilots who have been held captive by the Bosnian Serbs since 30 August are back in their homeland today. President Jacques Chirac led the celebrations at a military air base close to Paris as Captain Frédéric Chiffot and Lieutenant José Souvignet, weakened by more than three months in captivity, delicately disembarked from the plane that had brought them back from Bosnia.

The fate of the pilots had been a matter of great concern to the French people. President Chirac thanked President Milosevic of Serbia and President Yeltsin of Russia for their help in obtaining the pilots' freedom. France had made a final demand for the release of the two men on Sunday, threatening unspecified reprisals if they were not set free.

NEW YORK, MONDAY 11
Children are main war victims

The number of children who are victims of war is increasing at an alarming rate, according to a report issued by the United Nations Children's Fund (Unicef). *The State of the World's Children*, the organization's annual report, states that of all those who are caught up in war children are the most likely to be killed or exploited. Around 90 percent of victims of modern warfare are civilians as opposed to 50 percent during the last century. In addition to being less able to defend themselves, children face being victims of horrific war crimes or being drafted into armies. Lightweight weapons make them effective as nimble footsoldiers.

Unicef says children are main war victims.

PARIS, THURSDAY 14
Signing of Bosnian peace in Paris

Presidents Milosevic, Tudjman, and Izetbegovic sign the Bosnian peace plan.

The Bosnia-Herzegovina Peace Accord was signed today by the leaders of the three states that, over the past four years, have fought Europe's fiercest war since World War II. President Milosevic of Serbia, President Tudjman of Croatia, and President Izetbegovic of Bosnia signed the treaty. The ceremony was witnessed by President Bill Clinton, Prime Minister John Major of Britain, Germany's Chancellor Helmut Kohl, and Russian Prime Minister Viktor Chernomyrdin, who attended in the absence of the sick Boris Yeltsin.

A major condition of the treaty, the details of which had been hammered out in Dayton, Ohio, in November, is that a 60,000-strong NATO peacekeeping force, due in Bosnia next week, will have the right to take retaliatory action against any group or individual that carries out acts in breach of the cease-fire.

"I feel like a man swallowing a bitter but useful medicine, but I can assure you we are signing this peace treaty with sincerity," commented President Izetbegovic. President Milosevic said that the signing of the documents did not solve all the problems of Bosnia but added: "I am sure a common language can be found." (→ December 26)

WENATCHEE, WASHINGTON STATE, MONDAY 11

Pastor Roberson cleared of child rape and molestation

Pastor Robert Roberson and his wife Connie, the defendants in a controversial small-town court case, have been cleared on 16 counts of child sex abuse. Detective Robert Perez, who investigated the case, claimed that the town of Wenatchee was home to a sex abuse ring. Twenty adults are currently languishing in prison after sex abuse convictions.

Perez arrested the Robersons after they refused to give up their campaign for the release of Harold and Idella Everett, both of whom are still serving sentences for child abuse.

With the Everetts in jail, Perez and his wife became foster parents to their daughters, known for legal reasons during the case as D.E. and M.E. The two children were used by Perez as witnesses in the case to condemn Pastor Roberson as a man who indulged in child sex and molestation on the altar of his church.

However, Robert van Siclen, a Seattle lawyer, found from other children that Perez had used improper means to force them to testify against adults. It also emerged that Perez had twisted and bruised M.E.'s arm on the morning she had been due to give evidence. After being found not guilty, Pastor Roberson vowed to fight on for the Everetts' freedom.

Buffalo, New York State, Tuesday 12. The East Coast is experiencing its coldest weather of the year so far. The city of Buffalo had its heaviest-ever single day's snowfall on Sunday. Schools in the city have remained closed since.

Pastor Roberson after being cleared of sex offenses.

WASHINGTON DC, TUESDAY 12

Murder shocks army into investigation

The murder of two black civilians by two white soldiers in North Carolina last week has prompted the army to begin a massive worldwide investigation of its own ranks. It will undertake a thorough search for evidence of any right-wing extremist activity in its midst. The soldiers who shot dead Jackie Burden, a black woman, and Michael James, were white-supremacist skinheads whose rooms were covered in Nazi paraphernalia. All 510,000 members of the army will be scrutinized to discover whether they have similar leanings. Under army regulations, it is prohibited for military personnel to participate in the activities of racist organizations or in any other type of activity that violates civil rights.

Major General Larry R. Jordan will lead the inquiry, which will investigate all US army bases in America and throughout Europe and South Korea. There have long been rumors of white supremacist activity in the army, but a Defense Department official said: "The truth is, we don't have any evidence of any trends. It's all anecdotal information."

ROUEN, SUNDAY 10

Ukrainian ship captain jailed for the murder of eight African stowaways

A ship's captain and his second-in-command were jailed for life for their part in one of the worst atrocities at sea in recent times. Other members of the Ukrainian crew who took part in the murders of eight African stowaways were also given heavy sentences.

Nine Africans had hid in the Ukrainian ship's hold. When they were found, Captain Wladimir Ilnitskiy and his deputy, Valery Artemenko, ordered their crew to kill the stowaways. One Ghanaian, Kingsley Ofosu, managed to escape and hide. When the ship landed at Le Havre, France, he told authorities of the murders.

Ilnitskiy prepares to begin a life sentence.

NEW YORK, TUESDAY 12

Record Olympic deal for NBC

NBC will have a TV monopoly on the Olympic games for the first decade of the 21st century after signing a $2.3 billion deal with the International Olympic Committee. The biggest financial deal in international sporting history was settled when NBC agreed to pay cable and broadcast fees of $793 million for the 2004 Games, $613 million for the 2006 Winter Games, and $894 million for the 2008 Games. In August, NBC captured TV rights to the 2000 Games and the 2002 Winter Games. NBC also has the rights to the 1996 Games in Atlanta.

London, Saturday 16. The popular health supplement royal jelly should carry health warnings, say doctors, as it may harm asthmatics.

S	M	T	W	T	F	S
					1	2
3	4	5	6	7	8	9
10	11	12	13	14	15	16
17	18	19	20	21	22	23
24	25	26	27	28	29	30
31						

Vienna, 17
Far-right Freedom Party of Jörg Haider gains over 22% in Austria's parliamentary elections, making it Europe's most successful extremist party.

Jerusalem, 18
An Israeli television station pays $400,000 for an amateur video of the assassination of Yitzhak Rabin.

Seoul, 18
Trial opens of Roh Tae Woo, former President of South Korea, charged with taking bribes while in office.

Geneva, 18
The United Nations says that parts of North Korea are suffering famine, and that the situation will deteriorate during the winter.

New York, 19
A gunman shoots five people dead, including a 12-year-old boy, in a Bronx shoe store while apparently trying to steal a pair of sneakers.

Washington DC, 19
The President and Republican leaders in Congress announce that they will hold talks to try to resolve the impasse over the Federal budget.

Ohio, 19
Officials announce that Ross Perot's new Reform Party has failed to collect enough signatures to be put on the ballot in the Ohio primary.

Sarajevo, 20
NATO officially takes over peace-keeping in Bosnia from the UN.

Honduras, 20
Fourteen military officers are accused of human rights violations during the 1980s.

Warsaw, 21
The Polish prime minister, Jozef Oleksy, is accused by his own interior minister of having spied for Russia.

Grenoble, 23
The bodies of 16 members of the Solar Temple cult are found on an Alpine hillside. Fifty-three members of the same cult died in mysterious circumstances in October 1994.

MOSCOW, TUESDAY 19

Communists triumphant in Russian poll

Gennardy Zyuganov, Communist leader.

With two-fifths of the votes counted in Russia's parliamentary elections, the Communists have emerged as the dominant party in the next Duma. They are currently registering 22 percent of the votes counted, a figure that is unlikely to be too different from the final result, and which should give them over 150 of the 450 seats. In some industrial regions, where production has dropped catastrophically under democracy, the Communist share has been as high as 63 percent. The Communist leader, Gennardy Zyuganov, claimed that the result was "a complete rejection of the radical policy of so-called democratic reforms."

The results are a deliberate slap in the face for Boris Yeltsin. Of the reformist or moderate parties only Prime Minister Viktor Chernomyrdin's Our Home is Russia party has come close to 10 percent of the vote. Nevertheless, President Yeltsin can take some consolation from the decline in support for Vladimir Zhirinovsky, whose extreme nationalist Liberal Democratic party has so far gained only 11 percent of the vote – half the support that it won in the last Russian elections.

BOGOTA, THURSDAY 21

American Airlines jet crashes into Colombian mountainside killing 147

An American Airlines Boeing 757, on route from Miami to the town of Cali in southwest Colombia, crashed yesterday into a mountainside minutes before it would have reached its destination. The crash killed 147 of the mainly Colombian passengers. But to the amazement of rescuers who reached the wreckage earlier today, 17 people have been taken out alive. The plane was flying at 500 mph when it hit the mountainside.

The cause of the crash is unknown. The twin-engine 757 is one of the most up-to-date aircraft in regular use, and has an almost unblemished safety record. However, sabotage is not currently suspected.

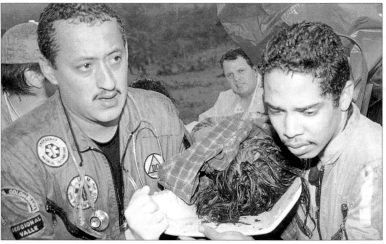

Rescuers carry a 14-year-old survivor from the wreckage of the crashed 757.

Washington, Tuesday 19. Oliver Stone's new film *Nixon,* starring Anthony Hopkins and Joan Allen (above), has been condemned by Richard Nixon's daughters as malicious "character assassination."

DELHI, SATURDAY 23

Hundreds die in school fire

Over 300 people are believed to have perished as fire swept through a temporary structure put up for a school prizegiving in the town of Dabwali in the north Indian state of Haryana. There were 1,300 people in the tent-like *shamiana* at the time, many of them children. Only two of the exits appear to have been left unlocked. As well as burns and smoke inhalation, deaths are attributable to injuries sustained in the stampede to escape.

LONDON, WEDNESDAY 20

Queen calls for royal divorce

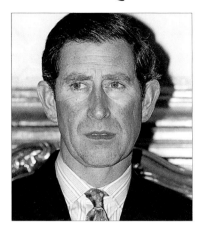

Reacting angrily to the continuing public revelations about the failed marriage of her son, Prince Charles, and Princess Diana, Queen Elizabeth has written to them urging a divorce. A statement issued tonight from Buckingham Palace said: "After considering the present situation the Queen wrote to both the Prince and Princess earlier this week and gave them her view, supported by the Duke of Edinburgh, that an early divorce is desirable. The Prince of Wales also takes this view and has made this known to the Princess of Wales since the letter."

Princess Diana has not yet replied to the letter. Constitutional experts said that a divorce would not prevent Prince Charles ascending the throne.

A family at war: from left to right, Prince Charles, the Queen and the Duke of Edinburgh, and Princess Diana.

WASHINGTON DC, WEDNESDAY 20

Senate gets tough on Whitewater

The Senate tonight passed a resolution to ask a Federal judge to order President Clinton to hand over fresh material relating to the Whitewater investigation. The papers are notes of a meeting in 1993 between the President's senior aides and his lawyers. The President has argued that the papers are protected by client–lawyer privileges.

Republicans are hoping that the documents will reveal that Mrs. Clinton was less than frank with investigators looking into her law firm's representation of an ailing savings and loan association. Senator Lauch Faircloth told the Senate: "It is becoming increasingly clear that Mrs. Clinton lied to Federal investigators." The White House say the papers will reveal nothing new.

WASHINGTON DC, TUESDAY 19

Holbrooke set to quit

Richard C. Holbrooke answers questions.

Fresh from his triumph in conducting the Bosnian peace talks in Dayton, Ohio, Richard C. Holbrooke has announced to Congress that he is to quit as Assistant Secretary of State for European Affairs next year. He said that he has recently married and wishes to spend more time with his wife. He is likely to return to the business world, where he has maintained active contacts on Wall Street between his diplomatic assignments, earning more than $1 million a year. Mr. Holbrooke first held diplomatic office under President Jimmy Carter.

NEW YORK, MONDAY 18

Wall Street tumbles 100 points

The Dow Jones today fell 101.52 points, its largest percentage fall in two and a half years. Wall Street is reacting to the continuing failure of Congress and the President to resolve the Federal budget crisis, and showing disappointment at the unlikelihood of an immediate cut in interest

Wall Street traders before today's close.

Bethlehem, Thursday 21. Palestinian police are cheered by enthusiastic crowds as they enter the administrative buildings of the town after the withdrawal of Israeli troops. This will be the first Christmas to be celebrated at this holy site under Palestinian control.

S	M	T	W	T	F	S
					1	2
3	4	5	6	7	8	9
10	11	12	13	14	15	16
17	18	19	20	21	22	23
24	25	26	27	28	29	30
31						

Arles, France, 25
Solicitor André-François Raffray dies. In 1965 he began paying a monthly pension to Mme. Jeanne Calment in return for ownership of her apartment after her death. Mme. Calment, 120, survives.

Ecuador, 26
Gloria Canales, 40, is arrested on suspicion of masterminding a network smuggling illegal immigrants into the US. It is alleged that she has been responsible for some 10,000 such border crossings from Central America each year.

London, 26
The British Government confirms that it has paid legal costs of around $60,000 to relatives of the three IRA members killed by the SAS on the Rock of Gibraltar in 1988.

Indianapolis, 27
Joseph Garner, 37, has been charged with murder after allegedly stabbing and dismembering his father before eating part of his brain to "release evil spirits."

Maryland, 27
Peace negotiators from Syria and Israel meet for face-to-face talks for the first time in six months, amid optimism that land-for-peace compromises will prove successful.

Beijing, 27
China's State Council issues a white paper praising the country's human rights record.

Moscow, 27
In defiance of American pressure, Russia pledges to continue nuclear and military assistance to Iran.

Washington DC, 28
The world's population grew by 100 million people in 1995 to 5.75 billion, the largest annual increase ever, according to a report published by Washington's Population Institute.

Bosnia, 28
Colonel Gregory Fontenot, commander of the 1st Brigade of the 1st US Armored Division, warns black GIs that Croats are racist, according to journalists covering the deployment in the Posavina Corridor.

BOSNIA, TUESDAY 26

Serbs request more time

Admiral Leighton Smith shares an umbrella with Momcilo Krajisnik in Sarajevo.

The NATO commander in charge of implementing the Bosnian peace agreement, Admiral Leighton Smith, has been asked by the Bosnian Serbs to allow them an extra eight months before they have to hand over their areas of Sarajevo.

Under the terms of the Dayton peace accord these areas are due to come under the supervision of French NATO troops on January 19 and Serb forces are to withdraw by February 3. However, Aleksa Buha, the Bosnian Serb foreign affairs spokesman, has asked that the Serbian pull-out be put back to the end of September at the earliest. Admiral Smith has replied that he is not empowered to renegotiate the peace agreement.

The population of the Serbian areas of Sarajevo is around 70,000. The speaker of the Bosnian Serb assembly, Momcilo Krajisnik, warned that fear amongst the Serbs in the city had risen to the point that they might be provoked into violent action if the deadline is not extended. Large numbers of Serbs are already quitting Sarajevo, even digging up the bones of relatives from the city's cemeteries to carry with them to Serbia.

Los Angeles, Monday 25. Dean Martin, straight man, film actor, singer, and famous drinker, died today at age 78.

NEW YORK, TUESDAY 26

Giants fans in snowball riot

Officials of the National Football League today confiscated the season tickets of 75 fans ejected from the New York Giants stadium on Saturday after a snowball fight during the game against the San Diego Chargers. Giants fans threw snowballs whenever the Chargers looked like scoring. As the snowballs contained ice 15 people were hurt, and one of the referees had to run for cover.

BELFAST, WEDNESDAY 27

IRA blamed for shooting

A man was shot dead last night on a Catholic estate in West Belfast as he sat at home watching television with his family. His three-year-old son who was sitting next to him was injured in the hand by flying glass at the same time. No group has yet claimed responsibility, but the IRA is believed to be implicated.

The 30-year-old-man, who is known to the police as a small-time criminal, may have been thought to be a drugs dealer. The killing follows two murders in the week before Christmas, and one earlier in the month, which were carried out by a group calling itself Direct Action Against Drugs, and which many believe is a cover for the IRA.

Tusla, Bosnia Monday 25. A Bosnian dressed as Santa Claus brings some traditional cheer by handing out candies to US troops at the NATO air base here. NATO troops taking up their positions in Bosnia were generally welcomed by local people.

SYDNEY, MONDAY 25
Riot at Bondi Beach party

The annual open Christmas party at Bondi Beach ended tonight in a riot as thousands of young people started fighting with each other, and then turned on the police. A record 20,000 people turned up to the event that, although only a few years old, is now regarded as a tradition. So much liquor was drunk that it took workers six hours to clear the bottles and cans.

Celebrating Christmas on Bondi beach.

ROME, MONDAY 25
Pope's address cut short through flu

The Pope caused alarm amongst the many thousands of Catholic faithful who gathered in St Peter's square today to hear his traditional Christmas message, and the many millions more watching on television. Looking ill and drawn, he faltered and stumbled over his words, and then cut his address short, apologizing to the crowd and withdrawing from the balcony. After 15 minutes he reappeared to say that he was not well but was getting better.

The Pontiff was also not able to celebrate the Christmas mass in St Peter's Basilica. This is the first time he has missed the service in the 17 years of his papacy. Vatican officials said that he is suffering from a fever and a stomach upset. He is planning to rest entirely for two days, and is not scheduled to make any further public appearances until New Year's Eve.

The Pope is taken ill at the window of his room overlooking St Peter's square.

JOHANNESBURG, TUESDAY 26
Flash flood kills hundreds

A severe flash flood has caused over 100 deaths in a black township in South Africa's KwaZulu/Natal province. Torrential rain late yesterday reached such a level that the Umsindusi River burst its banks and poured through the shanty town outside Pietermaritzburg. During one half-hour period 4 in (10 cm) of rain fell. So far 130 bodies have been recovered but hundreds more people are reported missing. The rain is still falling, hampering rescue efforts, and more is forecast.

Survivors search the wreckage by the river.

SPECIAL DOUBLE ISSUE

DECEMBER 25, 1995/JANUARY 1, 1996

TIME

INTERNATIONAL

MAN OF THE YEAR

NEWT GINGRICH

RENO, NEVADA, THURSDAY 28
Suspected bombers arrested in Reno

Two men were arrested today for questioning by FBI agents, following the discovery of a bomb similar to that detonated in Oklahoma City in April. It was planted at the Federal income tax office in Reno, but failed to explode. Experts estimated that it was powerful enough to have destroyed the entire building.

Ellis Edward Hurst, 52, and Joseph Martin Bailie, 40, residents of Gardnerville, 40 miles from Reno, were arrested in the course of wide-ranging investigations into a recent wave of violence against Federal government workers. The discovery of the bomb was the latest of four incidents in which Federal agencies in northern Nevada have been targeted.

According to officials, the methods used are consistent with the tactics of far-right activist groups. One of their main grievance lies in the fact that Federal agencies administer more than half the land in the western states. Orders have recently been issued to rangers working for the Bureau of Land Management to work in pairs and to maintain constant radio contact.

Some famous names among

Mohammed Siad Barre, **January 1**

Joe Slovo, **January 5**

Prince Souphanouvong, **January 10**

Gerald Durrell, **January 30**

Milovan Djilas, **April 20**

Jean Muir, **May 28**

Arturo Benedetti Michelangeli, **June 12**

Charlie Rich, **July25**

January 1, Mohammed Siad Barre
Barre was president of Somalia from 1969, when, as commander of the armed forces, he seized power. He was overthrown in 1991. He ruled over one of the world's poorest countries, beset by civil war and starvation.

January 5, Joe Slovo
Slovo, chairman of the South African Communist Party, was one of the intellectual forces behind his country's rejection of apartheid. In 1985 he became the first white member of the national executive committee of the African National Congress.

January 10, Prince Souphanouvong
Prince Souphanouvong, known as the "Red Prince" of Laos, led the Pathet Lao guerrillas against the right-wing government of his half-brother, Prince Souvanna Phouma, for more than 20 years. He became president of Laos in 1975 when communism was established, serving until 1986.

January 30, Gerald Durrell
Animal conservationist Durrell was founder of Jersey Zoo, where he bred endangered species. Author of 37 books

(notably *My Family and Other Animals*) and a dozen TV series, he used humor to popularize conservation.

February 5, Patricia Highsmith
American crime writer Highsmith spent most of her life in Europe, in particular England, France, and latterly Switzerland. In 1951 Alfred Hitchcock made a celebrated film of her first novel *Strangers on a Train*. Her most famous creation was the cultivated but amoral murderer Tom Ripley, whom she featured in a series of books.

February 9, J. William Fulbright
Arkansas Democrat, senator for three decades, and chairman of the Foreign Relations Committee for 15 years, Fulbright took a principled stand against the Vietnam War. He will be remembered for the study fellowships he founded and which bear his name.

February 22, Robert Bolt
Dramatist and screenwriter Bolt won an Oscar for the film of his play *A Man For All Seasons* and for his screenplays *Lawrence of Arabia* and *Doctor Zhivago*. He directed his second wife Sarah Miles in the 1972 film *Lady Caroline Lamb*.

April 10, Maraji Desai
In 1977 Desai, a Brahman from western India, became prime minister in India's first non-Congress Party government, formed by his right-wing Janata Party. He was a veteran of the movement that led to India's independence from Britain in 1947, and a devout Hindu, renowned for his high moral standards.

April 20, Milovan Djilas
Former right-hand man to Tito and a fellow wartime partisan, politician, and writer, Djilas became an outspoken critic of the Yugoslav system in 1954, when he rejected communism in favor of democratic socialism. He was an inspiration to other dissidents within communist regimes.

April 23, John C. Stennis
A Mississippi Democrat, Senator Stennis had the distinction of serving in the Senate for longer than all but one other Senator (Carl Hayden of Arizona) in the history of the institution. At his retirement he had served for over 41 years, and was particularly involved in military affairs. He was an old-style Democrat from the South, who started his career as a supporter of racial segregation.

May 22, Les Aspin
A Democrat from Wisconsin, Aspin served for 11 months under President Clinton as Secretary of Defense. He was first elected to Congress in 1970 with an anti-Vietnam War stance, but in 1985 he became chairman of the House Armed Services Committee.

May 28, Jean Muir
British fashion designer Muir had a mathematical approach that she once called "engineering with fabric." She showed her first collection in 1966, and in 1984 was honored by the Queen for her contribution to the fashion industry.

June 12, Arturo Benedetti Michelangeli
Reclusive and temperamental, Michelangeli was recognized as a supreme technical master of the piano. He often insisted that his own instrument be shipped to whichever concert hall he was due to appear in.

June 29, Lana Turner
Lana Turner was an actress who used her considerable physical assets to good effect in a successful film career. Figure-hugging garments led to her becoming

the many who died in 1995

Patricia Highsmith, **February 5**

J. William Fulbright, **February 9**

Robert Bolt, **February 22**

Maraji Desai, **April 10**

Ida Lupino, **August 3**

Phil Harris, **August 11**

Lord Home, **October 9**

Robertson Davies, **December 2**

"The Sweater Girl" and a popular pin-up during World War II. She starred in a famous version of *The Postman Always Rings Twice*, and was nominated for an Oscar as a neurotic mother in the film of *Peyton Place*.

July 25, Charlie Rich
Pianist, songwriter, and singer, in the late 1950s Rich was session pianist on the Sun label, for which he made his first solo records. International stardom came in 1973 with the first of a series of hits, "Behind Closed Doors".

August 3, Ida Lupino
Screen actress Lupino specialized in "siren" roles in such films as *High Sierra* and *Dangerous Ground*. She made her film debut at age 15 in *Her First Affaire* after being selected for the role for which her mother was auditioning!

August 11, Phil Harris
A comedy partner of Jack Benny in the 1930s, Harris was also a singing band-leader – the fast-delivery vocalist on such hits as "Smoke, Smoke that Cigarette." Harris became famous all over again in 1967 as the voice of Baloo the Bear in Walt Disney's *Jungle Book*.

August 17, Howard Koch
Koch achieved notoriety in 1938 as the adaptor for radio of H. G. Wells' *The War of the Worlds*, produced by Orson Welles, which caused panic with its realistic newsflashes about a Martian invasion. His immortality was assured when he became one of the three writers of the movie *Casablanca*.

September 3, Sterling Morrison
Guitarist Morrison was a founder member of the hugely influential but, at the time, commercially unsuccessful 1960s rock group The Velvet Underground. When the band reformed in 1993 Morrison was working in Texas as a tug-boat skipper.

October 9, John Cairncross
Guy Burgess, Donald Maclean, Kim Philby, Anthony Blunt – and John Cairncross, the "fifth man" in the British spy ring who met at Cambridge University in the 1930s and subsequently worked for Soviet intelligence.

October 9, Lord Home
The last aristocratic leader of the British Conservative Party, Home was prime minister for less than a year at the end of the Party's 13 years in government, before their defeat in the election of 1964. He subsequently became a distinguished foreign secretary.

October 23, Gavin Ewart
The wit of British poet Gavin Ewart was exemplified in a poem claiming that he had buried all his best work in a tin box, to be dug up in 50 years' time "to confound the critics/ and teach everybody/ a valuable lesson." There was a 25-year gap (1939-64) between publication of his first and second collections, and he continued to publish sporadically.

November 1, Brian Lenihan
Fianna Fail politican Lenihan held more cabinet posts in the Irish Republic than anyone else, attaining deputy prime minister before being sacked by Charles Haughey in 1990. This sacking followed "Dublingate" – revelations that Lenihan had lied in denying phone calls eight years earlier seeking a delay in the dissolution of parliament.

November 12, Sir Robert Stephens
Sir Robert was a versatile British actor who found his true greatness in the major classics. He was a Falstaff who showed the sad complexity beneath the roistering surface, and a towering King Lear in his last major role. He also gave a famous performance as Sherlock Holmes on Broadway.

December 2, Robertson Davies
Novelist, journalist, and teacher, Robertson Davies won widespread acclaim outside his native Canada. His fiction deals with moral conflict, and he was heavily influenced by the theories of Carl Jung. As a newspaper editor, he displayed a wry cynicism.

December 6, James Reston
One of the most respected US journalists, James Reston became a newspaper columnist in 1953. He set out to describe the ways of Washington so that the average American could understand how government worked.

December 22, James Meade
Meade was a British economist notable for his contribution to the ideas associated with John Maynard Keynes. He created an important method of assessing national income. In 1957 he became Professor of Political Economy at the University of Cambridge.

Page numbers in roman refer to main stories. Those in *italics* refer to brief stories in chronology panels.

PICTURE CREDITS

b= bottom, c= center, l= left, r= right, t= top

ASSOCIATED PRESS
: 66c, 81tc, 83tr, 88t, 89cl, 90cl, 94tc,
95c, 95b, 98tl, 98br, 104tl, 104br, 105c,
105bl, 106, 107c, 108c, 109c, 109cr, 110c, 110b, 111bl,
111bc, 111br, 112tl, 112b, 113tl, 113bl, 113tr, 114bl,
114bcr, 114tcr, 115tr, 115bcl

COLORIFIC:
115tcl

HULTON DEUTSCH/REUTERS:
8cr, 11tl, 14t, 18c, 19, 21cl, 21tr, 24br,
31, 33tr, 36tr, 46cl, 50cl, 53b, 54b, 56c, 57t,
84tl, 99cl, 114tcl

FRANK LANE PICTURE AGENCY:
78bl, 109br

LONDON FEATURES INTERNATIONAL:
114br, 115bl

PRESS ASSOCIATION:
97br, 105cl, 111cr

REX FEATURES:
1br, 6t, 12, 12/13, 13, 17c, 22, 24t, 25t, 25cr, 25bl, 26br,
27cl, 27bl, 27br, 28br, 29tr, 29tl, 29br, 30, 32t, 32br, 33tl,
33bl, 33bc, 34, 35t, 35bl, 36br, 36bc, 37t, 37cr, 38, 38/9,
39, 40bc, 40br, 41tr, 41br, 42, 43br, 43bc, 43bl, 44t, 45,
46br, 47tl, 47tr, 47bl, 48cr, 48b, 49cr, 49bl, 50cr, 51tr, 51c,
51br, 52c, 52c, 54cr, 55, 56t, 56br, 57c, 57br, 57bl, 58br,
58bl, 59tr, 61cr, 61b, 65, 66b, 67cr, 68c, 68br, 69b, 71br,
72, 73tl, 73cr, 73bl, 74br, 75cl, 75br, 76tl,

76br, 77, 78br, 79cl, 79cr, 80c, 81tr, 82tr, 82cl, 83tcl, 83cl,
85t, 86tr, 86cr, 86b, 87tcl, 87tl, 87cl, 87c, 87b, 87cr, 87crt,
87cr, 87crb, 87br, 89t, 89b, 91, 92b, 93tr, 93br, 94br, 95tr,
95cl, 96tl, 96tr, 96br, 97bl, 98bl, 99c, 99br, 100t, 100b,
100tl, 100lb, 101ct, 101c, 101cb, 101tr, 101crt, 101crb,
101br, 102, 103tl, 103tr, 103br, 104br, 105br, 107tr, 108b,
108t, 109b, 112t, 114tl, 114t, 114br, 115cl, 115tl, 115cr, 115bcr

FRANK SPOONER PICTURES/GAMMA:
1l, 1tr, 3, 4, 5, 6b, 7, 8t, 8b, 9, 10, 11br, 14cr, 15, 16, 17tr,
17tl, 17bl, 18t, 18b, 20, 21bl, 23, 25cl, 26t, 27tr, 28t, 29cl,
35cr, 37bl, 40tr, 41tl, 41bl, 43cr, 43t, 44b, 46cr, 47br, 48t,
49t, 50tl, 51tl, 52b, 53t, 54t, 57tl, 58tl, 59cl, 60, 61t, 64,
66t, 67t, 68t, 69t, 69cl, 70, 71c, 73br, 74t, 74bl, 75tr, 76cr,
76cl, 78tl, 78tr, 79t, 80t, 81br, 82br, 83cr, 84tr, 84b, 85br,
85bc, 86cl, 87tcr, 88b, 89cr, 90cr, 91br, 92t, 93tl, 93c,
94tl, 94cl, 96cl, 97t, 98tr, 99cl, 100/1c, 103bl, 107bbr,
107bl, 110t, 111tl, 111tr

TIME MAGAZINE:
115

TRH PICTURES:
32c, 81cl

**Dorling Kindersley would like to thank the fol-
lowing for additional editorial assistance:**
Fran Baines, Philippa Baker, Edda Bohnsack, Claire
Calman, Luci Collings, Maggie Crowley, Miranda
Fellows, Sue George, Mavis Lewis, Sue Leonard, Lorrie
Mack, Anna Milner, Christine Murdock, Flora Pereira